UNRECEIVED OPINIONS

Books by Michael Holroyd

Hugh Kingsmill: A Critical Biography
Lytton Strachey: A Critical Biography (2 vols)
Lytton Strachey by Himself (edited by Michael Holroyd)
The Best of Hugh Kingsmill (edited by Michael Holroyd)
Unreceived Opinions

Students and E

DATF

MICHAEL HOLROYD

Unreceived Opinions

"Seventeen copies sold, of which eleven at trade price to free circulating libraries beyond the seas. Getting known. (*Pause*) ... Never knew such silence. The earth might be uninhabited."

Samuel Beckett, *Krapp's Last Tape*

HEINEMANN : LONDON

William Heinemann Ltd
15 Queen Street, Mayfair, London W1X 8BE
LONDON MELBOURNE TORONTO
JOHANNESBURG AUCKLAND

First published 1973
Original material © Michael Holroyd 1968, 1969, 1970, 1971, 1972 and 1973
Collection, revisions and arrangement © Michael Holroyd 1973

cC

Printed in Great Britain by
Cox & Wyman Ltd
London, Fakenham and Reading

Contents

'Damn and "Blast"! The Friendship of Wyndham Lewis and Augustus John' was the Don Carlos Coloma Memorial Lecture given to the Royal Society of Literature, 30 November 1972. Most of the other pieces have (sometimes in a different form) appeared in: *The American Scholar, The Author, Book World, Encounter, Evening Standard, Harper's Magazine, Horizon, The Listener, London Magazine, New Statesman, New York Times Book Review, Publishers' Weekly, Queen, Spectator, The Times, The Twentieth Century.*

Introduction

My world is the world of words and of books. It is a crowded, shrinking place. Not long ago it had been larger, but part of our territory was annexed by 'media men' – a strange breed of animals and birds from television, films and even Senates and Parliaments. We do not much like this. There have been benefits negotiated with these new neighbours, treaties made: but we were better off before they arrived.

On almost everything we are split among ourselves and, further to complicate matters, we share our land with a curious race of links, *manqué'd* and rolls-royced, called publishers. We are immensely important and wholly without power. We are also tourist territory. No one knows or cares much what we really do, alone and among ourselves. Yet, in some wonderful way, there is still a kudos attached to visiting us, exploring a little of our country which we have exploited with roads of required reading for this purpose. People come and go all the time, like visitors to an open zoo, adding to our population problems but, so the links tell us, assisting our general economy. In these circumstances, we have come to exercise an influence that seems oddly inverted. No one, by thoughtfully reading our written words, is persuaded how to act, but many are persuaded to act so that they become reading matter themselves – an object, even a target, for the written word. In this sense, we tell ourselves, the pen is still mightier than the sword if only because, in an atomic age, the sword is just a stage prop.

This book is a complaint – a pessimistic, nostalgic and I hope not too rhetorical complaint against the conditions imposed on writers by society and against our defensive, over-simplified reaction to these conditions. Despite this, it is a celebration also of the plant of literature struggling in its not very fertile soil.

The pieces I have selected have been arranged so as to give a unity to the book. They comprise autobiographical essays that provide my credentials and misadventures; polemical pieces aimed at those whose 'concern' for the arts stops short at actually doing what is needed to help them; a quizzical look or two at the links and their partners, those sleeping beauties the booksellers; an attempt to revive interest in writers who have been victims, not through lack of talent but change in fashion, of our present system of literary government; a sidelong glance at some close relatives among fellow artists, and some consideration of our most esteemed representatives – a few of those who travel as diplomats in the unlettered lands beyond our frontiers.

It is, of course, just one man's view, passionately haphazard, which has gone to make up this unorthodox map of the writers' country. As a guide, it is intended to be part of an anti-tourist brochure which, I hope, will nevertheless tempt a few off the approved routes to explore the land itself more adventurously.

There is a test, designed by Talleyrand, to discover the sort of person you are. Imagine, outside your window, you see a fight taking place between two groups of people; do you instinctively help the losing side, or wait to see who will win and join them, or again send out to discover the cause of the fight and offer your support to those who are morally correct? Even unintentionally, I back the losers: and I offer this as my chief qualification to be a writers' unofficial trade unionist.

MICHAEL HOLROYD

Tinker, Tailor

At school, where I showed a small talent for languages, I spent my days studying science. It was a scheme specially engineered by my family who, after years of cautious investment in the tea business, had steered their finances towards the climax of bankruptcy. In the evenings, round the fire, we had seen our plantations on television as the Chinese, invading India, had happily trampled them underfoot. I could never, it was explained to me above the rumble of gunfire, expect now to inherit money – except, probably, in the form of debts: I would have to earn the stuff. Nevertheless, heavy mortgages and high optimism kept morale white hot at home, especially in the vicinity of my father, a man practised at turning defeats into imaginative advantages. It did not take him long to spot the bright side. Had I become a tea-planter, he assured me, I would rapidly have gone downhill. In a sense I owed my future to the Chinese; and in all probability my future, like that of the Chinese, lay with the atomic bomb: or some such thing – my father was not too precise. 'Now look here,' he would say at breakfast during the holidays, striking with enthusiasm a copy of *The Daily Telegraph*. Every day it seemed, a great cry was sent up through the advertisement columns of this newspaper for radiologists, bio-chemists, plasma-physicists, structural engineers. There were not enough of such men, my father declared, to go round. 'Put two and two together,' he urged kindly. So I returned to school a biologist.

It took me about two years to prove, undeniably, that I was no scientist. At the end of that time I had obtained, as it were, my QED. I was absolved and, with my head in the clouds, tailed off my school career with lessons in astronomy.

But the problem of my future remained. In my father's simple equation I had been not a solution but the remainder. It was not long before he re-phrased the quandary and came to a new, even brighter conclusion. No one, he stubbornly maintained, could argue as obstinately as I had done and not get paid for it. I must capitalize on this tiresome gift: I must take up the law.

So, on leaving school, instead of starting my National Service at an age when others were doing so, I was articled to a firm of solicitors at Windsor. It was a genuinely depressing office in the Dickens style – dark, dusty, full of awkward corners. Buses passed the door going one way to Dedworth, the other to Gravesend. In place of wages I paid them, with some justice perhaps, to employ me: but it seemed an odd contribution to the family predicament. My duties were unspecific – to sense how things were, to hang about, to sniff out the legal atmosphere. I practised making tea and coffee; I was shot at while attempting to serve a writ; I was accidentally locked, among carcasses, into a huge butcher's fridge (a huge fridge belonging to a huge butcher) which had been a subject of complaint. With time my misadventures grew. There was laughter in court when, on my first appearance, I sat next to a large metal radiator and released from it a jet of tepid water among the witnesses. There were tears on another occasion when our solicitor disappeared briefly into the lavatory and, in panic, I adjourned a complicated divorce case so that the disgruntled parties remained married a further six months.

In the office itself I was sometimes allowed to interview people. I don't know whether this is common to all legal practices, but we sucked into our offices a large percentage of madmen. They were sent, this class of people, scuttling up to the attic where I sat smartly before my blotting paper trying out poems. One old lady complained of nudity among the neighbours. On both sides, amid the cabbages, at twilight and even more revealing moments, they danced, she told me in a small voice, without clothes. They had constructed some kind of underground train service beneath her house and would make day excursions to one another, rattling the foundations. I made some notes, gave her a little of my tea, and we discussed ways and means of frustrating her naked entourage. It was not so much obstinacy as tact that was required at law.

But what I remember most vividly were the long afternoons, doing nothing. It seemed incredible to me that we should spend so many hours behind our desks, while outside the sun shone. It was a denial of life, the rigours of which occupied with profit so much of our working time. Occasionally I wondered why the staff did not rebel and flood out into the streets and parks. Myself, I was held in check by the sternest spirit of cowardice – in particular a fear of the open-air life that awaited me if I abandoned law: two years National Service in the army. This formed my chief legal incentive. If I could stick the law long enough, I thought, perhaps the army would melt away. One trouble was that my firm of solicitors had never encountered an articled clerk before, and did not know what to do. Eventually they transferred the guilt by paying me. I learnt nothing except, prudently, some details about the law of bankruptcy and something of the law of libel, both of which were to prove 'relevant' in literature.

As with science, it took about two years to demonstrate my unfitness for any branch of the law, after which there was no further escape from National Service. I wrote off enquiring about the possibilities, as an alternative to military service, of coal mining in South Wales or a Russian language course conducted in Cornwall; but the replies were discouraging. There was one more hurdle to fail. I did my best. With a pair of violet-tinted spectacles and an Irish walking-stick I advanced upon Reading, where I was to be examined medically. I had been up late the previous night recalling past illnesses and had mustered an impressive garrison of them. Water-on-the-knee and in the eye, bow-legs, an allergy to elastoplast: I revealed all, I sang. The result was a disaster. After a gruelling day I was graded 3, ensuring for myself not exemption but the choice of two years either as an army caterer or in the Pioneer Corps, digging field latrines. Throwing away my stick and spectacles I appealed, and admitting nothing beyond Church of England, was re-graded 1.

My first month in the army I spent at home. I had been ordered to report to a barracks in Winchester, but on arrival found that no one was expecting me or knew what should be done. They were not pleased, the sergeants and captains, and inclined, I felt, to blame me for the mistake. Fortunately there was one other person in the same predicament, a brilliant public school cricketer. He arrived an hour after I had, twirling his arms and knocking imaginary balls for six, and it was wonderful to see how everyone cheered up. Old scores were swapped in an atmosphere of great geniality, and eventually someone with rank called out: 'You two had better clear off home then.' The journey back was intensely happy.

Next time my welcome was more orthodox. I was to spend ten weeks' basic training at Winchester, but within ten minutes I knew I could not last it. I was too old, too slow, too terrified. Everything appeared to be done so loudly and at such a speed – it was astonishing to me how anyone knew what to do next: I could find no way of telling, except by watching the others and then doing fractionally later whatever they did. It is usual for 'intellectuals' comically to exaggerate their deficiencies as soldiers. This would be difficult for me – I was simply no good. I could always find reasons for doing things differently, and I could see no reason for calling a tree a 'bushy topped object' in order to achieve what was termed 'simplicity'. It was this quality of military simplicity that constantly foxed me. But over the ten weeks at Winchester certain changes gradually began to take place within me. I started to lose things: I lost the habit of reading, I lost all privacy and with this part of my own identity. At times I almost lost consciousness – at least I never felt quite all there. This was a help. I began to belong more to the platoon, to take on a corporate identity, answering, with a shout, to a number. The Michael Holroyd who had arrived at Winchester could never have got through those weeks. I was someone different.

Towards the end of this period I was sent to Andover for a War Office Selection Board Examination to discover whether or not I was 'officer material'. The answer seemed to me perfectly obvious in advance. Nevertheless, I wanted to pass. To be an officer promised, or so I imagined, an easier existence; to fail, even here, could only bruise my vanity. For it seemed to me then that the secret of all life was the courage to say the word 'yes'; whereas now I know it is the ability to say 'no'. The army taught me the wisdom of saying nothing.

The examination at Andover lasted three days and was divided into three sections: the paper, the vocal, and the muscular. At paperwork, which was my chosen medium, I hoped to score highly. I wrestled with the tactical questions very hard, advancing what I was afterwards told were many excellent reasons for all the wrong conclusions. There was, I believe, nothing I answered correctly. For someone who knew so little of military affairs, it was astonishing this knack I had for picking the loser.

At my lecture I spoke, interminably, on 'Sense of Humour'. No one, I was later promised, understood a word. It did not matter. What did matter was that I had spoken with confidence: unintelligible, unyielding, unamusing and unanswerable confidence – attributable to the fact that every word had been borrowed from someone else. The army, which is not badly infested with literary knowledge, failed to recognize my plagiarisms as I plundered on. People who had not actually heard my lecture warmly approved my choice of subject. 'Is a sense of humour necessary to an officer?' one major asked me, laughing, during my interview. I vigorously asserted that it was. 'Why?' The question travelled without curiosity, and I spoke, in reply, of a Sense of Proportion, of rubbing shoulders with people in all walks of life, of the fine tradition of British humour. Like languages (for which I once had some small talent) humour could take you anywhere. I spoke of Churchill and, in the pauses, I twinkled wryly. What I said contradicted almost everything I had proclaimed at my lecture, which treated humour as a means of apprehending truth. But it was the right answer.

There remained the physical problem: how to get a group of men up two trees and across a river without touching any area coloured white, and with the aid of a crowbar and two barrels – all in ten minutes: *Go!* . . . Had my life depended upon it I could not have succeeded. But we had, among our platoon of would-be officers, a burly marine. This giant, like a cart-horse, I loaded with wood, iron and flesh. He climbed, he waded, he ran, he swam. He was the apex of an upside-down pyramid of objects. His eyes and muscles bulged with unprecedented exertion, and we just did it – not by the correct method but simply through the superhuman efforts of this one man. The examiners were incredulous. This had never been done before, being obviously impossible:

but it counted. There was, however, a corollary to this feat. When it came to the marine's turn to lead our platoon over another series of hazards he failed through sheer exhaustion.

By the skin of my teeth I passed. They had given me the benefit of the doubt, but I would have to 'buck my ideas up', they said, in the future. I was as much surprised by this qualification as by the result. Another National Serviceman there was sceptical. He had been once before, told the truth, and failed. Now, quite cynically, he had lied and they had let him through. So it was all a sham. But at one level at least I disagreed with him. For surely what they were testing was our acting ability. As officers we should be called upon to act with conviction, to spread the pretence that there was no danger, the fiction that we personally hated the enemy and that they detested us. We had to act with the authority necessary to suspend people's belief in reality. As for the examination, they knew it was nonsense, we knew it was nonsense: but could we be trusted to keep the secret? That was the key question.

I returned to Winchester expecting very shortly to be posted on, like a parcel, to Eaton Hall, the officer training school near Chester. But again there was a delay. While the riflemen and corporals departed, I, together with one tuberculosis-suspect, stayed on. It was not a matter of health in my case but of loyalty. The authorities had just noticed that my mother was the native of a neutral country, Sweden: and they bristled. For months this information, copied on to countless forms, had rested harmlessly in their files, but now, in their imaginations, it sprang to life. Something would have to be done. The first thing they did was to promote me to lance-corporal; the second to confine me, as if pregnant, to the barracks until investigations could be made. The barracks were empty and there was positively nothing to do. I should have been in my element. Yet one of the things I had lost – something that had been much exercised in my legal days – was a talent for motionless inactivity. The sergeant in charge of us was a civil man and not accustomed to being a military nurse. We peppered him with questions. Did I look like a spy? Was TB contagious? He relented and, for the sake of peace, allowed us out. At once, by means I have fortunately forgotten, we acquired a Land-Rover and, replete with army petrol and with my new friend at the wheel, we patrolled the countryside – paddling in the sea, eating strawberries in Berkshire with my grandmother, or simply lying in the sun on St Catherine's Hill overlooking Winchester. We went occasionally to films and more occasionally to restaurants, and stared pennilessly at girls in the streets. These days and weeks, stolen from the march of time, were sweet and, being timeless, have remained with me while more 'important' events have melted away. But one morning I was sent for, told I had been cleared, and ordered to proceed to Chester: *soonest*. There was no time to say good-bye. I never discovered whether my friend had TB, and cannot now even remember his name.

The training course at Chester lasted sixteen weeks, but the atmosphere was very different. We strode about exaggeratedly swinging our arms, our chins forward, our heels biting into the tarmac, beneath the shadow of that portentous pile, Eaton Hall – an absurd and grandiose folly of a building erected specifically without purpose. Everywhere bustled bellowing sergeant-majors, effete captains with canes treading delicately on their toes, and majors with moustaches. 'Some of you will be lucky enough to see active service,' we were told. Was I the only one who found such sentiments preposterous? There seemed no way of finding out, for our ranks of officer-cadets were criss-crossed with complicated lines of snobbery (assumed rather than felt, I suspected) that prevented one of us from addressing another. The Guards could not accost the line regiments who were not tolerated by the Greenjackets who were hardly recognized by the Guards: it went something like that. Though the intention had been to instil us with a lively sense of competition, the result was fatuous. We reverted to the age of ten, squabbling over matters about which we had no experience, no real feeling and up to a few months ago no knowledge. The more tedious the subject, the more controversially we treated it.

If I was exempt from this epidemic, it was probably because I had been inoculated by my extra years. Another manifestation of my great age was less welcome. At Eaton Hall I met again a number of people I had not seen since my days as a biologist-astronomer. At school they had been my juniors: now they were senior. I had always imagined that, through ease and indolence, I had been reasonably popular at school. I had never mastered the trick of severity; I had abolished beating – could amiable inertia go further? But my smiles of recognition now went unanswered. I had become an embarrassment, and had to act the stranger with people I thought I knew – a situation that had some of the qualities of nightmare.

On the whole I do not remember Eaton Hall well. There was not the same rhythm of uniformity as at Winchester, nor any chance to be an individual: we were types. I was beginning, however, to appreciate something important – the power and value of my absence. By taking a little thought I was able within seconds partially to eclipse myself. I became the sun in the eternal night of barrack life, not missing exactly but always unseen. It became difficult to focus upon me. If I was alone in a room, that room was usually considered empty; and this pleased me well. My hand would shoot up with meticulous timing, barely too late for everything: I was the ultimate non-volunteer. On the parade ground I placed myself in the middle rank, and towards the middle of it. Since no one had learnt my name, there was almost no method of communicating with me. So they let it go. By the end I had become almost wholly invisible. In this way I slipped quietly into my role of officer and gentleman.

There was still the problem of into which regiment I should be gazetted. None of them were keen to have such an inconspicuous asset. I made investigations, my preference being to join any body of men sunning themselves peacefully on some neutral territory. I invented, Bunbury-style, an uncle who, I maintained, had served with distinction in one of these choice regiments, for this was the only way of answering, to military satisfaction, the question of why I particularly wanted to join it. Eventually, at the request of the former, I was transferred from the Greenjackets to the Royal Fusiliers, whose ultimate resting-place was Sutton Coldfield.

With the rank of second lieutenant in my brand new, reluctant regiment, I left Eaton Hall for three weeks' leave. It was 1956, a peaceful time for me. I led the life of a lapsed scholar, sleeping late and sleeping early, and day-dreaming through the intervals. But towards the end of my leave a suspicion had begun to invade me that all was not well. Somehow, I felt out of step. This feeling crystallized at a cinema one evening during the Pathé News, when I noticed some faces, furtive yet familiar, staring blindly from the screen. They belonged to comrades I had seen at Eaton Hall – I was sure of it. Their brave, trapped expressions, like zoo-animals', compelled attention. The commentator, suddenly very British, described the embarkation of the Royal Fusiliers for the Suez Canal to fight the Egyptians. It might have been, so far as I was concerned, some episode from ancient history. Like most serious, responsible people who do not wish to create trouble, I took no interest whatever in politics, being deaf to their music. When I read the newspapers I confined myself of course to the arts and book pages with, occasionally, a hopeful look down the obituaries. Rumours of war had reached me, but I knew it was none of my business and I had no wish to pry. But now, in this cinema, I felt obliged to do what my father had always been begging me to do: put two and two together. The answer was very alarming: I was a deserter. 'Could they shoot me?' I asked a friend who had safely completed his National Service the previous year. He considered the question far too long. 'I should think they'd grant you a Court Martial', he said, 'first'. Since nothing, militarily speaking, had the power of surprising me, I was totally credulous. Lying awake that night it did not seem impossible that they might want to encourage the others by putting a pistol to my head. At the very least I would be reduced to the ranks and given a long spell in some army jail. Next day I telephoned my adjutant, ostensibly on a small matter connected with dress. His reaction redoubled my apprehensions of the night. Cutting across a de-tailed query on buttons, he demanded to know 'where the hell' I was. Did I realize I had missed the war? I was to put myself at once under close arrest, then escort myself to the Tower of London where they would be expecting me. 'What shall I wear?' I persisted hopelessly. I had never heard the adjutant laugh before. 'It won't matter where you're going,' he said.

I arrived at the Tower of London later that morning and, standing to attention, was cross-examined by two senior officers. Why, they asked, had I not responded to the urgent telegram summoning me to active service? Because, I answered easily (grateful to have such a simple reply), I had never received it. Disbelief shone frankly in their eyes. Why had I not put two and two together? I still had no answer to that.

I spent that night in 'Napoleon's Room' at the Tower. The following day, unexpectedly, came a reprieve. The telegram, so far sunk without trace, had now resurfaced: it appeared that the adjutant, in the heat of war, had addressed it to himself. In these circumstances there was little they could do to me – except have me up on the minor charge of being improperly dressed. 'You are wearing the wrong buttons, Mr Holroyd. Kindly take a week's Orderly Officer.'

My week at the Tower was comparatively quiet. The only irregularity came as the result of a report in the *News Chronicle* that the Union Jack there was proudly flying upside down. This crisis, which I first took to be a practical joke, was quite beyond my reach, but before it could rise to a momentous level, a new job had been found for me. I was to travel to Dover and, high up on the cliffs there, enter Connaught Barracks. These premises, which had been empty since the Royal Fusiliers set sail for Egypt, were now to be put at the disposal of the refugees arriving from Hungary after the abortive uprising. It was Saturday evening. I hurried to my aunt – a lady who had once ridden to hounds – and extracted from her garage a very old bowler hat. Crowned with this, like a small black pimple at the top of my head, I descended properly dressed upon Dover. My instructions had been to make the refugees 'feel at home' on the cliffs. This was not only vague, I discovered, but a euphemism. For my job actually consisted of juggling with inadequate supplies of light bulbs and contraceptives so as to ensure that those Hungarians occupying unlit barrack rooms were protected with French Letters, while those left unprotected were bathed, like battery hens, in a permanent glare. The supplies were to be alternated each night. After a few weeks the Hungarians went forth – and multiplied.

Our battles now were ended. The regiment disembarked, flags wettened in the rain, and the band struck hopefully up. They marched, our boys, through the glistening streets of Dover; they ascended the cliffs and were greeted rather diffidently by myself in white gloves. I had drawn myself up outside the officers' mess in which I had rapidly re-grouped all the light bulbs, and kept saluting until told ('for heaven's sake') to stop. We had suffered, while abroad, twelve casualties, all of them rather remarkably shot in the back. At stand-to someone in a forward position would stretch or clear his throat, and a comrade behind, believing that the enemy were at last showing aggressive signs of life, would loose off a volley of bullets, wounding (often quite embarrassingly) some friend. All, however, were decorated with medals. I remember Anthony Howard showing me his a number of times before, rather ostentatiously, losing it.

The presence of Anthony Howard in the regiment was an oasis. In the law I had sighted islands of boredom; in the army I was marooned on the vast Continent itself. The boredom seeped down the walls of the officers' mess, saturated the atmosphere, infected our very souls. We lived in a void that was never painful while we remained motionless within its circumference, but which, after only forty-eight hours' leave, would appear horrific. One officer, I remember, whose room was above my own, practised coming to a halt. Over the year I spent at Dover that was all he did over and over again. 'One! Two!' he would call out, then bring his arm smartly down to his side and his heels together, bang! bang! For a second or two he would stand there, rigid, glazed. Then off round his room again: 'One! Two! Bang! Bang!' Only in Anthony Howard did I encounter someone to whom books were a part of life, and our conversations were like a private language. There existed between us, too, I realized, an unintentional rivalry as to who was more ill-adapted to this peculiar way of life – a contest usually settled in my favour.

What I had learnt at Eaton Hall, I perfected at Dover. At the end of my year I stood one day behind two sergeants in the same company as myself who had just read my name on a noticeboard. Was this Holroyd a new officer? they wanted to know; had he arrived yet? My technique had been simple. I acquired a board on to which I fixed some pages of blank quarto paper. Armed with this implement and an expression of the sternest vacancy, I would strut about the barracks, ostensibly from one place to another but in fact from my bed back to my bed. I dissolved into the background; I was the very substance of camouflage. According to Tolstoy, the chief attraction of military service is that it consists of 'compulsory and irreproachable idleness'. But idleness of this calibre requires energy. To appear busy is almost as demanding as actually being busy. The advantage to me was that I understood the appearance far better than the reality. My part contained two words of monologue which I left trailing in the wake behind me as I sped urgently back to my bed. 'Carry on!' I would cry. And they did. I spent so much time in bed, a damp and draughty spot overlooking the sea, that I caught lumbago and was seldom fit enough to attend sick parade.

For two months we left Dover to perform 'exercises' round Salisbury Plain. On bookish rather than military grounds, I was appointed A.D.C. to the Brigade Commander, that warrior-of-letters Brigadier Sir Bernard Fergusson.* He was a genial, imposing man, built like a tree but with a flashing monocle (like one my grandmother used to wear), belligerent whiskers and a caravan. I was required to find out what battles were being fought that day and then arrange for him to be driven to them. Shoulder to shoulder I would sit with him in the back of the official car, a map on my knees, discussing James Elroy Flecker and from time to time jerking forward, like some oarsman, to instruct the driver. Fortunately this driver knew the area extremely well. Even so, our progress was often haphazard, and however early we started we would arrive at some interval after the last shot had been fired. I began to wonder whether we should ever see a single hostility. At last, at midnight on Salisbury Plain, lost and alone, the Brigade Commander's patience snapped and he set me as a punishment to practising my salutes beneath the stars.

I seemed fated where Bernard Fergusson was concerned to do the wrong thing. When he invited me to dinner the invitation went astray; another time I took along Anthony Howard who lost his hat in the house, occasioning us all manner of dreadful misadventures in attempting to recapture it. On a third and I believe final occasion, I was put in charge of the drinks and told to 'organize' them. Everything had been poured into identical decanters and looked pale amber. I began preparing impossible beverages for the guests, all of whom were too polite to object,

* Now Lord Ballantrae.

though their expressions were painful enough. Suddenly Bernard Fergusson appeared before me, barked: 'I'll have my usual' – and vanished into an ambush of his visitors. I poured a stiff whisky, handed it to him – and with a gasp he spat it on to the floor. A ring formed round us as for a fight, while Fergusson demanded to know why I had given him a brimming glass of sherry-and-soda. At that moment, tripping over the carpet, L. P. Hartley came to my rescue. 'But I heard you ask for that,' he lied. 'I distinctly heard you.' During all my time in the army, this was the greatest act of bravery I witnessed.

I passed the last four months of my military career at the War Office. These were the first days of the amalgamation of regiments and the rundown of the army as a whole – 'streamlining' it was bravely called. In company with one other National Service subaltern, a nice intelligent man named Smout (whom I suspect of having later written a history of Scotland), I was put in charge of redundancy. We divided the country up, the two of us, and went to work. Since our recommendations were invariably accepted this was, I suppose, a taste of real power. Majors and colonels of all conditions would send us their forms giving reasons why they should stay or go. Sometimes they wrote in desperation, petitioning us not to fling them back into the civilian life they had never known; either that, or they would describe the joys of managing an egg farm in the Hebrides, a toy shop at Staines, or their qualifications for taking the cloth. It was ironic that the breed of person who had made much of one's life so uncomfortable over the past two years should apparently – and to some degree literally – be at one's mercy. But although I could appreciate the irony, the power itself was empty. As a driving force, power has never really moved me from a stationary position; and as a literary theme it seems to me less rich than love and death, in so far as it is separable from them. But at the War Office, power in all its emptiness enhaloed me – like a mirage that, seen clearly from a distance, vanishes once it is reached. The style and manifestations of it, however, adhered to me like a caricature of the real thing. I was given the rank of Temporary Unpaid Acting Captain: a dizzy pinnacle for a National Serviceman. And I lived up to it. On the telephone my voice was so unaccommodating that officers up to the rank of colonel felt it proper to address me as 'Sir': it was my finest hour.

Within minutes it was over: there were simply no more field officers to axe. One of the last, I noticed, had been a colonel in my own regiment, a moon-struck man with a cat, who became television critic for a fascist weekly. We had sent them all packing and now it was our turn, Smout's and mine. For a long time I had counted off the days till my release. Now, three weeks early, it came out of the blue, taking me by surprise. I was free.

What had I gained from National Service? Time: I had certainly gained that. At twenty-three I had a little more confidence – not much, but enough to know what I did not like. I had also saved a little money to buy myself more time in which to start writing.

I believe I also learnt something of the twin relationship between dullness and danger. The two appeared to stand at opposite ends of a line that had been coiled into a circle. Those who have some imaginative life of their own will sometimes, as a form of respite, unsuccessfully seek out the plains of boredom; it is only the others with a natural supply of inner tedium who try to lose it in 'exciting' or 'important' lives. The motto of the army, 'Service not self', seemed to me a dangerous one because it attempted to transfer to society the individual's blunted hopes of personal happiness. Since there is a tendency in every mass movement to reproduce the faults of the movement from which it is reacting, 'alternative' usually means the same. Recent radical and revolutionary groups are mostly attempts to escape from individuality into an ideal collective sphere where 'every man shift for all the rest, and let no man take care of himself'. In all the talk, for example, about Vietnam I have listened keenly for some admission of fear. Instead there have been endless words on ethics, humanitarianism, progress, and international politics. I longed for a bit of honest cowardice, for some humour, for something personal. What I heard was truth without sincerity: the canned stuff.

If it is true that we regret only what we fail to do, then this may account for my failure to regret those two long improbable years. But at each international crisis over the following two years, a practical joker would telephone me in the early morning and pretend to be our adjutant, or some War Office official summoning me back as a reservist. Then truly, for a moment or two, I would know fear.

In more specific matters I am still waiting for opportunities to exercise my full complement of military skills. Like Lord Reith, I have not been fully stretched. I was trained as Fire Officer and as officer in charge of Chemical Warfare, but so far have held my expertise in abeyance. My inability to drive any known vehicle did not disqualify my serving as Transport Officer, and I understand now that I could have awarded myself a driving licence, thereby avoiding the tortured business of passing my test.

In other respects the army did not greatly affect me. Inside the soldier had been the writer struggling not to get out. After National Service had deposited me back, like driftwood, on the slopes of civilian life, the writer began, very cautiously, to emerge. Those things I had lost in the army – privacy and the habit of reading – returned, so that I now enjoy them with greater relish. I still speak no languages; I still have difficulty over two and two, though I suspect that the right answer is often to be found by subtracting them. Responsibility and the duty and privilege of making decisions were reputed to be the special prerequisites of an officer: in which case I may have contracted an allergy to them. I have no passion to be married to responsibility, and I have learnt to postpone most decisions until the reasons for taking them have long disappeared. My campaign in the army was wholly defensive: it did little to prepare me for the real warfare of literary life.

The Slow Progress of a Biographer

The winter of 1963–4 was for me a crucial one. After two years' work, and a further two years of waiting, I had had my first book published: a critical biography of Hugh Kingsmill, the novelist, biographer and literary critic. But only two weeks after publication I was being threatened with an action for libel. The situation seemed perilous. My chief witness, Hesketh Pearson, who had first encouraged me to write, suddenly died. I could muster other supporters, but they would hardly figure as star witnesses. There was Malcolm Muggeridge, who had contributed a marvellous introduction to my book, but who had also attacked the Queen and whose appearance in court was guaranteed to stir up violent antipathy in any jury. There was John Davenport, the critic, who at that time had chosen to wear a prejudicial black beard. And there was William Gerhardie, the distinguished novelist, who had not actually published a novel for the last quarter of a century and who, besides denying that he spoke with a slight foreign intonation, would almost certainly turn up at the wrong court room or on the wrong day, however elaborate the precautions one took.

Altogether it was not a pleasant prospect. Yet my publisher, Martin Secker, who was nearing eighty, appeared to find the predicament wonderfully invigorating. It brought back to him, evidently, the good old fighting days of D. H. Lawrence, Norman Douglas and the early novels of Compton Mackenzie, all of whom he had sponsored. While the old man seemed splendidly rejuvenated, I, still in my twenties, tottered towards a nervous senility. For nights on end I would start awake from dreadful courtroom scenes – rhetorical but unavailing speeches from the dock – to the dreary horror of early morning and the next batch of solicitors' letters.

But out of this nightmare something else had been born. The first of the sixteen publishers to whom I had submitted my Kingsmill manuscript was Heinemann. Fortunately it had fallen into the hands of James Michie, the poet and translator of the Odes of Horace. He had liked it, had sent for me, and gently explained that were his firm to make a practice of bringing out books about almost unknown writers by totally unknown authors, it would very soon be bankrupt. However, I might become better known myself were I to choose a less obscure subject. Had I any ideas?

This was just the opportunity for which I was looking. Kingsmill, along with Philip Guedalla, Emil Ludwig, André Maurois, Harold Nicolson and others, had been categorized as one of those imitators of Lytton Strachey, whose literary reputation he had helped to bring into disrepute. In order to demonstrate the injustice of this charge I had to examine Strachey's books in some detail. To my surprise I found there was no biography of him, and no wholly satisfactory critical study of his work. Here, it seemed to me, there existed the real need for a book. James Michie agreed, and a contract was drawn up in which I undertook to make a revaluation of Strachey's place as a serious historian. It would be about seventy thousand words long and take me, I estimated, at least a year.

A year later I had arrived at a stalemate. I had read everything published by and about Strachey, and I had produced an almost complete manuscript. But I was very far from being satisfied. For I had come to the conclusion that Strachey was one of those historians whose work was so personal that it could only be illuminated by some biographical commentary. It was impossible, from published sources, to reconstruct any worthwhile biography. As for unpublished sources, Clive Bell had sounded an ominous warning. 'Lytton could love, and perhaps he could hate,' he had written. 'To anyone who knew him well it is obvious that love and lust and that mysterious mixture of the two which is the heart's desire played in his life parts of which a biographer who fails to take account will make himself ridiculous. But I am not a biographer, nor can, nor should, a biography of Lytton Strachey be attempted for many years to come. It cannot be attempted till his letters have been published or at any rate made accessible, and his letters should not be published till those he cared for and those who thought he cared for them are dead. Most of his papers luckily are in safe and scholarly hands.'*

This passage conjured up the picture of an almost impregnable stronghold through which I had to make a breach. But I had no doubt that within these fortifications lay solutions to many of the problems that my literary researches had raised. Why had Strachey been attracted to General Gordon almost, as it were, against his will? What was the peculiar mystery he hinted at in Albert the Prince Consort's marriage to Queen Victoria? What was the spell that obviously mesmerized him in Queen Elizabeth's powerful relationship with the Earl of Essex? There was something intensely subjective in such questions that could never be satisfactorily answered without a more certain knowledge of Strachey's own secret nature.

I knew none of the surviving members of the celebrated Bloomsbury Group, but I had been given the address of a certain Frances Partridge, a friend of Strachey's who had collaborated with him on the eight-volume edition of *The Greville Memoirs*. To write to her out of the blue and ask for assistance seemed as good a start as any.

I wrote. In her reply she explained that the person I should first get in touch with was James Strachey, Lytton's younger brother and literary executor. He was the key figure to any major critical and biographical study such as I wanted to carry out. For if he were prepared to co-operate then she too would be perfectly ready to help me, and so also, she implied, would most of Lytton's other friends.

I met James Strachey a fortnight later. In the meantime various unnerving rumours concerning him had reached me. He was a psychoanalyst, who had been analysed by Freud, had subsequently worked with him in Vienna, and who, during the last twenty years, had been engaged on a monumental translation of all the Master's works. This twenty-four volume edition, with all its maze of additional footnotes and introductions, was said to be so

* Also, I discovered later, E. M. Forster had written to Lady Ottoline Morrell (27 January 1932): 'No, I don't suppose Lytton will ever or should ever, get explained to the general public'.

fine both as a work of art and of scholarship that a distinguished German publishing house was endeavouring to have it re-translated back into German as their own Standard Edition. He was married to another psychoanalyst, Alix Strachey, author of *The Unconscious Motives of War*, a once-brilliant cricket player and avid dancer at the night clubs and now an authority on cow-boys. Together, I was inaccurately informed by Osbert Sitwell, they had rented off the attics of their house to some unidentified people on whom they had practised their psychoanalytical experi-ments to an extent where the wretched tenants no longer knew anything except the amount of their rent and the date it was due.

It was therefore with deep qualms that I approached their red-brick Edwardian house, set in the beech woods of Marlow Com-mon. I arrived at midday by a complicated system of trains and taxis, prepared for practically anything – but not for what I actually came across. Though it was cold and frosty outside, the temperature within the house seemed set at a steady eighty degrees Fahrenheit. No windows were open, and to prevent the suspicion of a draught cellophane curtains were drawn against them. There was an odour of disinfectant about the rooms. I felt I had entered a specially treated capsule where some rare variety of *homo sapiens* was exquisitely preserved.

James Strachey was an almost exact replica of Freud himself, though with some traces of Lytton's physiognomy – the slightly bulbous nose in particular. He wore a short white beard, because, he told me, of the difficulty of shaving. He had had it now for some fifty years. He also wore spectacles, one lens of which was transparent, the other translucent. It was only later that I learnt he had overcome with extraordinary patience and courage a series of eye operations that had threatened to put an end to his *magnum opus*. In a more subdued and somewhat less astringent form, he shared many of Lytton's remarkable qualities – his strange and subtle humour, his depth and ambiguity of silence, his sternly rational turn of mind, his shy emotionalism and something of his predisposition to vertigo. As he opened the front door to me, swaying slightly, murmuring something I failed to overhear, I wondered for a moment whether he might be ill. I extended a hand, a gesture which might be interpreted either as a formality or an offer of assistance. But he retreated, and I followed him in.

Of all his Stracheyesque characteristics, it was his silence that I found most dismaying during our hour's 'interview', as he called it, before lunch. I could not tell whether he produced these silences spontaneously, or whether they were in some manner premeditated. Had he heard what I said? Or did he disapprove of my remarks? Or again, was he pondering, indefinitely, upon some singular reply? It was impossible to tell. To fill the vacuum of soundlessness, I began jabbering nonsense.

His wife came in, austere and intellectual, very thin, with a deeply lined parchment face and large, deeply expressive eyes. We all drank a little pale sherry and then moved in procession past a bronze bust of Lytton to the dining-room.

Lunch was a spartan affair. Though extremely generous in spirit, my hosts were by temperament ascetic, and lived very frugally. We ate spam, a cold potato each, and lettuce leaves. In our glasses there showed a faint blush of red wine from the Wine Society, but I was the only one who so much as sipped any. My hosts solemnly tipped theirs down the sink at the conclusion of the meal. After the spam, some cheese was quarried out from the cold storage, and some biscuits extracted from a long row of numbered tins ranged like files along a shelf in the kitchen. Everything, spam, potato, lettuce, cheese and biscuits, was, like the windows, swathed in protective cellophane.

During lunch we talked of psychoanalysis – not the subject but the word, its derivation and correct spelling. Should it have a hyphen? Did it need both the central 'o' and 'a'? It was a topic to which I could contribute little of brilliance.

After lunch, Alix Strachey excused herself. She was going up-stairs to watch a television programme for children. Recently she had decided to learn physics, she explained for my benefit, and found these kindergarten classes very instructive. James said nothing. In silence we filed back the biscuits on the shelf, poured away the rest of the wine, re-inserted the cheese into its wrappings and into its frozen chamber. Then James announced that we were to visit the 'studio wilderness', a large building with a stone floor, standing some ten yards to the rear of the house. He put on boots, a scarf, gloves, a heavy belted overcoat down to his ankles, and we started out on our journey. The 'studio wilderness' housed much of Lytton's library and collection of papers. The bookcase along one of its walls was filled with French and English volumes going back to the year 1841. In the middle of the building were two great wooden tables piled high with boxes and files, and on the floor were littered innumerable trunks and suitcases – all full of letters, diaries and miscellaneous papers. Cobwebs and a pall of dust blanketed everything. Spiders – of which I have a particular horror – scuttled about the walls and floor, or swam suspended from the ceiling. James stared at this carefully accumulated debris with a sort of fascinated wonder. He had made Herculean efforts to organize it all, but by now it had got the better of him. He felt sometimes like putting everything in the fire, or sending it off to the archives of some distant university. But instead he stored every item, however minimal, and had persistently done so for the last thirty years. It formed a peculiar family museum, with special emphasis on Lytton. He was waiting for a time when civilized opinion should have advanced far enough to make the revelations which these papers contained acceptable to the public. One of the ways he would determine whether such a time had yet arrived was to be the reaction of any potential biographer. I was not the first to approach him. Several years before, Guy Boas, the teacher and author, had done so. But it had not worked out. Boas considered the material far too scandalous for publication. James Strachey suggested he might get the book printed in Holland, but Boas, not liking to risk it, had backed down. Then Michael Goodwin, editor of *The Twentieth Century*, had applied, had even been permitted to start his research, but had soon vanished, driven, in James's opinion, insane by the whole project. Much pioneer work had been done by Professor C. R. Sanders. Finally, a certain Professor Merle had come over from Paris and been allowed to take back a large number of confidential microfilms of Lytton's letters in order to compose a thesis for the Sorbonne. So what I saw in front of me was only a fraction of the total quantity of material. There was still more besides, James added, in his study. We must go there now.

We travelled back and went upstairs. The study was a long rectangular room surrounded on three sides by books and gramophone records and a narrow window running above them. At the farther end of the room stood a desk on which lay the intimidating engines of James Strachey's *œuvre*. Two massive metal radiators, to which I politely extended my hands, turned out to be stereophonic loudspeakers – James was an authority on classical music, especially Haydn, Mozart and Wagner, and contributed notes and commentaries for Glyndebourne. Above the fireplace hung a portrait of Lytton relaxing in a deck chair, painted by Carrington. Next to the fireplace was an armchair, draped in cellophane. James showed me more papers, including his own correspondence with Rupert Brooke, and several reels of microfilm that the French professor had not taken with him. 'Do you *still* want to write about Lytton?' he at length inquired. I replied that I did. 'I see,' was all he said.

I left the house late that afternoon in profound depression. The mass of unpublished material had exceeded my wildest dreams, and made my previous year's work seem all the more futile. But I could not think I had made a good impression. It appeared likely that I had been wasting my time.

Forty-eight hours later I received a letter from James. He and his wife had decided to assist me so far as possible. But there were practical difficulties. Since 'this Freud translation business is in a rather specially hectic state', they were both bound to avoid being diverted. Therefore, I would have to bring my own food and drink each day. There was also the problem of travel. I should have to journey up and down by a complex of trains and buses. However, if I could face such horrors as these, I was free to start whenever I liked – preferably before the snow set in. I would be allowed to the 'studio wilderness', and permitted to inspect anything in the house itself.

So began what, for the next five years, was to prove not simply the composition of a large book, but a way of life and an education.

I started work at Marlow in October 1962. The hexagonal room where we had first had lunch was given over to me, and as soon as I entered it I would strip off as many clothes as I thought practicable, begin reading through the correspondence, copying out sections, taking notes. From time to time there was a knocking at the hatch which communicated with the kitchen. I would open it to find a steaming cup of coffee and a number 3 biscuit, presumably left by Alix. From time to time James would quietly manifest himself from the doorway on the other side of the room, stand there awhile regarding me, deposit some notebook or sheaf of papers he had just come across: then disappear. Apart from this there was little to disturb me – occasionally some music from the radiator-like loudspeakers upstairs, and very occasionally the sound of scuffling feet from the top floor tenants descending the stairs. Nothing else.

Very soon I realized that I had stumbled upon what must be reckoned one of the major caches of literary papers in modern times. Lytton was never an eloquent conversationalist and had been allergic to the telephone. But he had loved to write and to receive letters: he was one of the last great correspondents. Here, in holograph, typescript and microfilm, were nearly all his letters, preserved since the age of six, and the letters from his friends, many of them internationally famous as painters, philosophers, novelists and economists.

All this was tremendously exciting. But it posed for me equally tremendous problems – problems of how to treat this colossal quantity of unpublished documents and of how to organize my life around it. Near the very outset I had to make the difficult decision that the subject was worth several years of uninterrupted labour and a coverage of about half a million words. And I had to persuade my publisher that I had made the right decision. James Michie had left Heinemann, but I was fortunate in that David Machin, his successor, was equally sympathetic. I outlined to him my plan. I intended to try and accomplish four things – to provide a selection of the best of Lytton's letters; to attempt a completely original reappraisement of his work; to present a panorama of the social and intellectual environment of a remarkable generation; and to write a definitive biography. These four ingredients I would endeavour to shape into the polychromatic design of a huge conversation piece around the figure of Lytton Strachey. 'Discretion', Lytton himself had once said, 'is not the

better part of biography.' I should not be discreet. My purpose
was to fuse an imaginatively kindled re-creation of the inner life
of my characters with the rigorous documentation and exactitude
of strict biographical method.
Part of a biographer's research can have about it an inevitable
sameness. When one has examined ten thousand letters, one may
be forgiven for eyeing the next ten thousand with a certain
lacklustre. Undoubtedly, while I was ploughing through Lytton's
early and most plaintive correspondence, with its microscopic
details of faulty digestion, illness, apathy, self-loathing and all the
unhappy qualities that made up what he termed 'the black period'
of his life, I did feel seriously infected with many of the same
ailments. If symptoms like these were posthumously contagious,
then my next subject must, I resolved, be some athlete of astonishing virility and euphoria. However, Lytton's unusual character,
with its curious contradictions and complexities, soon began to
exert over my imagination a potent spell. I became absorbed in his
life, and over the years I was writing my book I do not think I
was ever more than half aware of the outside world. The world
in which I lived so intensely was that of the Bloomsbury Group
during the early part of this century. My work held something of
the excitement of an archaeological discovery. The vast *terra
incognita* represented by the Strachey papers seemed like a miniature Pompeii, a whole way of life, that was gradually emerging
into the light.
Luckily, too, the routine of my research was widely variegated.
One of my most interesting finds took place in the basement of
51 Gordon Square, the Strachey family's home from 1919 to
1963. The house was being vacated, and had been bought by
University College, London. But I had been given authority to
explore everything. On my first visit I noticed a tablet in the
entrance hall listing the various members of the family with the
captions 'In' and 'Out'. The word 'Out' had been slotted against
those who (some of them half a century ago) had died. By the time
I finished reconnoitring the basement, the dustmen had turned up
to carry off the rubbish for burning, and I won a fierce tug-of-war
with them for Lytton's bulky, long-lost Fellowship dissertation,
120,000 words long, on Warren Hastings. Among other things I

came across that day was a letter in the illegible Gothic hand of Sigmund Freud, written on Christmas Day 1928, and setting forth in great detail his thoughts on Lytton's *Elizabeth and Essex*.

The research was enlivened, too, by a great deal of travel in order to record impressions of people and places. One of the first things I did on leaving Marlow was to fly to Paris. There I met Gabriel Merle, a charming and taciturn French scholar, who allowed me to carry off the microfilms he had been lent by James. These microfilms contained Lytton's correspondence with his family, with Virginia Woolf (unabridged) and with Duncan Grant and Maynard Keynes. The latter were especially valuable, since the originals had been placed under lock and key with a strict embargo that they were not to be seen until 1986. Having negotiated the customs and returned home, I hired from Kodak's a huge black machine, like an astronomer's telescope, and fed the reels of microfilm into it. For two months my life orbited round this monstrous object, which stood in the centre of my one-room flat, dwarfing the furniture. I ate, slept, washed and dressed under its shadow. And for twelve or fifteen hours a day I would sit projecting the films on to a screen, and copying down anything I needed.

Later on I travelled through France and inspected La Souco, the house overlooking Monte Carlo, which had belonged to Lytton's brother-in-law, the painter Simon Bussy, and where Lytton had often stayed and worked. It was deserted when I called, with a notice that it was up for sale. So I boldly made my way in and explored until captured by a voluble French neighbour who accused me of being a burglar. My French not being up to providing a truthful explanation, I gave her to understand that I was a prospective purchaser, and in the guise of a man of wealth was lavishly entertained by her.

A number of people had disliked Lytton Strachey – Harold Nicolson, for instance. I went to see him in his rooms at Albany one evening. He was sitting in a chair when I entered, open-eyed and apparently examining me very critically. He said nothing. I stood before him shuffling my feet, shifting my weight from one to the other, murmuring something about the uncontroversial weather. He continued to glare. Suddenly a sort of convulsion ran through him, and he blinked. 'I'm afraid I've been asleep,' he said. 'Would you like a drink?' I said that I would. But the question was evidently academic, more to satisfy his curiosity than my thirst. We began to talk. Lytton, he told me, had resembled a bearded and bitchy old woman, rude rather than witty in society, injecting with his unnaturally treble voice jets of stinging poison into otherwise convivial gatherings. After about a quarter of an hour he looked across at his own large empty glass, which stood on the table between us, and asked: 'Another drink?' Hesitantly I agreed. But once again he made no move, and since I could see no sign of drink in the room, we went on talking. Ten minutes later his gaze again fell on the glass, this time with a sort of dismayed incredulity. 'Do you want *another* drink?' His tone was so sharp I thought it prudent to refuse.

Next day I told this story to Duncan Grant. Without a word he leapt up and poured me out a strong gin and tonic. The time was half-past ten in the morning.

Another near-contemporary of Lytton's who was reputed to disapprove of him was Bertrand Russell. He invited me to Plas Penrhyn, his remote house in the north of Wales, high up on a hill overlooking the Irish sea. There, in the drawing-room, he regaled me with mildly indecent stories of Frank Harris and Oscar Wilde, showed me the typescript of his then unpublished autobiography and several Strachey letters. Had he disliked Lytton? I asked. No, he answered, never. And so smiling, diminutive and gently nostalgic did he appear that it was scarcely possible to believe that he had fiercely upbraided Lytton for having degraded G. E. Moore's ethics into 'advocacy of a stuffy girls'-school sentimentalizing' – a piece of invective that earned him a withering rebuke from E. M. Forster.

When I first started on my quest for Lytton, Frances Partridge had intimated that James Strachey's approval would guarantee me the help of many other friends. And so it turned out. Over the years I met or corresponded with over a hundred people, and the great majority of these co-operated with me very fully. This was all the more remarkable in view of the highly inflammable material that was involved. For here was I, a total stranger from a completely different generation, proposing to investigate their past lives with a probing intimacy. It was only through detail, I argued, that the extraordinarily complicated relationship surrounding Lytton could be properly presented. I was setting out to do something entirely new in biography, to give Lytton's love-life the same prominence in my book as it had had in his career, to trace its effect on his work, and to treat the whole subject of homosexuality without any artificial veils of decorum – in exactly the same way as I would have treated heterosexuality. To have done otherwise would have been to admit tacitly a qualitative distinction, and tended to perpetuate prejudice rather than erode it. But my plan depended for its practicability on the co-operation of a band of mercurial octogenarians. It was for all of us a daunting prospect. 'Shall I be arrested?' one of them asked after reading through my typescript. And another, with deep pathos, exclaimed: 'When this comes out, they will never again allow me into Lord's.' In particular, it says much for the courage, candour and integrity of Duncan Grant and Roger Senhouse that, despite the shock of its unexpectedness, they did not object to what I had written. Each of them had been central to the understanding of a part of Lytton's life. But neither, perhaps, had appreciated the full extent of the role he played in Lytton's emotions until he read my account based largely on what Lytton wrote to other friends. It was hardly surprising that this sudden revelation of a new dimension to their friendship should be the cause of some agitation. But neither of them put any obstacle in my way, and Duncan Grant set his seal of approval on the first volume by drawing, for its jacket, a magnificent portrait of Lytton, which he later generously presented to me.

By the crucial winter of 1963–4, I had reached in my first volume what is for me always one of the most difficult stages in a book. I was two-thirds of the way through it. A great deal remained to be done, but the temptation to relax slightly, together with the accumulating strain of the Kingsmill affair, made the last third very arduous. I had often been haunted by fears that I would not be able to do the book, that it was beyond me. Now these fears multiplied alarmingly. Like a snail, I inched my way forward, writing in the mornings, typing or doing extra research work every afternoon. This last section of the book took me almost a year to finish, and by the time I had done so, my two index fingers, the only ones I used for typing, were raw.

I returned to Marlow in the autumn of 1964, taking with me the typescript of volume one. While James unhurriedly read through it in his study, I worked below preparing for the second volume. Occasionally, in the late afternoon, the electricity supply would fail, and the regime became candles in champagne bottles. James did not say much while he was reading the typescript, but when he had completed it his reaction was devastating. I had, he felt, been far too adversely critical of his brother. He suspected that I harboured an unconscious dislike of him, probably on moral grounds. This suggestion seemed to me utterly fantastic, but there is no appeal against the accusation of an *unconscious* attitude. One's natural rejoinder – that one is totally *unconscious* of it – seems only to corroborate the allegation. For my own part, I had come to feel that James resented from an outsider any criticism – even in the form of qualified praise – of Lytton, to whom he had been very intimately attached. 'I'm in a bit of a conflict,' he told me. On the one hand, he explained, he had grown rather friendly towards me, but on the other he rather violently objected to many passages in the book. He didn't enjoy being unpleasant to someone he liked. What, therefore, were we to do?

What we agreed to do was to go through the book syllable by syllable, trying to hammer out a mutually acceptable text. In return for what he called 'a bribe' of five hundred pounds, I agreed not to publish this first volume until I had finished the whole work. Both volumes could then be brought out together or with only a short interval between them. Despite James's generosity, this was undeniably a hard blow. I felt like a marathon runner who, on completing the course, is asked whether he wouldn't mind immediately running round it all over again.

I returned to London, to my portable typewriter, the one-room flat and the start of another quarter of a million words. Over the next two and a half years James went through both volumes, in microscopic detail, twice. I stayed with him and Alix a number of times in Marlow; he occasionally came to London; we exchanged about a hundred and fifty letters; he sent me over a hundred pages of closely written notes. When he was especially cross, I noticed, he would switch from blue to red ink, and on one fearful occasion the envelope itself was addressed in red. Nothing escaped his attention. One character had 'short' not 'small' shin bones; 'extrovert' was a word that derived from Jung and not from Freud, and was therefore meaningless; another person's ability was not 'considerable' but '*very* considerable'; 'pratter' was a mistyping of 'prattle'; and so on. These notes, queries and comments took up an infinite amount of James's time. But they were of incalculable value. By nature he was severely uncommunicative, yet now he was being provoked into divulging all sorts of information known to practically no other living person, that would, I believed, greatly enrich the biography. Sometimes, of course, we could not agree. In these cases I stuck to my guns and put James's dashing comments in the footnotes.

In April 1967, very shortly after having completed his final notes, James died suddenly of a heart attack. I felt stunned. I had thought he would live to at least a hundred. Although he would on occasions rant and rave over something I had or hadn't written, all our differences had been argued out in the best of spirits. His mind and scholarship could certainly appear daunting, but they were mixed with a humour and gentleness that were unforgettable, and that made working with him an education in civilized behaviour.

Readers of the biography might well deduce from some of the footnotes that James disliked the finished book. Happily this was not so. He was never one to pretend to opinions that were not absolutely his own, so that I knew it was true when he told me at the end he appreciated my seriousness of purpose and approved of the structure and length of the book. The figures and situations, though not always as he saw them, had seemed to force their way through, he said, by a kind of continuous pressure of permeation. And some of the narrative, especially towards the close, he praised highly. Since I had never blindly accepted his opinions, and since I knew his approbation extremely hard to win, nothing could have delighted me more.

A Plaque on All Your Houses!

On Monday, 22 November 1971, amid scenes of rejoicing, a new blue plaque was unleashed in London. It was far from the gentle ceremony one would usually associate with unveilings. Being intimately involved in the affair, I can reveal that much had gone on behind the scenes that can only now be told.

It was the spring of 1967 when the idea had first come to me. At that time I could imagine nothing against it. I was too inexperienced to know that this was to define its chief weakness. The scheme, I believed, was acutely simple: to erect, in memory of Lytton Strachey, a G.L.C. plaque on his house in Gordon Square.

The long history of this plaque illustrates a law in modern society as sophisticated as anything discovered by Mr Parkinson and Dr Peter. After four and a half years of exhaustive tests we have found that the rate at which anything gets done depends upon the force of opposition you can summon against it. For without this spirit of opposition, things are starved of the very oxygen of controversy: they are dead. People, it seems, never act: they react. Therefore one must launch upon the very measure one seeks to implement an onslaught so embittered as to provoke a violent chemical reaction in favour of it. This is social politics at its most practical.

But four and a half years ago I was wholly ignorant of this power of paradox in modern politics. When the Greater London Council first welcomed my simple proposition in a spirit of generous enthusiasm, I felt no dismay. Nothing could serve as a better index of my naïvety. The project was further confounded from the start by the approval and support of the press. Not a word was raised against it. Since it seemed as good as done I dismissed it from my mind: and so did everyone else.

We had assumed, some of us, that we would see the plaque raised to its position before the end of the year – that is, almost exactly four years ago. But without opposition this proved impossible. We had nothing to push against and we could work up no momentum: we had the sensation of falling, of sinking in a sea of goodwill.

The autumn came and went, and so did winter, spring and summer. It occurred to me that in this very postponement might lie our salvation if, as it were, we could put it into reverse. Might it not even be used as a catalyst to alter the rate at which arrangements were being made for the plaque, without of course altering the plaque itself? Was not this continual delay an outrage, a scandal? Surely we could breathe some interest into the business through the very suspense of that boredom which now so thickly encrusted it. For, after a year, I was already becoming aware of the essential chemistry of politics. I see today, however, that by itself postponement is not enough and that it was impractical of me not to seek to alter the plaque. Had I suggested – *demanded* – that the blue plaque be coloured red or, better still, green and shaped like a flower, there would have followed such a postbag of complaints, such a whirlpool of journalism, that a blue plaque would have appeared overnight as if by magic. I still had much to learn.

But I had good teachers. Throughout 1968 and 1969 I learnt enough to keep the plaque alive, if not to make it fit for the street. No natural birth is without some labour pains, and we strove to bring about the necessary difficulties. From the symptoms, if they were acute enough, we reasoned, the initial cause would eventually develop. I may take some personal credit, I believe, for confusing the issue with recommendations for alternative sites and even, from time to time, alternative people. The G.L.C. redoubled its efforts by replacing the man who was dealing with plaques with what was termed 'half a man' and by giving the issue a 'priority' stamp – their lowest classification. They did more. They refused, during the dustmen's strike, to answer correspondence; they insisted, during the post strike, upon written confirmation of telephone calls; and sometimes, in the intervals between strikes, they so addressed their envelopes that they were delivered to themselves. Had it not been, during these dark years, for this perpetual bustle of delay, muddle and red tape I am confident we would have no plaque today.

Strachey's ninetieth birthday came and went, and we all grew older. But by now we had ambushed an army of new people – publishers, architects, authors and other specialists – into superintending the birth. If we could summon up second, third, fourth and even fifth opinions, then it stood to prejudice that one of them must be against us. The chances, with so many actors in the scene, of staging a quarrel or contriving a resignation mounted rapidly and so did our spirits. Everyone agreed that this was what we needed. But it was difficult, despite this feeling of co-operation, to find anything about which to disagree. 'Have you any other ideas?' one publisher wrote desperately in the summer of 1969. One had been for a play by Beckett; another for holding an unveiling ceremony with nothing to unveil and counting upon a collective hallucination. Either the audience would imagine it saw the Biographer's New Plaque, or else, if it did not, its sense of being made to look foolish would express itself in just the sort of anger and resentment we had been trying to stimulate for so long. Anger, of course, is energy; and energy is essential to achieving anything. My own suggestion, for Mr Geoffrey Grigson or Dr Leavis to be given the honour of conducting this pleasant duty, was not taken up, since it was only one of many brainwaves being put forward at this period. But it would almost certainly have been tried at some stage during the next decade or so. For with so many experts now involved there seemed no reason why, even if the confinement lasted another nine years, we should not still witness a successful delivery: perhaps, if his writings had attained by then sufficient unpopularity, on Strachey's hundredth birthday.

Politics is the mother and father of difficulties, and where they do not exist it is vital to invent them. The architect's department, for example, twice redesigned the non-existent plaque – a millimetre this way, a millimetre that – for reasons of ecology. The G.L.C. reinterpreted its policy of not erecting plaques until at least ten years after the death of the person concerned: they made it twenty years. But this brave move failed when it was discovered that by now Strachey had been dead for almost forty years. He seemed to be moving beyond the reach of all of us. Undaunted, they then dug up a piece of useful geography: Gordon Square, that metropolitan lair of the Bloomsbury Group, was not in Bloomsbury at all, but Camden. This seemed promising.

The reports, however, during these years were often dismally optimistic: the plaque was 'in the pipeline'; the plaque was 'agreed in principle'; the plaque was ratified, endorsed, confirmed and occasionally even declared imminent. More and more people, more and more departments were brought in to amass thicker and thicker files of bizarre correspondence about the elusive plaque. I moved house; several of the publishers merged; the Clerk to the Council died or at least disappeared; the plaque remained constant. Every two or three weeks one of us would write to another to assure him 'I will keep you informed of any results' or, with more pathos, to ask 'I wonder if you have any more news?' 'We are still waiting,' came the inevitable reply.

It was only when London University, who owned the site in Gordon Square, entered the arena that a real sense of emergency clothed the proceedings. After all our efforts, it appeared at last that we might have hit upon a body of men who were genuinely unco-operative. It was a stroke of purest good luck. People began to speculate as to whether they would put up the plaque and then knock down the house, or knock the house down before endeavouring to put up the plaque. There was an air of fresh excitement, as at a horse race. And throughout the suspense and speculation London University played it marvellously cool. On all occasions they were as silent as the grave.

Many of us had done much over these long years to prepare the ground which by this time was richly fertile. But who was responsible for the stroke of genius in finally planting the seed I do not know. Like all acts of genius it seemed supremely simple afterwards. Mysteriously it was reported in the newspapers that, following a long search, 'a legal complication' had been found. We could not believe our good fortune. We held our breath. No one denied it. Everything had long been prepared, and now everyone worked against the manufactured legality as if it were time itself. There was no longer any question of priority: this was urgent. All the possible objections we had ourselves discovered were passed over to our pacemakers, the legal department, for they must not fail us. Nor have they. So finally, when the legal objection arrives at Gordon Square, the plaque will be there to meet it.

Barabbas through the Looking-Glass

One of the fascinations in writing the lives of authors is to explore the relationship they had with their publishers – and then compare them to one's own. Of the two writers whose biographies I have written, Hugh Kingsmill and Lytton Strachey, one was uncommercial, the other, after much struggling, highly successful. Their experiences with publishers differed widely.

After his first book, *Landmarks in French Literature*, which was brought out as one of a series by Williams and Norgate, Strachey stayed for the rest of his career with a single publisher. Kingsmill stayed with no one for long. There were few London publishers from whom he did not extract, at one time or another, an advance, very often for one of his anthologies, which he would foist on whoever was bringing out his most recent book. This was his standard way of dealing with the option clause in his contract. Having the advantage of possessing no business brain, he was inclined to treat any money given to him in advance as a quite separate matter from the royalties themselves – a sort of pledge of faith that had no connection with eventual sales, and that it was quite unethical to deduct later on. After all, he once pointed out, they were very tiny amounts – more of retreats, really, than advances.

In their financial aspect, publishers were *in loco parentis* for Kingsmill – which may explain why, in spite of all his infuriating habits, they continued to find him endearing. With rugged optimism, he expected to get from them what his father, Sir Henry Lunn, was unwilling or unable to hand over himself. And, from his point of view, he managed them very ably. From Jonathan Cape, Robert Hale and Macdonald he certainly received advances without getting around to supplying any books, and from Methuen he received a number of such sums.

'Annually when our auditors checked our books,' wrote Alan White of Methuen, 'I was asked by my boss to account for these sums. Piqued by his tone, I said tartly that works of the imagination could not be written with mechanical regularity. He stared a full minute at his papers, and then remarked, without the trace of a smile (though he was not without humour on subjects unconnected with business), "Works of the imagination is right."'

But when at last a book was produced, it was written so well, and sold so badly, that the publisher and Kingsmill himself were reduced to despair – at which moment another anthology was born. He was, in the words of Rupert Hart-Davis, 'the publisher's nightmare'.

It was Rupert Hart-Davis who, while he was working at Jonathan Cape, commissioned Kingsmill to write his autobiography. The late Jonathan Cape told me, when I was writing my biography, that in his opinion Kingsmill was neither a very pleasant personality nor a writer of any great talent, but on further questioning admitted never having known him or read his books. Rather naïvely, perhaps, I pressed him to explain his views, at which he pointed out that Kingsmill had never completed his autobiography, for which he had nevertheless received money. With a flourish he then handed me the original contract with the air of a magistrate producing a criminal document. Choosing to overlook the several years that had elapsed between the date on the contract and Kingsmill's final illness and death, I exclaimed, 'But he died!' Mr Cape looked at me coldly for what seemed a very long time. 'And whose fault was that?' he demanded.

It was his unending money difficulties that drove Kingsmill to use his publishers so desperately; and it was his irresponsible attitude that persuaded publishers not to commission from him those very books that he would have written best. The sort of author who replied to their letters on the backs of writs was not, they reasoned, quite the proper person to entrust with a major literary undertaking. They were wrong, though their attitude is understandable.

Strachey was cushioned against the awful poverty Kingsmill experienced and, largely for that reason, inspired his publishers with greater confidence. He was recommended to send the type-

script of *Eminent Victorians* to Chatto and Windus by his friend
Clive Bell. 'And how very strange to be published by Chatto and
Windus!' he had himself written to Bell four years beforehand, just
after Bell's little book, *Art*, had been published. 'I thought they
did nothing but bring out superannuated editions of Swinburne
variegated with the Children's Theological Library and the posthumous essays of Lord de Tabley.'

Nevertheless it was to Chatto and Windus that *Eminent
Victorians* was sent. Its two readers, Geoffrey Whitworth and
Frank Swinnerton, were 'as excited before publication as the
world was after it'. But after its publication, on 9 May 1918, almost
the only people from whom Strachey heard nothing were the
publishers themselves who, in the quaint way publishers have,
assumed that the author's interest in his work had ceased on
publication day. They had brought it out at the price of ten-and-
sixpence, allowing Strachey 15 per cent of this on the first thousand copies sold, and 20 per cent thereafter – this for what, to all
intents and purposes, was a first book! They had also undertaken
to pay him a £50 advance on the day of publication, but the weeks
went by and nothing happened. 'It's rather awkward,' Strachey
nervously admitted to Clive Bell. 'Ought I to write to Geoffrey
Whitworth? Perhaps if I'm patient it'll all come right – but
perhaps not.' Soon afterwards a letter from Geoffrey Whitworth
did turn up. It made no mention of the advance, but it contained a
phrase that deserves to become a publisher's classic. *Eminent
Victorians*, he explained almost with regret, was selling so well
that 'we are being *forced to think about* a reprint' Strachey
commiserated, but also brought up the matter of the non-
existent advance, and by return post received a cheque with
apologies.

After this false start, the relationship between Strachey and
Chatto and Windus grew to be extraordinarily cordial. They
were always seeking out ways and means to pay him extra money
(without any prompting from Strachey), always improving the
mouth-watering clauses in his contracts and subsequently breaking them for his increased benefit. They pressed him not to hurry
with his next book, they offered to grapple with the tax authorities on his behalf; they sent him innumerable dust jackets and

alternative bindings from which he was invited to select his favourite; then out of the blue they wrote to congratulate him in general terms, on nothing in particular, and urged him, for his own protection, to submit all negotiations to the Society of Authors. They even arranged for him to witness the printing of his books, though the moment he appeared all the machinery broke down and came to a halt, much to their confusion – and probably to Strachey's relief.

And Strachey, too, was the last word in courtesy. He invariably made pressing inquiries after the health of the partners (even the retired ones), apologized for the slightest delay and for the legitimate correction of proof copies, recommended a friend of his to join the firm, would not listen to offers from other publishers. Perhaps best-selling authors still enjoy relationships such as this. But for the rest of us it is something to savour in all its charm, and to marvel at long and deeply.

Barabbas, then as now, is the exceptional, not the typical publisher. But the difficulty of the author-publisher relationship must always be that their interests are sometimes identical, sometimes directly opposed. As every publisher knows, the maladies most incident to authors are egocentricity and paranoia. Blinkered by these, the author cannot understand why his publisher should be so skilful before signature of the contract, so inept after publication day. The combativeness of some authors, it seems, puts the publisher on his mettle; while the vast dough of the public reduces him to slumber.

Traditionally, as every author knows, incompetence is the special talent of publishing. Once it was an occupation for gentlemen, ex-debutante secretaries and an office cat, and the incompetence was leisurely, decorative. Now it has been invaded by computers that give out rows of x's instead of the elusive sales figures, by the interests of television and newspapers. The resulting chaos is energetic, formidable, but usually not unfriendly. I have been in one publisher's office where a director was dictating a letter on the most modern machine to a French colleague in Paris, while that colleague sat next door discussing with a fellow director the very matter about which he was being simultaneously consulted only a few feet away. Yet not a smile breaks, not an eyebrow lifts, not a forehead creases at incidents such as this – they are everyday affairs.

My own experience with Strachey's publishers probably catches the correct balance. Very generously they allowed me to work in a large office, going through Strachey's letters. They gave me much information about his books, put me in touch with other people who knew Strachey. They could not have been kinder. Three years later, when my book was about to be published, they expressed astonishment, and some indignation, that I had never bothered to consult them. After all, they pointed out, they would have welcomed me in their offices, shown me Strachey's letters, put me in touch perhaps with one or two people who knew him.

So in my experience, the publisher is less of a Barabbas than a Mad Hatter.

Research for another biography took me shortly afterwards to America. There, I discovered, they employ far more professional methods to achieve similar ends. The incompetence is considerably more skilful, the paranoia more fiercely stylized. Many of the author-publisher difficulties have been done away with altogether by a single brilliant stroke: they have done away with the author. More and more books are attributed to retiring politicians and soft-drink companies, and since no ex-President or industrial millionaire can be trusted to construct two consecutive paragraphs, this means that their books are put together and packaged up by committees. These committees consist chiefly of editors, so that at long last books may be said to be written by publishers themselves – a development that neatly cuts out the middle man and helps to explain why today there are so many more writers than readers.

For a visiting author there is one particularly odd experience. He can be introduced one morning to, say, Mr Bob Jones of Doubleday, only to be re-introduced to him that same evening as Mr Bob Jones of Random House. The publicity, editorial, sales and administrative staff of a publisher can change within a few hours, and often does, so that the author is confronted fairly regularly with rows of strange faces, all busy doing what their predecessors did, and all boasting tremendous titles. In a sense this is a system of promotion. Resignation or the sack, it's all the same – they all go elsewhere for more. But if you wait long enough, I believe, you will see them come full circle, sitting at their old desks and assuming their old identities as if there had never been a lifetime's interval.

Three experiences that I enjoyed will show, I think, how the paranoia of authors is maintained at the highest possible level. I had come to do some research work at a certain library. My way had been prepared by a voluminous transatlantic correspondence, in the course of which I had filled in countless forms, forwarded innumerable copyright statements and generally become what is called 'fully documented'. But at 4.30 p.m. on the day I arrived, the Keeper of Manuscripts gave notice of his retirement, which was to take place at exactly 5.00 p.m.

His successor was a man of precarious availability. He was said to be so busy that he had practically no time left for work. All the same, this did not greatly worry me, since I was obliged to remain working at the library several weeks, the information I had been given by letter being very largely and categorically inaccurate. One morning the telephone rang, and I was told that the new Keeper was available. I put my papers in my briefcase, rose to my feet, took a few steps toward the door, only to be told, 'He's no longer available.' It needed, evidently, the split-second timing of a French farce to catch him. Later on I waited at the corner of a passage, saw him hurry into his office and nipped in behind.

'I expect you know why I'm here,' I cried. But no, he guessed not. I explained everything from the beginning, seeming, as I spoke, to see the words ricocheting from his head.

'Could you put it all in writing?' he asked, when I had finished.

'But it's already in writing,' I protested, 'in our correspondence.'

He shook his rock-like head. 'That's in the form of letters. What we want is a memorandum. Set it out as a memorandum – and post it to me.'

His last words were, 'If you get it to us immediately, we won't act on it at once.'

Another library at which I worked was on a university campus. All around, we were told, were examples of student unrest. But why, our librarians wondered, were *we* being ignored? Why was the catalogue still unburnt, the windows intact? Such neglect was humiliating, and something must be done about it. After a week of persistently unbroken peace, the librarians could endure it no longer, and decreed that we should *act* as if under student siege, take part in a sort of tactical exercise without troops. The doors were locked, and we came and went by a series of extended tunnels, past German literature and the cataloguing department of an adjacent library, to emerge several hundred yards away at what turned out to be an area of maximum danger – all this, much to the bewilderment of militant students who could not account for this Falstaff's army of broken-down scholars perpetually streaming past.

To help finance work such as this, I had agreed to lecture at one or two universities on the subject of biography. My first lecture was scheduled for midday. I arrived punctually and was met by my host, a distinguished professor of English literature. We proceeded to the hall where I was to talk as the clock struck twelve. It was empty. 'We'll wait a few moments,' the professor said, 'for stragglers.' We waited for twenty minutes, but no one straggled. The professor then rose and introduced me in fulsome terms. At the very back of the hall a white-coated coffee lady, on duty to refresh the crowds after the performance was over, settled herself down comfortably. The professor eloquently completed his introduction and I climbed to my feet. About half-way through the lecture, a straggler appeared in shirt-sleeves, stared several moments at this nightmarish spectacle, and stumbled out. I continued doggedly to the end, the professor formally thanked me, and the three of us drank cups of palpitating coffee. 'I could see,' he remarked, 'how it would have gone down better with a larger audience.'

Almost always a writer's audience in America is theoretically very large, but in practice tiny. This is one aspect of the paradox at the centre of American life, and for authors its most striking feature is the sale-or-return system. According to Jacques Barzun, the country is going through a cultural boom; and according to Julian Mitchell, its intellectual and artistic life is far superior to Britain's. The paradox lies in the fact that, despite these manifestations of higher civilization, the people themselves are in the process of an evolution in reverse. From the Cadillac back up into the trees is, perhaps for all of us, only a small leap. One of the main signs of this regression is the loss of language as a means of communication. Television and radio are possibly the worst in the world, and the most used. Successful books apparently sell in hundreds of thousands, but a recent survey has shown that practically none of the people who generously buy these books read them. Prestige is all. Many authors' sales, in fact, never again approach what they were before publication day, when the returns start coming in; and in one case I heard of, they actually exceeded the number of copies printed.

So the atmosphere, though stimulating, bases its stimulation on hope continually deferred, and the writer's best policy, here as elsewhere, is to keep his own company, and to allow his publisher to keep his illusions.

Harvard on my Mind

When I arrived in New York, a Day of National Mourning was declared. After months, even years, of painful endeavour, General Eisenhower had triumphed over his military doctors, and died. The macabre rumours of heart transplants, of the possibility of replacing every organ and item of his body in order to construct a replica Eisenhower, were reluctantly silenced. It was not even suggested, as has recently been the case with President Kennedy, that he was not wholly dead at all, but had been spirited away to some remote island as an anonymous medical monster. People were content that he should die, rather than persist as a corpse kept afloat by modern chemistry.

The Day of Mourning wore a mild carnival atmosphere about it. Everyone had liked Ike. He had the kind of humdrum virtues most people could easily recognize. Above all, he was not a politician. Even his military failures, such as the decision not to advance on Berlin, were largely political miscalculations. For that matter he was not really a front-line general either; he was certainly not a writer; in fact he was not a lot of things, and this reassured people. Everyone agreed he was just 'a nice guy'.

After a brief deceleration, a moment spent lowering flags, life scurried on as hectically as ever. In New York people are busy, all day, about being busy. Morning and afternoon they hold meetings and wring from themselves the decision to hold other meetings on the same subjects but on different days. These meetings are therefore self-perpetuating, forming an American nightmare that can end only with the conclusion of the world itself.

On the secular side, meetings are a kind of business social event. A coffee break, an accidental encounter in a passage, cocktails at four – these are meetings. But there is also a religious awe attached to such events. Like miracles, meetings may occur at any moment whenever two or three are gathered together. I was even told that, for especially senior executives, it was possible to induce a state of holding-a-meeting while quite alone and invisible to their colleagues.

The conditions in which most businessmen live may help to stimulate these hallucinations. They sit, acre after acre of them, floor upon floor up to the level of the very clouds themselves, in artificial daylight cells, like factory animals, fed on Vitamin D and other nourishing substances, and producing whole litters of gorgeously typed notepaper for their files.

There is not much cruelty in these establishments. If their quarters are cramped, the chairs in which they huddle are well-designed, the air that is perpetually belched out at them, hot and homogenized. But for the sentimental foreigner there is a pathos in their lives. Windowless, they cannot see (and in some cases appear to have quite forgotten) what it is like outside. They do not know if it is cold or sunny, dry or raining – and this, as one wanders into their offices, is always their initial welcome. 'What', they ask, 'is it like outside?' Then, almost before one can reply, a cell door slips hermetically shut and one finds oneself involved in the ceremonies of another meeting.

What it is like outside is brown and loud. Even the green trees and grass are, if one examines them, brown; even the most automatically-geared cars are loud. The feeble cries of preservation societies are drowned as the remaining brownstone houses crash to the ground before the advancing skyscrapers. In an affluent society, such as America, nobody can afford anything, least of all a house. Businesses buy everything, build everywhere. Tremendous empty showrooms, gigantic wildernesses of lobbies with chandeliers, mosaics and *objets d'art*, priceless and valueless, rise up to be admired in all their magnificent obsolescence.

But the people who trek across these ornamental wastes live mainly in apartments far away. Apartments are not what the British understand by flats. They are more like prisons, solitary confinement areas that often confine more than one person. These prisons, which the population exchange daily for their office cells, have all the paraphernalia of the normal jail. They are terrifically locked-and-bolted; they are guarded by men in uniforms, men with bulging revolvers like freakish genitalia; they are claustrophobic, dark, and perhaps character-building; they have unopened and even unopenable windows: and they are in any case too high to jump from.

Once inside, you may hear the continual noise of police sirens, the call of the ambulances, the wail of the fire trucks above the ordinary hooting and screeching. So you feel safe from the unmentionable, but so often mentioned, atrocities that are going on by popular demand outside.

But I was not content to remain indoors. The heat and restriction drove me out and often unintentionally I went to many of the most dangerous localities at the most critical hours. I followed fire engines to non-existent fires; saw police cars roar round in circles, play at dodgems with the ambulances. Having read an article by Alan Brien in which he told of a train conductor being shot, I took with some nervousness a train. It was a smooth journey. I travelled by plane, several planes, but not once were we hijacked. I seemed to lead a charmed life. Once I read in an English newspaper of a violent episode involving many people, some armed. I had been there at the time and could remember nothing unusual. The papers report this sort of calamity regularly, and New Yorkers, much to the benefit of their psychiatrists, live in a state of unintermittent tension. The authorities have even arranged – a marvellous scenic effect – for smoke to issue by day and by night through the manholes in the road. This greatly heightens the suspense by giving the impression of some volcanic eruption for ever imminent. The pantomime is complete.

It is an Alice-Through-the-Looking-Glass world. The symptoms come first, of pain, pleasure or fear; the events, so I discovered, come afterwards. Within the fear lies a longing. So the scene is set, the cast assumes its roles, and the villains are awaited not in vain.

By contrast with New York, the atmosphere of Cambridge, Massachusetts, appears calm. True, Boston looks as if it has recently gone through a blitz worse than London's, but this is only the start of a modern redevelopment programme that will in due course convert it into a stereotyped American city. There is far less bustle and aggressiveness, fewer prognathous gum-chewing jaws, less noise and more green. To travel the odd two hundred and fifty miles from New York to the city of Cambridge takes less than an hour by the shuttle, yet for me it was a journey from comparatively sprightly youth to crabbed old age. Plus-fours and purple face: that is my uniform now.

The day I arrived at Harvard, the student riots broke out. Two weeks before the papers had been full of biographies of Eisenhower. Now they were cluttered with the riots. This news belonged to a different era, and with Eisenhower's death the period of transition between them seemed finally over.

From the end of March there had been strong rumours that militant students intended to seize University Hall, an administrative building in the middle of Harvard Yard. The only thing that appeared to be delaying them was some motive for doing so. Should it be a protest against bloodshed overseas? Or should it involve starvation on the African Continent? Or, again, could it be joined to some local issue that might have the advantage of attracting more attention to the locality? If necessary, some argued, it could be converted into a demonstration of support for something. Controversial issues in the neighbourhood were hard to discover, but eventually two main ones were drummed up.

The first of these concerned the Reserve Officers Training Corps (ROTC), which some students, particularly the so-called 'Students for a Democratic Society' (SDS), wanted abolished. The second called for an end to Harvard's expansion programme which involved the tearing down of 182 workers' homes in Roxbury to make room for the Harvard Medical School extension, and of other apartments on University Road to make way for what was termed 'the Kennedy complex'.

The formulation of these resolutions was a brilliant move on the part of SDS. Their case was unanswerable – literally so, since there was none to answer. In all their statements – and there seemed to be several hundred of these a day – they employed what became the best cliché word of the revolution: *demands*. Their reasoning was beautifully simple. Since there could be no logical answer, how, logically, could there be a question? Instead, let us say, of asking some bachelor whether or not he has stopped beating his wife, you demand that he should instantly stop – or get beaten himself.

The two demands could not logically be acceded to for the following reasons. The ROTC was essentially a voluntary affair from which the university had already removed curricular credit. If ever there was a fine non-issue, here was it. As for the Harvard expansion demand, this very neatly presupposed a building plan that did not exist. It also referred to a new Kennedy School of Government Building which not only did not exist, but, in so far as it had even been mooted, was for another type of building to be erected, in the indeterminate future, on a piece of land some distance from the houses cited in the SDS demands.

But the most brilliant revolutionary move of all was to make these demands of the Faculty of Arts and Science, with which they had nothing whatsoever to do. So that, even had the demands been subject to negotiation (which they weren't), such negotiations must have been meaningless.

There remained one further piece of revolutionary logic for the democrats to apply. After the students voted against taking over University Hall, they at once took it over. Armed with red bicycle chains, padlocks and anatomical placards reading 'Put Your Body Where Your Head Is' they marched in, pushing out five deans who happened to be there at the time. 'The building is occupied!', they declared. When a non-comprehending nuclear physicist inquired whether it wasn't large enough for both of them to occupy, he was slung over an SDS shoulder and evicted.

They then set about bursting open the files with crowbars and looting various confidential papers that were later published to advantage in the anti-Establishment paper. *Old Mole* and elsewhere. Altogether it was an exemplary exercise in revolutionary procedure, creating, among many other things, a totally new interpretation of copyright.

The next move was up to the faculty. They showed themselves at least the equal of their opponents. Already they had made sure that all the personal records of the Faculty of Arts and Science and of every member of the freshman class, together with many important financial papers, had been kept in the building that they were pretty certain must be seized.

They were now faced, these philosophers, biologists and political economists, with a deliciously agonizing ethical dilemma. Was the situation one that would justify force? And if so why, what kind of, and when? It was a quandary that could have entranced them for the rest of the semester, and many semesters to come, long after the occupying students had left to become directors of their fathers' banks and automobile firms. Unfortunately the faculty wasn't allowed this luxury – and bitterly its members resented this.

Without consulting them, the Harvard administrators, through Franklin L. Ford, Dean of the Faculty of Arts and Science, told the students to leave within fifteen minutes or be evicted by the police and face charges of trespass. Symbolically, it was decided to make this announcement through a loudspeaker so weak that few of the crowd could overhear it. Possibly, from all points of view, this was just as well, since five hours later the position remained unaltered, the students meanwhile having organized various meetings indoors with their girl friends. As the hours passed, a faint aroma of marijuana floated out on the cool night air.

It had been open to the President, Nathan M. Pusey, to end the affair almost before it had begun. Had he called the faculty, pulled them from their beds if necessary, explained that 'demands' were being made of them under duress, but advised them nevertheless to vote on these 'demands', it is inconceivable that they would not have applied for a court injunction. Instead, he called in the police on Thursday morning at 5 a.m., once it was light enough for the cameras to operate with maximum efficiency. Dean Glimp announced: 'You have five minutes to vacate the building.' But his words, issued through an instrument called a bullhorn, were smothered in the fog of pot, drowned by the thin chanting of 'ROTC Must Go' – much praised subsequently as an example of revolutionary music.

There were 400 policemen, about half of them State Troopers trained in riot control, the other half metropolitan police from the Boston, Cambridge and, I believe, the Roxbury area so zealously championed by the occupying forces. The former acted perfectly well; the latter used more force than was necessary. One way or another, the building was cleared of 'kids', in fifteen minutes – about the same time that it had taken them to remove the five deans.

The action now was over, and the talking could begin in earnest. To regularize the situation the students at once called a strike, at the same time rather cleverly censuring Pusey (who was not a policeman) for the police brutality, and calling for his resignation. The next step was for everyone to form himself into a committee. These committees were known by mysterious letters that pretended to aim for simplicity but very nicely thickened the prevailing confusion. Very much in demand as chairmen were people whose names were so improbable that anyone who did not know them personally might have thought they stood for the titles of new action groups – Fainsod, for example, whose organization many ingenious professors spent hours crossword-puzzling over.

Few of these committees were officially recognized by other committees. But some spectators felt when President Pusey appointed an ultimate Committee of sixty-eight students and faculty members to offer him advice of a general sort, that the parody was a little heavy-handed. Up to then he had been considered a man of astonishing humourlessness and ideal for his job – which was fund-raising.

It was a bad spring for trees and grass at Harvard this year. In February the branches had cracked under the weight of snow, and the ground was blanketed with it. Now, in April, everything was white again with the accumulated garbage of Xeroxed statements from every committee. They were pinned to the bark of trees, piled high in drifts along the roads, everywhere unread and unreadable.

The main job of these committees was to meet. These meetings were of two kinds: those indoors, at which everyone sat down and no one was permitted to say anything except on a point of procedure: and those outside, at which everyone stood up, and spoke in unison on non-procedural matters. In the latter category it was permissible to use fists. I saw one ROTC officer, who had strayed ox-like into a most tastefully arranged mock Vietnam graveyard, very properly sent spinning by the combination punches of an outraged pacifist. The sight of this helped me to interpret the total feebleness of the pro-Vietnam militants throughout this campaign. Surely they were convinced that more students were becoming trained in combat technique than at any other time in the history of Harvard.

The police had now, since leaving, become the main issue, and the students' latest demand was possibly the wittiest they had yet devised. 'Our demands are: We condemn the Administration for its unnecessary use of force,' the strike resolution of 10 April read. That was a good one for the faculty to ponder. Another fresh demand was for the dropping of all criminal charges against those students arrested. But with this the professors had an easy time. After several days, and several million words, they agreed. Since they were, once again, in no position to implement this, and since their recommendation would almost certainly have an adverse effect on the judiciary of Cambridge, their position was simple. The judge, when approached, took in fact the most extraordinary view. Certain people had allegedly broken the law, been arrested and released on bail. These people, he seemed to suggest, were subject like anyone else to the laws of the country, which could not be blinked simply because it suited them. The law would therefore be applied fairly, impartially and without discrimination. There was no reasoning with such a man.

To read the students' manifestos, to attend their interminable non-negotiable discussions day after day, were strange experiences. To begin with, the subtlety of their tactics quite escaped me. On the surface they were totally inarticulate, repetitious beyond all belief, unable to string together two coherent sentences. What lay behind these performances I wondered; what was the purpose of all this self-importance and self-congratulation that coated the congealed porridge of their words?

It was only when I tumbled to the fact that it was not what they said but what these grunts and meaningless stammerings implied that I could appreciate their skill. For here was Harvard, in its 332nd year, the most admired college in all America, whose students, apparently, were without any education. If rudeness were the substitute for talent, intelligence or honesty, then they would endeavour to be rude at all costs – and let the world draw its conclusions. Of all the gambits in the entire revolution, here

surely was the best – and one they played for all it was worth.
Undoubtedly it constituted by far the most serious onsalught
upon their teachers.

How could the faculty reply to such tactics? They were not
long in deciding. They elected to stage a series of highly amusing
parodies of the students' meetings, and to interpret their inco-
herence as a form of soul-searching so profound as to be incapable
of being conjured into words. They took the seriousness of this
to the very point of caricature, producing an optical illusion, in
which, if justice was not done, at least it was seen to be done.
The demands of the students, however, were changed with such
readiness that very often their professors were engaged in pre-
tending to debate claims no longer being made of them. Thus, let
us say, if they were first required to paint their faces green, they
would be discussing with great scholarship the precise shade of
green, and whether green stripes or blotches were permissible,
at the very moment when the students a few hundred yards away
were clamouring for red faces – which they eventually got.

To hear the faculty meetings was, one student told me, an
experience similar to that of reading Shelley for the first time.
Certainly it could be described as educational. Wassily Leontief
(Economics) spoke of 'very wide extenuating circumstances';
George Kistiakowsky (Chemistry) suggested that it was 'much
too soon to render any judgments'; Alexander Gerschenkron
(Economics) spoke at length on the freedom of Western Europe
and his special theory of ancient Roman law; Harry Levin
(Comparative Literature) excused himself for striking a personal
note, but went on to say that his need was to gain the students'
confidence by presenting them with a tape of the faculty's
deliberations.* All this, and very much else, was orchestrated to
alternating laughter and applause. But I waited in vain for someone to suggest, as a solution to the problem, the transference of
the workers allegedly threatened by Harvard expansion to thè
now discredited ROTC buildings.

But there was one man in all this display who seemed woefully

* Professor Levin, it is only fair to record, strongly disputed this account. For
his, and other people's objections (together with my reply) see *Harper's Magazine*, November 1969, pp. 6–14.

ignorant, perhaps even wilfully so, of the new revolutionary spirit. This was Franklin L. Ford, Dean of the Faculty of Arts and Science, one of the people fortunate enough to have been thrown out of University Hall on the first day of the crisis and to have his private correspondence blazoned across the newspapers. In his speech he was curiously handicapped by eloquence, in his arguments by reason, and in his pirated writings by an excellent prose style.

On Wednesday, 16 April, he collapsed with a stroke and was removed to hospital. As one uninstructed in revolutions, I felt that here was the chance all so-called moderates had been waiting for to launch their counter-revolt. Was there not, I reasoned, cause for real indignation, real anger? Was there not the opportunity for a blasting invective against those 'non-violent' extremists who had so harassed Ford as to give him a stroke? And would not this invective, if powerfully done, alienate those 'sweet sincere kids' everyone was talking about, who had been led astray by SDS? Surely now was the moment to unconfuse them.

What actually happened was altogether different. The moderates moderated, and did nothing. The extremists held a fiery debate in which the problem of whether to send a message of sympathy to the hospital was made the subject of an interesting moral dilemma. At first I was surprised at the lack of reaction to Ford's tragedy, until the position was explained to me. The word 'violence' does not mean what some of us might think. Poisoning someone, pressuring them until they lie half-paralysed in a hospital – that is not violence, and to imagine so is mere girls'-school sentimentality. Violence is confined to certain regions, notably Vietnam, and to policemen's batons, notably on the heads of 'radicals'. Violence is something that can be seen – and is seen every day on television and in the newspapers. There is nothing subtle about violence, unless it is the fact that we need it in order to protest. The proper response to it is not compassion, but plenty of good moralizing. No wonder the moderates thought so little of Ford's predicament.

The rest of the Harvard story is already well known, especially the way in which racial discrimination was successfully introduced on to the campus in a form that should remain permanent – a notion that (mixed with an attractive dash of anti-semitism) was spread by the press and nicely exploited soon afterwards by the non-violent student soldiers of Cornell, who set up a 'banana republic'.

One aspect of the Harvard affair was especially appealing, and that was how students and faculty members came so closely to resemble each other. You could hardly tell them apart. Their comradeship was best exhibited on Monday, 21 April, when, at midday, both parties decided simultaneously to stage a 'mill-in' of battle-scarred University Hall. The place swarmed with historians, astronomers, football players.

Once they had filled it to bursting point, they held discussions on two matters that had somehow failed to be included in any of the earlier demands: Vietnam, and the place of the university in society. The rigours of tedium that they so fearlessly confronted were to some extent offset by their crowding into a single large room, the floor of which was known to be unsafe. Six hours later they dispersed, unbloody but bowed.

The curtain now has fallen – but only temporarily. In the closing moments, after almost everyone had left for their summer vacations, the suspension of sixteen students was announced. This should surely inspire the opening scenes next autumn in this admirably-plotted farce.

One failure at Harvard has puzzled many commentators. How was it that the SDS did not spread its militant message of freedom to the people of Cambridge and Boston? I can now reveal that there was such a plan. One SDS member proposed haranguing the workers, and another suggested that a good time to choose would be the lunch-hour. But neither of them, nor apparently any others, knew at which time the workers had their lunch, so the plan was abandoned and the workers stayed in the troughs of ignorance and hostility.

Recently I've heard several criticisms of the parties involved. The faculty has been compared to Chamberlain in his dealings with Hitler; they have been accused of not knowing the difference between government and pedagogic hair-splitting; and it was said of them that their one pathetic desire was to get the students to love them, to achieve which they fell over themselves in sacrificing everything from their principles to their President. As for the revolting students, their more formidable ambition was to fall in love with themselves. Since infancy, it was intimated, they had been grossly overindulged, and they longed to find some opposition to their will. They had gone to college for reasons of social prestige, and had no interest in their subjects, no belief in the past or the future. They wanted it now – but what 'it' was they did not know. Freedom they already had, a freedom to do almost anything or nothing in particular. They were lost in a vast and empty desert of freedom.

People who talked like this were crusty old diehards belonging to the vanished Eisenhower age. Having been on the scene of the riots, which inspired so many repeat performances up and down the country, I can pay sincere tribute to the amazing stamina of those concerned. They achieved much: a new language of obscure 'meaningful' beauty; new sartorial fashions including labels and red ribbons that gave them the air of undelivered parcels; a new logic that went beyond Wittgenstein or Ayer; the pressing into service of qualities long supposed to have been useless or even harmful – colossal tedium, undismayed humourlessness, prejudice, insensitivity and many others.

But it is probably just as well that Eisenhower did not live to see this. Such a glorious spring upsurge of biological politics could never happen at West Point, which is still in the panty-raid stage of evolution. Or could it?

My Aunt's Library: A Paranoid Manifesto for International Book Year

During the Second World War my aunt would take me for long drives. A small determined figure, she sat perched high up at the wheel of an enormous van with myself, aged about six, beside her; and together we roved the wilds of Berkshire and the Home Counties in search of prisoner-of-war camps. As soon as we spotted the friendly barbed wire we would head straight for it, pull up, and unload from the back of the vehicle whole shelves of books to rain down on the heads of our captive German, Italian or even Japanese audience. As part of the war effort our peregrinations seemed endless, continuing in all weathers and until late at night when my aunt was relieved by another lady, the owner of a chocolate factory.

On some days, perhaps at times when the roads were absolutely impassable, my aunt would promote her patriotism at the telephone exchange, offering gratuitous library advice during many an otherwise unliterary conversation. Though I never caught her reading, she was one of those people who, metaphorically speaking, 'are never without a book in their hands'. With her it was a private virtue: she read in bed and scarcely, she boasted, ever slept. Her bedroom was her library – even the bed itself rested on books. She was surrounded by them night and day. Indeed they had become part of the furniture in the house, used to prop things up, keep doors open, keep doors shut, support windows, raise tables. At this period of economy and crisis, books could meet almost every emergency: they lined the air-raid shelter; they afforded protection. We read, the Holroyds, for Victory!

But the war could not go on for ever. Eventually, when the enemy were let out from their camps to go home, there was less call for the mobile library; and at last none at all. The old van was halted and my aunt abandoned, without protest, the telephone exchange. As the roads became filled with hooting and fuming non-readers, she very sensibly forgot how to drive. She also found, now that there was no world war to occupy her, less time to read. It seemed a sign of the new age we were entering, where books were read to kill time by people who preferred it dead. Finally, though persistently taking out books through force of habit from the wheelless library in the town, and even grilling them a little in the oven in case of germs, my aunt never got round to opening them. Although still, in a sense, never without a book in her hands, she had joined that vast army of non-readers.

Worse still, books began to vanish from the house. They were buried when the air-raid shelter was filled in, and they were no longer needed as furniture. A broken window pane was replaced not by Kipling's *Jungle Book* but by a flat piece of glass; a bed rested with fearful symmetry on four even legs; doors no longer obeyed books but locks, keys and even handles. Now that we had just enough money for such things, books were vanishing; they had lost so many of their uses.

What had happened in my aunt's house provides a perfect microcosm of the postwar book world. It also indicates, I believe, what is needed to bring books back into public demand: nothing short of the declaration, roughly speaking, of a Third World War. Authors have been the casualties of peace. Never have books done so well as between 1939 and 1945, according to the publisher Philip Unwin, when almost no one was writing them and there was no paper to print them on. Many a writer in the past twenty-five years has sidled guiltily into the foreign territory of a book-shop to ask, anonymously, for a copy of his own work and been politely told: 'The author, I'm afraid, is dead.' And in the wider sense this is perhaps true. Books are easy to kill, though in a publishing climate that appears to favour the survival of the fattest, they may look robust enough. I have known a book murdered, or at least hideously maimed at birth, by a single letter of the alphabet. 'Your book is not available,' Hatchards wrote to

Cecil Roberts a month after publication of his autobiography. How many other customers, I wonder, are told 'not' instead of 'now'?

Here is a question that might profitably occupy our statisticians. They owe us something. 'The men of letters have fallen; the men of numbers have risen,' Philippa Pullar has told us. What the men of numbers have written about the men of letters makes very confusing reading. Speaking, like ventriloquists, through their dummy computers, they have announced that, in the last twenty years, more books have been published than during the whole previous history of mankind. One hesitates to think where, placed end to end, they could lead us. Every year there are still more books published, yet the authors' individual sales have slumped dramatically. The economics of the book trade baffle the un-literary. A survey recently conducted in America has revealed that almost no one who buys books actually reads them: like my aunt, they have not time. They will read them; they intend, almost certainly, to do so this year, next year, sometime . . . or else they will give them at Christmas or on birthdays to other non-readers. Meanwhile the books themselves are on display, for whereas reading is anti-social and like other forms of muscular idleness provokes guilt, display is fashionable.

Characteristically book-buying is far heavier in America than in Britain where there is a higher proportion of readers. These, of course, are catered for by the free public libraries, a system that does not exist to the same extent in America which has developed instead the Book Club business. The quickest way to kill books in America, so the argument runs, would be to make them freely available, since American enjoyment depends to a masochistic degree upon the spending of money. It was probably with this in mind that Penguin Books Incorporated of America have boldly advertised their editions of my books in the States as 'Not for sale in the U.S.A.'.

In terms of books America and Britain are the obverse of each other, an American 'bill' signifying a British banknote, and a 'check' a bill. But in both countries the standard of literacy has never been higher, and it has given rise to a transatlantic society where we are all at sea; where, though no one actually reads, everyone writes. The only logical conclusion to be reached from these accumulated statistics is that the principal purchaser of any general book must be its own author – possibly too its principal reader. Publishing a book has become almost wholly a private affair, an act of narcissism.

Whenever illiteracy is seriously undermined the way is made open for the cult of non-word communication. Among the most prolific modern authors are those who confidently proclaim that the day of the book is over. Such men as Marshall McLuhan and Asa Briggs have gained immense literary reputations broadcasting the death of literature. And, despite some implied contradiction, there is much truth in what they say. We require in those we reverence some element of magic. But magic is banished by the commonplace. In an age when the currency of words is always being devalued, awe has been inflated to awfulness. Writers now are ordinary and everywhere – can there possibly be enough food to feed them all by the year 2000? 'Women will write novels to while away their pregnancies,' predicted Somerset Maugham; 'bored noblemen, axed officers, retired civil servants fly to the pen as one might fly to the bottle. There is an impression abroad that everyone has it in him to write one book.' And if one book, why not others? The number of authors, like the number of unemployed, threatens to engulf us, for in the public mind the two are not unconnected. We are crowded out with people promising, when they have 'time' or are good for nothing else, to 'write a book one day' – and, in the case of politicians, actually implementing this threat. They have joined, barely in time, a sinking ship.

Everyone writes: but still not everyone writes books. Unless it is part of one's professional salaried career, unless it will belong to the educational market, writing a book today is a deliberate act of eccentricity. It is a waste of that precious commodity time, which, as everyone knows, in the algebra of modern life equals money. No efficiency expert, no ponce of productivity, could possibly condone it. Lord Eccles, our Minister for the Arts who has himself wasted time, has told us what attitude we should adopt to the full-time author: we should ignore him – perhaps he will go away. It is advice that the country, authors included, seems very ready to follow. For in the 1970s men of letters are the undeserving poor. Less than fifty years ago, as Mr J. B. Priestley has often reminded us, it was all very different. In the days of Belloc, Chesterton, Shaw and H. G. Wells they were looked up to as public figures. Now an author 'goes public' at his own considerable risk.

My own small attempts at doing so are, I feel sure, average ones. In Yorkshire, at a grand literary luncheon that involved the feeding of the five hundred readers in the county (more pessimistic reports put the number nearer a thousand), I was stationed at the end of a long tall corridor that had been built entirely out of unsold copies of my books. It was an impressive, an undeniable spectacle. The plan was that, like a Bank of England cashier, I should implant my signature on every volume sold. A bottle of ink stood ready at my elbow, though I had not expected I would need to refill my pen. In the event I did not need to open it. The five hundred – or perhaps thousand – passed hurriedly between the Scylla and Charybdis of Kingsmill and Strachey, and vanished, unbooked, into the twilight.

If this was an average experience, it is possible that in my next public performance I may have achieved something for the future – a happening worthy to be included in the *Guinness Book of Records*. This took place at the much-advertised Book Bang in Bedford Square. Throughout the country this festival of books had been proclaimed, debated, financed. Slogans appeared on buses and in undergrounds; newspaper reports, radio programmes, television features were devoted to it. In a literate society, news of books travels incredibly fast – sometimes in one ear and out the other in a split second. But though illiteracy is rare it may still be found flourishing densely in certain branches of John Menzies and W. H. Smith, the country's two leading booksellers. They have, I believe, training centres specifically for it, situated in the country. It was at Smith's for example, in what they call the book department, that the assistant, eyebrows raised, returned a customer's inquiry about Book Bang (which had opened to ear-splitting publicity that week) with her own query: 'Who published it?' This should have warned me.

I arrived in failing light and pouring rain and was met by my Quixote of a publisher. We paddled towards a barrow which had been loaded with a few sodden copies of my books, and took up our positions, like out-of-work gardeners, at each end. No one came. It was as if we contracted, like leprosy, a raging book virus. From the warm dry interior of a tent, sounds of a rival attraction – Coco the Clown – floated out to us. We shivered, held our ground. Eventually, in a desperate bid for attention and in defiance of various bye-laws, my publisher commandeered a megaphone through which he bellowed out, with a calm air of panic, that the famous – the world-famous – biographer was even now signing copies of his books. 'Roll up!' he despaired. 'Roll up!'

The rain pelted down and no one rolled up. Then, through the gloom, a heavily mackintoshed figure emerged with a bundle. He splashed towards us – I drew my pen – he unpacked and produced from the bundle my book which, he declared, he wanted to return as not being worth the paper it was written on – a statement which, in the downpour, became increasingly objectionable. Haughtily I refused to buy it back: he insisted, and a fierce tug-of-war in reverse developed between us during which, in a brief moment of triumph, I inserted my signature,* High above us, two strangers

* This sentence earned for the author the coveted Ellerbeck Literary Award, consisting of a non-transferable Meat Token for one pound of Best Steak, and a copy of *The Harpole Report* by J. L. Carr. In an explanatory letter 'George Ellerbeck', a family butcher of Kettering, explained: 'Although you may not have heard of the Ellerbeck Literary Award you will be pleased to hear that you have won it. The Prize is awarded at infrequent intervals and *you are only its* third recipient. The circumstances are that Mr Carr who makes a living by writing is one of my customers and pays me in part with unsold works, known I understand as Remainders. These I give to better customers in lieu of my customary picture-calendars. Mrs Ellerbeck who goes to the WEA class and is not averse to a bit of literature suggested some years ago that I award one of these copies as an Encouragement to another member of the Literary World, this to be known as the Ellerbeck Prize.

'We decide who it is to be from the most graphic and telling picture of the cultural world outside Kettering that we read during the month after that Mr Carr delivers his books and we settle with him. Sometimes it is a complete book that Mrs Ellerbeck has been reading and sometimes it is only a few lines. In your case it is only a few lines but I hope someday this will encourage you to write a book about it.

'I came across these lines in some newspapers that Mr Timpsons saves us for outer wrappings. It describes you wrestling in the dark beside a wheelbarrow of sodden volumes and cleverly inserting your signature in a book a dissatisfied struggling in the dark, in waves of optimism my publisher kept up his insistent chanting. At length the anonymous reader rolled off, leaving my battered book behind him: I had scored minus one.

Some public events are fractionally less humiliating than others, but because the author of books is an obvious eccentric he attracts the attentions of other obvious eccentrics. 'I have been reading your book on Lytton Strachey', one fan wrote to me after my biography was published, 'and I do think you have done a service to humanity in general by showing how far degradation can go ... one can only be truly thankful that one never met him ... he set the worst possible example. Homosexuality is not being "civilized" or "rational". It is the filthiest trick ever devised by man: it is anti-social, it often leads to cancer.'

This is a fairly representative reader's approach; but from professionals too one can receive bizarre treatment. Wishing to know whether a certain well-known manuscript library in America held any documents I needed for a book, I wrote to enquire – and almost at once received no answer. After a tactful interval of three months I wrote again. This time the answer was swift and co-operative. Yes, the librarian replied, from the catalogue it did appear they had one unspecified item that might be useful. I promptly wrote offering to pay whatever was the regular fee, and eventually was rewarded by the arrival of a luxurious folder complete with a covering letter explaining that, on reconsideration, since only one item was involved, the library had decided to waive its usual charges. A warm glow of gratitude invaded me as I opened the folder – only to find within, beautifully copied and immaculately presented, my own original unanswered letter stamped with a warning that I did not have copyright permission

---

customer was attempting to return to you. As a tradesman this has happened to me and I can appreciate your courage and skill.

'I have removed the dustjacket for two reasons. As I store them in with my carcases they have a slight taint and also I am told that without the jacket it will be harder to sell.

'Mrs Ellerbeck and myself intend to look for more of your writings whenever Mr Timpsons brings in his newspapers. Meanwhile good luck to you. Yours truly George Ellerbeck.'

to quote it. The methods of the Harvard School of Business had struck again.

Such methods accompany one's research. Letters in *The Listener* and *New Statesman* asking for information concerning Augustus John, about whom I am writing a book, elicited en masse three replies. All three began with a brief paragraph stating that about Augustus John they could tell me nothing. They then came to the meat of the matter. One, from a septuagenarian clergyman exiled in France, asked if I were that 'nice-looking curly-haired boy' he had known in Winchester in 1912 – he had often wondered what had happened to me. Another, from a single woman in Sevenoaks, explained that she knew what a hard time authors were having these days and was therefore enclosing a list of valuable coins – farthings and the like. Finally there was the man whose sister (now dead) had once eaten in the same restaurant as John, though not, he volunteered, at the same time. In return for this advice he requested that I recommend him to my publisher as an indexer, his chief qualification being that he was remotely descended from Sheridan who, if he might venture a literary judgment, was a far better subject for a biography than John.

Such reactions were not confined to Britain. In America, where I enjoyed a book tour of nationwide secrecy, a similar letter appearing in the *New York Review of Books* and *The New York Times Book Review* provoked two answers. 'I have nothing to offer in the way of Augustus John', the first read. 'I'm certainly not Swiss, nor American, nor British. I don't know if you are familiar with the Swiss Germans. If you are perhaps you'll appreciate this little verse I composed in one of my more lucid moments:

Montreal I surely miss
From Zurich though I'll never flee
For today I met a Swiss
Who doffed his hat and spoke to me.'

The second reply was wholly in prose. It had arrived in New York from Surbiton in Surrey via the American Embassy in Monrovia – 'a long way' the writer guessed. It comprised an offer of help. In Surbiton public library there rested a copy of John's autobiography *Chiaroscuro* published by Jonathan Cape and still in print. From this my correspondent could 'scribble out some notes. We had a few days of summer here. Now back to winter.' At which this good woman of Surbiton concluded: '*Now get that book going!*'

It would be wrong to make fun of such people. They are our fans. Together with a platoon or two of thesis-maddened graduates, they constitute our volunteer army of supporters, depleted certainly, but not yet wholly extinct.

Although there is plenty of neglect, there is little failure. Either royalties or prestige, these are the choices. You will not find best-sellers prominent within the reference books of modern literature: this is their neglect. You will find books that are long out of print by authors who have long ceased to write: that is their success. Cyril Connolly's ten-year test has been ploughed up to form just part of a fallow period. The dole, the accumulating rejection slips – these contribute to that Puritan hell we must experience to qualify for entry, posthumous if need be, into the heavenly pantheon of literature. Our fantasies, our obsessions, have become our sweetmeats.

But sweetmeats are for peacetime, and the time is now for war. Nineteen hundred and seventy-two has been declared by Unesco as 'International Book Year'. In America and throughout Europe great fairs and junketings of all sorts are taking place, and in Britain we have a first British National Book Week in November. To help us celebrate and promote this portentous event, our controversial leader, Lord Eccles, has contributed the sum of nothing – a kind of parting gift. With this in the bank, added to plenty of zeal and ingenuity, the National Book League is working round the clock manufacturing 'buttons and the like'; they are standing by for 'calls for advice and help'; they plan, I can reveal, a revolutionary happening, set to music, underneath Hungerford Bridge; they are fully determined to give away, free of charge, incomplete books in order, they admit, 'to provoke the casual reader'. In Northern Ireland there is to be a bus; and at Gillingham an Aladdin's Cave, with wine.

All this is admirable: but should it stop there? I suggest that we should seek to reach back to the wartime state of affairs that existed in my aunt's house thirty years ago. Of course we can no longer count on a captive audience of Germans, Italians or even Japanese. We have only ourselves. We stand, as in 1940, alone and should employ similar tactics. We must sell on the beaches, in the fields and streets; we must sell in the hills; we must never remainder. My aunt's van, and hundreds like it, should once more patrol the avenues of Berkshire, move in convoy through the Home Counties and even farther. That spirit which fired the Victorian missionaries in Africa one hundred years ago should now fill our publishers' travellers pushing forward to the un-lettered Akenfields of Britain and abroad.

It is well known that, on the completion of his book, an author's fancy lightly turns to thoughts of sales – some publishers wish it would do so earlier. If we are to come anywhere near his expectations we must revolutionize our methods of distribution. It is all right for Hatchards or John Sandoe, for Dillons, Heywood Hill, Blackwells or Heffers to specialize among their customers in readers. The big stores must think differently. With all cynicism and sincerity I recommend them to advertise books as multipurpose objects – the shy girl's shield in the train, the short man's leg-up, the snob's affidavit. These objects must be sold, as Jilly Cooper might easily say, by book or by crook. Why should a public that apparently cannot tell the difference between Stork margarine and butter know the difference between a book and anything else? We should rewrite our epigrams. Logan Pearsall Smith's 'People say that life's the thing, but I prefer reading' must be revised to 'We're only here for the books!' The country must go to work on a book – we have the syllables to give them the slogans. *The Times*, surely, had the right idea when to an article on import duty it gave the title: 'Free Intercourse in Books'.

If the currency is silliness, buy, grow rich, then sell. It cannot be difficult to spread a sense of wholesome shame among those who inhabit a naked house, a house divested of books. To build houses without bookshelves should require unobtainable planning permission. If the reason why books do not sell is that they are not instant, then they must be made new, bright and absolutely instant – at once. For as even Paul Hamlyn showed us, the only way of getting rid of large quantities of books is to pretend that they are not books (in the narrow sense of reading matter) at all. Our real customer, our customer of the future, is the non-reader. He is not scarce. It is no more part of the bookseller's business to consider the reading of his wares than it is that of a salesman at the Bed Centre to investigate the use to which his client puts her purchase. Both, unless invited, are intrusions.

But where books actually exist anything may happen. They are like time bombs, and we should plant them everywhere. Who knows that one rainy day when the television fails, the radio collapses, the telephone lines are down, all transport hit by strikes and the country finally comes to a standstill, that someone, somewhere, will not at last pick up a book, and open it?

Censorship

Members of Parliament today have exclusive access to a curious library. No volume is entitled to rest upon its shelves that is not obscene, and whose obscenity has not been guaranteed by a Court of Law.

In this fact lies much of the philosophy of censorship, now again called into question by the apparently radical recommendations of the sub-committee reporting to the Arts Council. For throughout history it has been the potential readership of a book, not its intrinsic merits, that has determined its fate. All those, the argument runs, who for reasons of tender age, feebleness of mind or lack of education are semi-literate, will be depraved by indecorous literature, and will be incited to emulate the anti-social behaviour of the characters about whom they read. But Members of Parliament are too sophisticated, in the truest sense of that word, to be corrupted, or further corrupted, by obscene writing, and may read their fill. The continuance of a censorship system will, therefore, always stand as a rebuke to our standards of popular education, of which, ironically, books are seen to be the chief agent.

Donald Thomas's history of literary censorship in England from the fifteenth century to the present day is a serious and largely entertaining book.* For the most part he has steered a successful course between the aridity of legal history and the evasiveness of grand generalizations about the 'spirit of the age'. His narrative is crammed with facts, statistics and law. But it is enlivened, too, by the many exploits of those often eccentric extremists who campaigned for and against various forms of censorship; by some interesting pictures not always

* *A Long Time Burning* by Donald Thomas.

strictly relevant to the text, and by the appendix two hundred pages long containing illustrative material. Although we may read here 'The Story of Sinful Sally' and 'Here lies John Penis', the scholarship, high price, small print and lack of paragraphs will prevent this book ever becoming private Parliamentary reading.

As Mr Thomas makes clear, the type of writing we censor alters from century to century according to what we believe will threaten the political or social stability of the country. 'The nature of political censorship at any given time,' he writes, 'depends on the censor's answer to the simple question, "What are you afraid of?"' Today we no longer punish blasphemy or sedition because we do not fear atheism or expect civil war.

But it is a fallacy to suppose that censorship is in decline. 'D' notices and the Official Secrets Act testify to our growing sense of insecurity in international affairs; we live, self-consciously, under extraordinarily severe libel laws; the Race Relations Act of 1965 makes racist literature a criminal offence; and even the Prices and Incomes Act of 1966 promises fines of up to £500 for writings that encourage workers to strike.

Perhaps the greatest change has been in the apparatus of censorship. If we wish to communicate ideas on any wide scale, we have to rely on editors, publishers, and the producers and controllers of radio and television, who must approve the type of dissent we express. The technology of the twentieth century enables really unfashionable or unnewsworthy opinions to be silenced by the most effective means of all – by ignoring them.

Mr Thomas is especially stimulating – I do not use the word pejoratively – on the topic of pornography, for which he has a certain fondness. Pornography, he argues, is anarchic and will be suppressed in one form or another by all governments. Since it thrives on suppression, it is assured of a long life. Nowadays, its main function is to ridicule the comic yet sinister puritanism of mental hygiene made popular by D. H. Lawrence, and the whole school of thought which insists that literature should be morally edifying. 'It is the recognition of something more than the darker side of human nature that while the propagandist of the new order prophesies that the heavens shall declare the glory of man, he hears at his shoulder a derisive chuckle.'

One objection to pornography is surely that, because it is fundamentally a fantasy fiction, it may increase the amount of otherwise avoidable suffering. Possibly because this is not scientifically demonstrable, Mr Thomas never really considers the contagious unhappiness of pornography.

Unlike the Arts Council committee C. H. Rolph is by no means in favour of abolishing censorship altogether, and might well maintain it for some of the pornography so vigorously championed by Mr Thomas. His book* is a journalistic and much slighter work, though it covers some of the same historical ground. By giving us summaries of a select number of court cases, some of them *causes célèbres*, others of legal significance, he traces the development of the obscenity laws up to their present state of well-intentioned confusion, and patiently exposes the rather tortuous logic responsible for this confusion.

But he is not content with the facile job of uncovering legal discrepancies, and goes on to suggest what could, and could not, be done to rationalize the present system. His proposals seem sensible and liberal, but he finally confesses himself to be in 'a hopelessly equivocal state of mind'. For the increase in permissiveness, of which the easing of our literary censorship is a part and of which censorship is a part and of which, intellectually, Mr Rolph approves, has brought about an assault on our privacy that he finds emotionally very disturbing.

The difficulty of reconciling literature with any kind of censorship is that, by their very nature, they are opposed. Censorship is a social phenomenon, concerned with the reaction produced by any piece of writing on a significant number of people. Literature is an individual matter, and should be valued not for its moral or educative influences, but simply for what it is. To justify or condemn good writing for its uses is about as narrow as to appreciate an oak tree for the amount of firewood it will produce.

In a reasonably civilized environment, the censorship laws should not greatly hamper the free flow of literature, because it

* *Books in the Dock* by C. H. Rolph. Foreword by John Mortimer.

is involved with the whole human condition and not just the condition of the state.

How small, of all that human hearts endure,
That part which laws or kings can cause or cure.

Fallen Men

The theme that Mr John Gross has chosen for his book is apparently simple and unexceptional.* Beginning in 1802 with the launching of the *Edinburgh Review*, the first periodical to emerge 'as a really powerful institution, a major social force', he traces some of the major changes that have taken place in the world of that now extinct specimen, 'the man of letters'.

In the last 150 years the literary scene has altered out of all recognition. Writers are no longer the romantic creatures they once were. On how many occasions have we all heard some tired businessman declare that he too would write a book some day, once he had time to spare from more important affairs. Not everyone can play the piano, or paint (except, of course, abstract painting); but there is no one who cannot take up his Biro, and write. While the level of literacy remained low, writing was magic. The paradox is that as the writer's potential audience has risen, so his prestige within the community has sunk. Once authorship was a vocation; now it is part of industry, of exports.

This change in the public's attitude to authors was already detectable in late Victorian times. When, in 1883, Trollope revealed in his splendidly honest autobiography that he laboured at his novels with businesslike efficiency, readers were appalled and ceased to buy his books. The status of writers in society has never recovered.

But Mr Gross is not primarily interested in status. His book examines not society's opinion of its authors but certain authors' attitude to society, to social change, and the cultural ideas with which they sought to permeate society. Whether these ideas were

* *The Rise and Fall of the Man of Letters* by John Gross.

put into general effect, whether they were ever heard or understood except by a small section of other writers, seems unimpor-
tant. The world of the literati is a small enclosed place, and its
frontiers with the actual world closely guarded. They do not even
speak the same language.

Within this private community Mr Gross is a most skilful and
engaging guide. He discusses those magazines from the *Edinburgh
Review* to *Scrutiny* that provide examples of the taste of the day;
he follows the development of literary criticism from the didactic
tone of the early Victorians to the more relaxed age of what
H. L. Mencken called 'beautiful letters', and eventually to the rise
of English studies in the university curriculum. He does not
pretend to deal with literature, but with the literary climate 'in
which creative writers could work to the best advantage'. For this
reason we are introduced to Arnold the critic, not the poet;
to Carlyle the prophet, not the letter-writer; to the T. S. Eliot
who edited *The Criterion*, not the man who wrote *The Waste
Land*.

To chart the backwaters of literature, and to examine, through
the lives and work of journalists, editors, teachers and inter-
preters, the shaping and the eventual disintegration of nineteenth-
century culture, may seem a pretty thankless task. But Mr Gross
has a strong sense of individual life, and his brief critical and
biographical studies are amazingly complete. The narrative is
always brisk and stimulating, and carries his daunting accumulation of knowledge very lightly. As a critic he is severe but genial,
fair-minded but forthright, very conscious of pitfalls that might
be pointed to by other critics.

Although he successfully avoids the temptation to oversimplify,
or to stick labels on people, his theme demands some concessions
to classification, to the treatment of writers as portents or fugle-
men. Carlyle's style, for example, with its half-humorous, half-
poetic fascination is denuded of all originality when explained by
the fact that 'unprecedented social realities called for new modes of
speech'.

Mr Gross is at his best when dealing with individual critics. He
subjects some of Dr Leavis's work to a vigorous commonsense
analysis that it is ill-suited to sustain; and his brief portrait of

Edmund Gosse makes one hope he will write the new biography of Gosse that he rightly says is needed.

Contrasting the literary scene of the 1920s with that of the 1930s, Mr Gross is puzzled that it should have been so apolitical. Critics one hundred years from now may well be astonished at our obsession with the sociological aspects of literature. For it is not what writing can give to the community but what one person's experiences within that community can give to literature that is important. Nor is it the task of the writer to fix the destiny of kingdoms but to see what he personally may achieve. The literary scene may certainly act as a catalyst to some writers, but it is often no more than a place where people who have abandoned the isolated struggle to realize their full potential land up.

One of Mr Gross's aims is to show the role of literature in public life. But he also knows that literature is fundamentally inegalitarian. The public therefore do not enter his book; they have no place there except indirectly via those writers who may be thought of as the representative spokesmen of their day, or as embodying standards that were later to be popularly upheld. Those who are simply for all time, such as Emily Brontë (chronologically a Victorian, though in no other respect), do not appear at all. *Wuthering Heights* is not a novel of social change; 'The Visionary' not a poem that relies in any way on the literary scene of the day.

Mr Gross has succeeded in giving us a memorable panorama of the literary background since the beginning of the last century. But his book is a strangely provoking one. There is hardly a page which is not enjoyable and acute, but because his terms are never precisely defined one is never exactly sure of where he is heading. What, for example, is a creative as opposed to a near-creative writer? Can a critic, historian or biographer as well as a novelist or poet qualify for creativity? What, above all, is or are English studies, to which Mr Gross finally directs us?

On this topic he is disarmingly frank. Neither he, it appears, nor anyone else knows, for 'the fundamental uncertainties about what the subject is, and how it should be taught, have not by any means been dispelled by the increase in academic numbers or by advances in scholarship'. Obviously, he adds, the very heart of the subject is research. But 'as for purely literary research, nobody quite knows what it means'.

The first qualification of a good critic, according to Mr Gross, 'will always be an interest in literature for what it is, rather than for the ends which it can be made to serve. But the second qualification, no less essential, will be a commitment to the life which lies beyond literature, by which it must finally be judged.' Mr Gross appears to have both these qualifications in a high degree. But what does he mean by 'life'? Not, surely, a sense of community but of emotional life. This is what his hero Dr Johnson possessed above all other qualities. But what Johnson understood by life is precisely what has ebbed out of modern criticism before the tide of comparative literature.

For Mr Gross literature is an enjoyment, not a discipline, and his criticism is unacademic in the best sense. There are many rousing, heart-warming passages in his book which should ensure that, although it so accurately mirrors the age in which it has been written, it will survive well into other ages.

PLR

(1) Oh Lord, Miss Lee!

Authors are angry now. The patience, the politeness of years has been exhausted. In the history of modern literature their mood is unique, and the sort of action that they are now being forced to take is without precedent. Most of them feel that they have been betrayed. For this they blame, personally, Miss Jennie Lee.

It is a story of frustration and misfortune, going back as far as the year 1951. For it was in this year that the novelist John Brophy proposed a scheme whereby each reader would pay a borrowing fee of one penny for every volume taken out of a public library, this fee (after certain deductions for administration) to go wholly to the author. 'Brophy's Penny', as the scheme became called, represented the first practical attempt to ease a situation that had become so serious that it threatened the end of professional authorship as we have known it in the past. It also signalled the beginning of an extraordinary campaign.

Up to then, authors and librarians had been natural allies. The authors' best hope of success lay in getting the librarians' co-operation. But their predicament was so critical and, as time passed, grew so much worse, that they rounded on the librarians for not giving them more positive support. This was unjust, and aroused much antagonism. Hard things were said. Sir Michael Sadleir proclaimed that 'free libraries are living off the charity of authors', and several other writers were tempted into denigrating the whole race of librarians.

Although not fully alive to the poverty authors were suffering, most librarians had not been indifferent. Now their attitude stiffened. Their reaction to all Public Lending Right schemes tended to be instantaneous, automatic, hostile. After all, why should they expose themselves to further insults? Why should they show eagerness to discuss a matter that seemed to involve only more work for them, and more money only for the people who had abused them? A great deal of the authors' rancour came from their impotence. Librarians they could wound and be wounded by. The battle appeared real, and was fought at times with some of the bitterness of a civil war. But the Government, their real enemy, they could not touch. And the Government ignored them.

Nevertheless between 1951 and 1964, almost wholly under the direction of the Society of Authors, a tremendous amount of constructive work was done. Memoranda, pamphlets, debates, newspaper articles, radio programmes and lectures poured out in an apparently endless flow. In February, 1959, the Roberts Report into the structure of the library system was published. This yielded many valuable statistics, and, armed with these, Sir Alan Herbert charged into battle on behalf of the authors.

The Herbert Memorandum, published in March 1960, reviewed the whole subject anew, listing the difficulties, summarizing the authors' case, and proposing what action might be taken. The impact on public opinion was considerable, and as a result two Public Lending Right Bills were drafted. The second of these Bills – modified from the first – was presented to the House of Commons on 23 November 1960. It was talked out on 9 December and again on 10 March 1961.

Still the pressure was kept up. Deputations, meetings, booklets and a Motion on the Order Paper in the House of Commons led to the sudden introduction by the Conservative Government, on 24 June 1964, of the Public Library and Museums Bill. Time was extremely short, but David James, the member of Parliament for Brighton, immediately put forward in the House certain amendments designed, *inter alia*, to add Public Lending Right to the permitted library charges, and provide for its administration. Supported by a tiny band of Conservatives, and no Labour member at all, David James took every form of action open to him. The result was – nothing. When the Bill became an Act of Parliament on 31 July 1964, there was no mention in it of Public Lending Right.

Summing up the total achievement after thirteen years of vigorous crusading, Sir Alan Herbert announced: 'We have won no medals. I have done myself much material damage by the time and toil that I have, like others, given to the cause. But I do not regret it. Most men now know what we want and why; some at least feel guilty about it, and I believe the heart of the people is with us. But in Whitehall, in Parliament, we have got nowhere, and I have nothing but frustration to report.'

In the autumn of 1964 the Labour Government was returned to power. Sir Alan Herbert lost no time in drawing their attention to the militant mood of authors. In a lecture, delivered to the Royal Society of Literature on 10 December, he said: 'The word "Lecture" suggests a mood of philosophic calm, the contented, contemplative talk of the cloister. I feel neither contented nor calm. For more than five years, the Committee of Authors and Publishers . . . have been using sweet reason and balanced argument. After more than five years we have nothing whatever to show, except a nice letter from the last Prime Minister [Sir Alec Douglas Home] . . . Personally, I am tired of sweet reason. We are entitled now, I feel, to anger – and, if possible, action. Action, alas, is difficult, authors cannot strike, they can only suffer and swear.'

But, at this very moment, when the troughs of pessimism were deepest, we were suddenly lifted clear of them by Hurricane Jennie Lee. Indignation gave way to fresh optimism; the swearing died away; all hopes revived. Sir Alan Herbert had received another 'nice letter', this one from Jennie Lee herself, who was later appointed Joint Parliamentary Secretary of the Ministry of Education and Science. It was an impressive title, and she made an impressive speech. 'It is very much the business of an enlightened Government,' she declared, 'to see that he [the artist] does not die from discouragement.'

Miss Lee had been asked to survey Government activity in the field of the arts and amenities, excluding sport. The Government, she claimed, wanted to establish a more coherent, imaginative and generous attitude to the arts in Great Britain. 'Who will help us now?' Sir Alan Herbert had cried. Miss Lee had answered him – or so it seemed.

A Policy for the Arts, a white paper published in the spring of 1965, promised that the question of Public Lending Right would be examined 'in consultation with the interested parties'. Soon afterwards, Miss Lee received deputations from the Society of Authors and the Publishers Association. At both these meetings she affirmed her belief in the essential justice of PLR and welcomed any scheme that would not involve charging the borrower in order to preserve the freedom of the Public Library Service. She was believed. On the promise of what she had said the new Literature Panel of the Arts Council set up a working party, intended to represent all the interests concerned, which began studying the whole subject again, in order to make recommendations that would satisfy Miss Lee's requirements.

While this work was being done, Miss Lee continued to make encouraging noises in and out of the House of Commons. The matter was receiving serious attention by the Government, she had told Lord Francis-Williams. He had no reason to suspect she might be joking.

In the summer of 1965 came the most encouraging sign of all. It was then that Miss Lee told the Performing Right Society; 'I think you are doing a wonderful job . . . I am hard at work at a similar scheme for authors.' This was the first time the comparison had been officially admitted. It looked like a great advance.

No wonder, then, that publishers, authors and booksellers fêted her. She was to be seen at concerts, at fashionable art exhibitions, at new bookshops, smiling confidently. 'In spite of pressure of affairs', she even managed to keep an engagement to attend an informal meeting of the Independent Publishers Group on 29 June 1966, when she was presented with a memorandum on Public Lending Right. No one protested, when Charles Skilton, in his introductory speech, declared that 'she had created an image of a passionately involved Minister of the Arts, and it was as such that they welcomed her'.

In this disguise, she was welcomed everywhere. 'If I had my way, all Ministers would be women,' growled Mr. J. B. Priestley. It was here that she at last made what was obviously intended to be a major speeech on the prospects of PLR legislation, and as such it deserves what she herself would call 'careful study'. She was, she said, a bookworm – or at least she supposed she was. Books were her first love. In office, her task was to provide 'more living room' to all the arts and artists. 'But I do confess that, for me, books are the magic. They are the beginning.'

Such sentiments led her back to tales of misty nostalgia. She recalled her youth in a mining village of Scotland, with its library near the railway crossing. She recalled Dunfermline – it cost twopence on a bus to get there. The library at Edinburgh University, she added, meant nothing to her – in comparison, that was, with the Carnegie Library in Dunfermline. She spoke of children generally and of deprived ones in particular. The local library, she stated, ought to be a child's home from home. Many libraries were now becoming 'art centres'. She welcomed this. It rejoiced her heart to see 'lively librarians' who could act host to the whole cultural, artistic and intellectual community. It was what she liked to call 'democracy in depth'. At the Ministry they were 'doing their little bit' to help. They had sent out some circulars 'expressing the hope' that everything would be all right.

Everything would be all right, presumably, one day. But perhaps the most difficult thing to get right, she admitted, was PLR ... 'If anyone thinks it is easy, he knows nothing about it.' But they *must* find a means of being fair to the author. If they did so, the real architect of the legislation would be Lord Goodman who, with his committee, had had a great deal of work and worry. But she wished to say to all who wrote, published, criticized, sold – and to the few who bought – books, that it was far from being a neglected side of the work of herself and her colleagues. 'I can assure you that I will be proud indeed if, even in the most minor respect, I can be associated with this type of legislation, which will encourage something which I regard as the real potential of this country.'

Lord Goodman was present at this lunch. In spite of knowing a great deal about PLR, he didn't think that putting it into effect should prove especially difficult. His reply was short. The necessary legislation would be achieved, he said, if it had the support of the Government.

The Arts Council report on PLR was ready by April 1967. It was sent to Miss Lee, who returned it asking for certain revisions that, in essence, consisted of shortening it from forty-four to thirty pages. In its revised form it was sent back to her in October 1967. Her ingenuity was evidently now at an end. So she sat on it, and continued to sit on it, *and is still sitting on it now* in February 1969.

Throughout 1968 she had often been questioned as to what she was doing. On 21 March she told Mr Paul Channon, her opposite number in the Conservative Party, that the report was being carefully studied – and this became for a long time her way of describing her sitting position. Mr Channon again asked whether she would *please try* to come to some conclusion about it in the near future. There was no laughter in the House, no uproar, when she declared: 'I am most anxious to come to a conclusion that would meet the legitimate claims of the authors . . .' With a credulity that now seems ridiculously excessive, many of us still persisted in believing her.

The following month, on 13 April, Mr Ben Whitaker asked her if she would introduce legislation to enable PLR to be financed by means of a lottery. Miss Lee said she had nothing to add to her earlier reply.

She has had nothing to add over the last nine months, except the magic and meaningless word 'discussion' behind which she now hides. It has been a completely sterile period. In the nicest possible manner, she had nothing to add at the Brighton Conference on 24 September. 'I know,' she was pleased to say, 'that some of you have been bothered about the lending right pamphlet. . . . The pamphlet was sent out as a basis for discussion, and you would be . . . helping me, if you read it with the greatest care and if you enter into the dialogue. Obviously we have got to see that we do more justice to our authors than we have done in the past.'

To this nothing, Miss Lee added a further nothing in a letter dated 8 November, and sent to Miss Elizabeth Barber, the General Secretary of the Society of Authors. 'What I said at the conference was that there was not at the present time a Government commitment to the scheme proposed by the Arts Council. This is a fact. . . . I went on to say that the Arts Council has carried out its duty in making recommendations and publishing a discussion pamphlet. What the Government now wants is the reactions of all interested concerned people . . . I have never made any secret of my support in principle towards the scheme of library royalties but a very considerable sum of money is involved and there are many differing views on the subject. Certainly at the present time it will be most difficult to implement the scheme but meanwhile I hope that discussions will proceed . . .'

So, after being encouraged to believe that positive action was to be taken in the near future to remedy an admitted injustice, we have been advised to return to the contented, contemplative talk of the cloister, to sweet reason and balanced argument, to where it all started long, long ago.

I stand amazed at the impertinence of this suggestion.

Who will help us *now*? Mr Paul Channon, Miss Lee's opposite number, certainly made a very splendid speech during the Public Libraries and Museums Bill debate. But it is not so difficult to speak when you do not have the power to act. Everyone agrees we should be helped. Sir Alec Douglas Home was going to help us once. Does he remember, I wonder, writing to Sir Alan Herbert promising to get PLR considered by Edward Heath 'who is designing our future policy'? That was in November 1964. We have yet to hear from him or from Heath.

In her last public utterance on this subject, Miss Lee has said that she knows some of us are bothered about PLR. But she is wrong. We are not bothered. We are exasperated; we are sickened. The anger that was dammed up and falsely diverted over four years ago has now swept back with redoubled force. It is almost impossible adequately to convey the digust that is felt for you, Miss Lee, without some drastic change in the law of libel. You tell us that the time has come for discussion. We tell you that the time for discussion is past. My desk is piled high with records of all the useless discussions that have gone on now for almost twenty years. The Arts Council report was produced *as the result of discussions* between all the interested parties except the librarians, who declined to join them. But they have discussed the report since it came out. The only person who has discussed nothing is yourself. We have listened for something constructive from you, we have strained our ears against the vacuity of your utterances.

For us there is nothing left to say. We have thought of the librarians' and of Parliament's objections, we have thought of everything, and we have grown hoarse speaking about it. We decline absolutely to discuss it further for your entertainment. Everything that can be said by us, has been said, and is available in print. The time has now come for abuse, for bloody-mindedness. That is the only new authentic contribution left for us to make. You don't respond to lobbying; you respond to bad manners – these are what you inspire; these are what you, and others like you, have made the stuff of politics. Very well: you shall have them. But must we really throw ourselves in front of race horses, chain ourselves to library railings, make damn nuisances of ourselves, flood the press with oft-told grievances till the public cries out with the sheer boredom of it all and begs you to do something so that they can enjoy a little peace? Is this what you think of as a 'lively' cultural scene?

We have flattered you (my God! how we have flattered you!) and you have not smiled on us; we have spoken well of you, even behind your back, and you have merely turned away from us; we have believed you, and you have misled us. Did you not say it was the job of your Government to see that the artist does not die from discouragement? Miss Lee, this country's authors *are* dying, slowly, painfully, from *your* discouragement. You are the Minister with special responsibilities for the arts. Have you exercised those responsibilities?

We wonder if you know the facts about us. We know the facts about you. You hit the headlines when you deferred your pay rise, temporarily continuing to receive five thousand pounds instead of the full six thousand three hundred and seventy-five pounds a year due to you. We were reported on the back pages when, in 1966, Richard Findlater's pamphlet *The Book Writers: Who Are They?* came out, revealing the income of our authors. Do you know what our authors are worth, Miss Lee? Statistics can make dull reading – these were eloquent. According to an independent survey carried out by Research Services Ltd, only one author in six earns more than £1000 a year from his books, one in ten between £500 and £1000, and the remainder very much less – many only thirty shillings a week. If books are, as you said, the beginning, after four years in office you have not yet begun.

Many have congratulated you in the past on persuading Parliament to increase the amount given to the arts. Your ears ring with their applause, so that you cannot hear perhaps a note of protest. But if you have expected gratitude, you may be bewildered by the suspicion that, among artists themselves, you are, at best, a laughing-stock. You had thought yourself, possibly, the great friend and patron of the artist, and it is open to you to reflect that all patrons attract bad treatment. Is not a patron, Miss Lee, someone who looks with animation upon men struggling in the water, and hails them with words of encouragement? But we are not waving, we are drowning – and your fulsome ovations embarrass us.

The damage you inflict is more serious than you can know. We were prepared to enter into your crackpot schemes. We would not have objected to your putting our libraries on ice and to our wearing coloured hats as we skated round the shelves for the greater gaiety of the populace – if it had got us anywhere. But art is not the community jamboree of your fancy, Miss Lee, it is often a lonely occupation, and artists are mostly isolated people, working by themselves. They need the rhythm and mood of the age behind them if they are to produce their best work. In the case of authors, that rhythm and mood is set against them. Your central failure to do anything about this may actually endanger the quality of our literature.

You have said, Miss Lee, that the object towards which you are working is the establishment of a great open university in this country. We are your protesting students. You think because we are few in number that we cannot influence people. You are wrong. We will use radio, television, and every paper in the country. At the sound of your name the rafters will ring with derisive laughter, as at the word 'mother-in-law' in a music hall. You may think we cannot strike. But we can create the essential conditions of a strike, we can create an intolerable situation that *everyone* wants to be rid of. You think we are without real power. But again you are wrong. The publishers have power where we have not, and they are our allies. The National Union of Journalists is composed of writers also, remember. Our books are made

by printers – printers who print *Hansard* for you. They, too, are
our natural friends.

This is the opening shot of a war that is about to break on your
head, Miss Lee. There is time, still, to avoid total hostilities, if you
act quickly. But we cannot delay long. How long did you think
we would wait? Oh Lord, Miss Lee, how long?

(2) Oh Dear, Lord Eccles

Dear Lord Eccles,
             This is the second open letter of which you have
been recipient – some would say victim – in the last two months.
On 7 July 1970 in the *Evening Standard*, Simon Jenkins wrote to
inform you that, in your new post as Minister for the Arts, you
had two tasks of top priority. These were: first, 'to get money out
of the Treasury'; and secondly, 'to get the public lending right
scheme for authors off the ground providing them with some
revenue from the use of their books in public libraries. This
injustice,' he added, 'has gone on long enough and need continue
not a minute longer.'

Mr Jenkins had no doubt that, in both these jobs, you would be
successful. It is a pleasant prospect. When you achieve the first,
you will be able to establish, without difficulty or delay, a tax-
free system such as writers now enjoy in Eire. The beauty of this
scheme is its administrative simplicity; its justification, the
encouragement of creative work which, in the present climate, is
dangerously undernourished.

When you are successful in setting up a practical PLR scheme
you will have remedied an ancient grievance of which your pre-
decessor, Jennie Lee, often spoke, but which remains, and will
always remain, a blot on her record. To judge from press comment, nothing became her office like her leaving of it. Almost at
once, as if by magic, she was translated into a Baroness; and she
annihilated those who had criticized her for having no sense of
humour by announcing that she intended to become a writer. It

was a spirited performance. The papers were full of compliments, both generous and bewildered. Despite her having obtained a personal swing against her at the General Election of roughly three times the national average, Lord Goodman felt able to celebrate her as 'not a great intellect', a woman who could claim to have 'no profound knowledge of the arts', yet one who had made 'no enemies and countless friends'.

Much of this fanfare, ostensibly addressed to Miss Lee, was in fact directed to you, Lord Eccles. People were anxious that money should continue to flow towards the arts. 'It is the hope of the Writers Guild of Great Britain,' pontificated its President, Carl Foreman, 'that Miss Lee's successor, who comes to his new post with so much to recommend him, will continue along the fruitful lines already established.' This letter appeared in *The Times* above another from an American mouth organist who proposed attaching Miss Lee to you as a 'roving ambassador for the arts'.

Over the past few years, while the Conservatives were in opposition, we argued our case to the sympathetic Shadow Minister for the Arts, Paul Channon, who, in due course, turned out to have been, in disguise, a Parliamentary Secretary for Housing and Local Government. Your appointment was warmly welcomed – as the *Guardian* put it 'first because the job has survived, and secondly because Lord Eccles has got it'. And *The Bookseller* commented that everyone who had heard you speak at book trade functions 'will have no doubt that this is an appointment full of promise for the future'.

Was I alone in feeling some nervousness at your appointment? I don't think so. Beneath the forced-up euphoria one can detect a degree of uncertainty. People pointed to the Prime Minister's tendency to play the organ, and your own habit, between spells in office, of taking up your pen to write moral autobiographies. These seemed to me insufficient grounds for confidence. I based my doubts upon the evidence of your past record.

This record, in connection with PLR, is not encouraging. In the summer of 1960, when you were Minister of Education, you invited a deputation led by Sir Alan Herbert to go and see you. I must tell you, Lord Eccles, that they did not know why they had been invited, that when they came out they stood about and wondered. You had had nothing to offer them – saving the ritual sympathy politicians in office so lavishly distribute to those in need. You warmly assured Sir Alan Herbert that the Government could do nothing to help; you warned him that charging the borrower – a measure which at that stage was not being advocated – was out of the question; and you urged him to contact the representatives of the local authorities, with whom, you emphasized, you had no influence whatsoever. You were extremely friendly. Tea was drunk in cups, and you volunteered the information that you were preparing a Public Library Bill to which amendments could be made. That, of course, was in 1960. The deputation did not see the Bill till 1964: and much good it did them.

While you were out of office you wrote small books. In one of these, *Life and Politics* (1967), which argues that our problems in this country are moral, not economic ones, you wrote: 'Such small pockets of poverty as remain in Britain will be cleared within a few years.' This, too, is a pleasant prospect. But had you read, I wonder, Richard Findlater's pamphlet for the Society of Authors, *The Book Writers: Who Are They?* It was published the year before your book; it is still in print; and it is more relevant to the writer's predicament now than ever. These are your New Poor, Lord Eccles: they are your responsibility now; their economic problems comprise your moral problem.

Last year (1969) when Jennie Lee was under attack for not yet having implemented a PLR scheme, you were one of the first to gallop up to her defence. I have just re-read what you wrote then. It is a curious piece of dialectics. You exonerate Miss Lee from having put into practice a scheme that, in all the details you enumerate, had never even been submitted to her. Readers of your statement were overcome by much the same bewilderment as Sir Alan Herbert's deputation nine years earlier. What trickery was this, Lord Eccles, to raise up a PLR scheme of your own fantasy, and demolish it with such relish? A close reading seemed to suggest that you were in some state of confusion, not to say ignorance, as to what was going on. You had been sent shortly beforehand a synopsis of the actual PLR project, yet you had seen fit, without reading a word of this, to enter the debate. It was a colossal impertinence. Had anyone been taken in, he could have been seriously misled as to the facts. But when these facts were pointed out to you by Elizabeth Barber, you fell strangely quiet. Did you blush, I wonder? Did you apologize? You did not.

But your intervention displayed more than eccentricity; it showed a genuine flair for prejudice. No one but an author, you wrote, 'with his head in the clouds', would imagine that the Minister with responsibility for the arts had in fact the responsibility we attributed to her. The voting of money, you pointed out, was a Cabinet decision. Could you really have thought we did not realize that? The real question is who, if not the Minister for the arts, has the responsibility, Lord Eccles, for persuading the Cabinet? It is now you who have this moral responsibility – the Cabinet's responsibility is merely economic. And the real decisions, as you have reminded us, are moral ones.

No one would deny that there are complexities involved. The most equitable scheme – that of paying the author a royalty every time his book is borrowed – is as yet perhaps the least practical to administer. The easiest to administer – that of paying the author an extra royalty every time a public library buys a copy of his book – is less equitable, ignoring as it does all those authors, many of them old, whose books are out of print but still read in libraries throughout the country.

Very early in October, just hours before the three months you gave yourself have expired, there will land on your desk a completely new PLR scheme. It is not long, and it is quite simple, so we hope very much that you will be able to read and understand it. We have laid aside all previous schemes and, with them, all the old objections. This one has been devised by Graham C. Greene, Michael Gilbert, Victor Bonham-Carter representing the Society of Authors, and Ronald Barker of the Publishers Association. It recommends that the best basis for PLR payments would be a royalty calculated as a percentage of the published price of each book supplied to public libraries during the year. It is totally distinct from library charges, and so will not attract the hostility of the librarians themselves – indeed I am sure many of them will support it since their objections in the past have been technical, not ones of principle.

There can be nothing to prevent this scheme, or another better one, from coming into immediate operation except the failure of the Government to make available the two or two and a half million pounds that it needs. So everything seems set fair. But because of our bitter experiences over the past twenty years, and the complete ineffectiveness of reasoned argument to gain results, what might be called a ginger group, under the redoubtable head of Giles Gordon, has been formed to go into action should our claims yet again be set aside. For the unhappy conclusion arising from the apathy of successive governments is, as the historian Robert Skidelsky has pointed out, that 'good argument gets you nowhere: only direct action does'.

Yet we would be easy to disarm. None of us want to waste our time petitioning for support, imperilling marginal Conservative seats at by-elections, pressing for a work-to-rule on *Hansard* and preparing even more combative measures. We simply want to write our books, and be paid for the use of them so that we may continue to write to the best of our ability. To deny us this any longer is to rob us of our livelihood.

(3) Private Reading, Public Justice

'"How Things Don't Get Done". On this theme there must be a million Whitehall memories, tales of folly, deceit, conspiracy, frustration,' wrote Sir Alan Herbert in his recent autobiography. 'But here, I believe, is a classic. In all my years of battles about the libraries this was the deepest disappointment, the most miserable "might have been", Whitehall at its worst.' It is a tribute to the vigour and wit of the campaign which A. P. Herbert led for so long that few people can have any doubt of what he was writing about: Public Lending Right, the scheme whereby authors would be paid for the use of their books in libraries.

This year (1971) marks the twentieth in the campaign. Throughout this long time authors have battled on 'with as much effect as a bird or bee trying to penetrate a window-pane', to use

A. P. Herbert's words again. But, he adds: 'It is now at least recognized and understood all round the world.' The symposium which Mr Richard Findlater has skilfully edited,* and which is most appropriately dedicated 'to A. P. H.', consists of ten contributions from librarians, publishers, a literary agent and of course authors themselves. Each contributor confines himself to some aspect of it about which he is particularly well qualified to deal. Mr Victor Bonham-Carter, gives a concise history of the campaign up to last summer. His account is a model of restraint – more a whisper than a shout. But what he has to tell us of the patient injustice meted out by successive Governments makes one want to sit down like a dog and howl, as D. H. Lawrence once wrote, 'in soul-lacerating despair'.

Mr Peter du Sautoy, a past President of the Publishers Association, examines the pattern of book-buying and book-borrowing in this country and explains why publishers have consistently backed authors' efforts to get PLR accepted as a straightforward matter of equity; Mr Hilary Rubinstein, a partner in A. P. Watt the literary agency, illustrates the significance PLR would have especially with the average writer, 95 per cent of whose sales are to libraries; Mr Raymond Astbury gives us an admirable history of the Public Library Movement and shows how the introduction of PLR would add to the important contribution libraries make to our cultural life; another librarian, Mr K. C. Harrison, tells us of schemes that are already in existence in other countries, and of their relevance to Britain; Mr Michael Freegard, General Manager of the Performing Right Society, draws a valid parallel between Performing Right (whereby musicians receive royalties for the communication of their work in public) and PLR and demonstrates that public lending is equivalent to public performance. He also gives authors fresh heart by describing the once 'insuperable' obstacles that were overcome, the insurmountable problems that were solved during the lengthy and arduous struggle to gain this right.

None of the contributors are primarily concerned with the details of how PLR should be established: that, after all, is not their job. Over the years scheme after scheme has been submitted

* *Public Lending Right* edited by Richard Findlater.

to the Government which by now has a rich supply from which to choose. The onus of selecting some reasonable version now rests with Lord Eccles. No one would seek to deny that there are some difficulties involved in working out a just and practical plan. In the past, the subject has been bedevilled by all sorts of red herrings being dragged across it – most recently the question of library charges which, though it could be tied to PLR, is in fact a completely separate issue. To devise a scheme that is absolutely perfect in all its details may indeed not be possible, but this can be no reason for continuing to tolerate the injustice of no scheme at all. As John Fowles, the novelist, writes: 'The essential, surely, is to get the principle accepted; no complex proposal like this can spring perfect into being. It will have to be regarded as experimental and alterable in its first years . . . What we cannot settle for is continued public apathy; and this leads me to my own deepest conviction in the matter. I believe that for novelists at any rate PLR is wanted almost as much psychologically as financially.'

What all the contributors do, as Lord Goodman writes in his introduction, is to demonstrate 'that authors in this country – and many other countries – are living under a library system which works injustice to them'. Into the ears of politicians it can never be repeated too often that PLR is not a disguised subsidy to authors who have failed to make a living out of their profession. To establish it would not be some act of charity, not even some form of patronage but, as Angus Wilson urges, 'a matter of justice'. It is obviously absurd that authors should be read by tens of thousands of people who borrow their books free of charge and who benefit them not at all. The ordinary novelist, biographer or historian receives a return on about one tenth of his readership. The facts are, as Richard Findlater points out, that 'most of the people who write books earn less than half the national average wage from their authorship'. Everyone concerned in the production and distribution of books from the printer to the bookseller earns a living from them with the exception of the authors themselves, without whom the trade would not begin to exist. Who can deny that this subsidy of British readers by British authors is ludicrous? What other profession would tolerate such a system? What other profession would not strike to obtain justice and, by striking, get it? But authors, as John Fowles reminds us, 'can't strike; we can only be struck. Every time you borrow a book from your public library.'

The essays in this symposium are all based on indisputable facts, sometimes on statistics, on the belief that reason, which has successfully got us nowhere over the last twenty years, must in the end prevail. It stands to ... well, it stands to reason. None of these contributions can cause offence: except one. Mr Findlater closes his symposium with a memorable polemic by John Fowles. Read this, and you will understand why that most genial of men, A. P. Herbert, sickened by the politicians' contempt towards those who (so they believe) cannot hold Governments to ransom, finally lost his temper. 'I wish to rub the nation's nose in it,' he wrote. 'I wish to leave behind me a fair but filthy record of the nation's neglect and meanness.'

The root of our problem now is frustration. It seems to us that, in dealing with Governments, good manners, reasonableness, words themselves are no longer in currency. Logical argument has been as valuable in this campaign as bows and arrows in a nuclear war. If I wish to communicate with Lord Eccles I am made to feel that I can do so not by speech – unless it is to be the chanting of slogans – but by energetic movements of my feet and hands. To explain that PLR is a matter of elementary justice, long overdue, I must use my feet for marching; my hands I must use for throwing home-made bombs, for burning books – that, the most illogical act of all, may very well prove the most eloquent. This will be news; this will embarrass important people; this will swell our ranks with those who enjoy our methods and don't care about our ends. Only by dangerous and ridiculous measures can we hope to be promoted above stairs, as it were, and be classed as people with whom some politicians feel they can communicate. As mere law-abiding scribblers, we do not rate such privileges. After all, one would not discuss one's business affairs with one's butler – why then should Lord Eccles bandy words with artists and writers? Up to now he certainly has not done so. The case, as Lord Goodman says, is 'unanswerable'; but it requires an answer. Now.

(4) My Lord's Potato

At his first press conference in July 1970, Lord Eccles, our new Minister for the Arts with the optimistic title Paymaster General, demanded: 'Give me three months and we will do something.' He was referring to Public Lending Right, the scheme whereby authors would receive payment for the use of their books in libraries. 'It was,' he joked, 'a hot potato.'

Three months went by, and then another three, and then three more. Lord Eccles was not idle – he was not even joking. In August it was reported that he was 'already concerning himself' with the subject; and as early as the New Year a spokesman on his behalf promised that 'the subject is one very close to Lord Eccles's heart'. A hot potato so close to the heart must have been uncomfortable and, amid lessening applause and mounting laughter, he was everywhere urged to deliver himself of it. For, contrary perhaps to what he had expected, the potato had lost none of its heat. It was, if anything, growing hotter. Had Eccles, people wondered, got an asbestos heart – or no heart at all for the impoverished author? But then, after nine months' confinement and a visit from Lord Goodman, he finally gave birth: to a working party.

There had been working parties before in the long history of PLR – there had even been working parties to report, in some cases, on the reports of other working parties. So it was not surprising if some authors and publishers were sceptical. However, this working party was said to be different: it was the ultimate working party to end all others – and, in truth, we could not stomach others. The Government had virtually committed itself to acting on its findings.

One of the effects of setting it up was to silence the more militant campaigners who were beginning to talk of putting up PLR candidates – Kingsley Amis, perhaps, or even Margaret Powell – at by-elections in marginal Conservative seats. For while the working party worked, to do anything except talk would be seen to be unreasonable. So they fell silent, waited, but did not forget. In December last year, at the conclusion of a debate in the House of Commons, it was resolved 'that the House urge Her Majesty's Government to bring their examination of Public Lending Rights to an early conclusion'. The campaign was then entering its twenty-second year.

Today, after fourteen months' labour, the working party has produced its report. It is, mercifully, a short document. There have been those who, up to now, have felt suspicious of what they were up to. Were not some of its members sworn enemies to the very principle of PLR? Were not its terms of reference exceedingly narrow – simply to consider how PLR might be implemented by amending the Copyright Act 1956? Had they not been begged quite specifically *not* to recommend 'particular courses of action'? A rumour had even spread to the effect that their meetings were being orchestrated by an official, specially appointed by Lord Eccles, who, though deaf, had an insuperable stutter. How could anything good come of all this?

Something good has come. The minuses seem for the most part to have cancelled one another out. The very limits of their task made it impossible for opponents of PLR within the working party to raise objections to the report. It is unanimous.

The report, which is carefully argued, identifies two alternative methods of running PLR. The first is a surcharge system which involves adding a charge to the published price of all copyright books when sold to a library. The second is something entirely new called Blanket Licensing which, until our computer system has been improved, seems the most practical scheme devised. Under this system, which is analogous to the way in which performing rights are already exercised, libraries would be licensed to lend copyright works under the amended law on payment of an annual fee. This would be issued by a collecting society called *The Authors and Publishers Copyright Association* (APCA); and in addition an independent tribunal would be set up (on the lines of the Performing Right Tribunal) to safeguard public interest and arbitrate on matters of dispute.

The mechanics of this scheme are extremely simple and do not involve the librarian in any burden of administrative work. Each book is identified by its publisher with a PLR symbol and a machine-readable slip for processing by computer. When the book is bought by a library, the slip is merely detached and sent to APCA. The money from the annual fees is then distributed as an additional royalty based on the price of the book, 75 per cent going to the author and the rest to the publisher. To operate this method reasonably will cost four million pounds, £500,000 of which would be required for administration.

It is quite a good system – it is not perfect. All authors must be seriously disappointed that no practical method has been found for benefiting older writers, often in the most need, whose books are already on the shelves. Nor is it absolutely equitable in terms of actual loans. At least in the short term there is a danger too that librarians will buy fewer books. But if the licence fee is paid out of the library's total expenditure and not exclusively out of the book fund (which is only 25 per cent of their turnover) then the effect should be very small – after all, the four million represents only 5 per cent of library expenditure as a whole.

Though this report is hardly inflammatory, one may be sure it will provoke a shrill reaction among those to whom PLR has always been a red rag. It will be pointed out that authors are asking for double the amount they wanted before. Had successive Governments not been so incredibly dilatory, it might have been cheaper. But the cause of this rise is not simply inflation: it is that the Blanket Licence can apply to all libraries, not simply public libraries.

It may be lamented that Agatha Christie will grow richer – and so will other best-sellers without her talent. Yet if their books are in constant demand why should they not benefit? They have the right to pay income tax, surtax. PLR is neither a reward for literary merit nor a charity: it is a means of commercial justice.

There will be many hares put up for us to chase – that the money is more urgently needed for slum clearance; that the borrower should be charged; that 'Brophy's Penny' must be re-introduced; that PLR will encourage more bad books to be written; that library lending does (or does not) discourage book buying; that writing is its own reward; that the price of books should be increased or decreased, and authors gently assisted by patronizing State grants. For years such irrelevancies have been shot at us. The time has come to ignore them, to shrivel them up with absolute contempt. The patience with which they have all been answered again and again has become abused.

Authors do not spend time seeking money; they desperately need money in order to buy time in which to work. But there is something even more important at stake: the currency of words. We have been accused – even by literary editors – of being 'frenetic and intemperate' over this cause. If this is true, then it arises from our bitter experiences over many years. Politeness, reason, good argument, moderation: we have overspent these, we are bankrupt. We have seen how others get results, and we are determined to get results ourselves.

It is difficult to see how any Government can avoid acting on some of the implied recommendations in this report. In the past, Jennie Lee was vaguely confused by good intentions over the issue. I do not see the same hindrance in Lord Eccles. We have returned his potato to him. It is ready for eating. But if it is not to be eaten, we shall know where to put it.

Some British Tradesmen

In about 1960, while writing a book about Hugh Kingsmill, I called on Mr Jonathan Cape who had published Kingsmill's *Frank Harris* and commissioned from him an autobiography. My hope was that, besides discovering some material at Cape's useful for my book, I should also find the book a publisher. My biography, I hinted broadly, might very well appear on Cape's list in place of the autobiography Kingsmill had never lived to complete.

Jonathan Cape listened to me stonily, said little and shook his head – not up and down as I was willing him to do, but from side to side. Whenever he did get a word in, it was, so it seemed to me, an attempt to steer the conversation towards more general literary topics. Did I, he asked at one point, know my Dickens? I could force this question into the context of what I had been saying only by interpreting it as some reflection on Kingsmill's life of Dickens, *The Sentimental Journey*, about which I hastened to give my opinion: a brilliant book, but not wholly successful.

'Not wholly successful', Jonathan Cape echoed, and began to elaborate on this theme which seemed much to his taste. Whatever risks he, as a publisher, might be prepared to take, his partner Mr Wren Howard would never for a moment consent to publish a literary biography of a not wholly successful dead author. He was therefore powerless to help me. He paused. Did I know *David Copperfield*? 'It was one of Kingsmill's favourite Dickens novels,' I urged quickly. If I could see Mr Howard, I persisted, maybe I could convince him of Kingsmill's value. Jonathan Cape shook his head, again the same way. 'He would tell you what I have told you. It's a system we have. Do you know Spenlow and Jorkins?' Only then did I realize that whichever partner was absent would always be unsympathetic; that there was no hope.

It is characteristic of Mr Michael Howard's industry that he has ferreted out this interview, and alludes to it in his fine commemorative volume of the firm.* With strict observance of its half-century, he publishes his book exactly fifty years to the day after Cape's first publication, Doughty's *Arabia Deserta*, appeared. That book they owed to T. E. Lawrence, a passionate advocate of Doughty's; and in subsequent years, books by and about Lawrence towered like Himalayas along the uneven range of their publications.

To judge from his correspondence, Lawrence must have been a tiresome author with whom to deal, but where best-sellers are involved it is very wonderful to witness how forbearing publishers can be. Besides Lawrence, Mr Howard allows us glimpses of several other authors from the Cape list: B. Traven, for example, who seems to have been almost invisible; Mary Webb slapping her publisher's face; that 'bounder' Ian Fleming so neurotically poised between uncertainty and professionalism; Laurence Housman, at the age of eighty-seven, querulous at the top of an apple tree. Inevitably, though sometimes the two are the same, we hear more of best-sellers than best-writers: two pages on John Lennon, none on John Stewart Collis. But Mr Howard reveals that Cape rejected William Golding's *Lord of the Flies*, Orwell's *Animal Farm*, and an early work by Samuel Beckett. He also retells the famous story of the case against Radclyffe Hall's *The Well of Loneliness*, but I was disappointed to read nothing of Wyndham Lewis's *Roaring Queen* which Cape, fearing a libel case, withdrew at proof stage and which has still never been published.**

The history of Jonathan Cape is largely that of its two founders, Cape himself and the author's father, G. Wren Howard. Of these, by far the more dominant personality was Jonathan Cape. He was a shy man, emotionally and, as many authors can testify, financially. In manner he could be formidable; in business unyielding; always he was hard-working, and almost always, one suspects, more popular with women than with men. In bringing him

* *Jonathan Cape, Publisher* by Michael S. Howard.
** *Roaring Queen* will be published by Secker & Warburg. 1973.

vividly to life and making him, without false sentimentality or special pleading, a sympathetic character Mr Howard has achieved a portrait comparable to Arnold Bennett's bookseller in *Riceyman Steps*.

Cape saw publishing as an occupation for tradesmen, and authorship, one can only assume, as one for gentlemen. A good book he defined as 'one that sells a hundred thousand copies'. Yet he had a sort of hearsay weakness for fine writing. On the whole it was the outside of books that interested him most. His reverence for literature is difficult to pin down, but perhaps it may accurately be described as the opposite of that contempt arising from familiarity. The trouble, of course, was that literature is as independent of commerce as it is of morality. Most of his literary judgments, delivered with great authority, were vicarious, and he depended, like a ventriloquist's dummy, upon the opinion of that great publisher's reader Edward Garnett. His relationship with Garnett was never easy, and he seems to have resented this dependence upon him. But he was far too good a businessman to let him go.

He relied, too, upon Wren Howard who evolved ideas on book design, established disciplined and unobtrusive formulas of typography. With his neatly bristling, slightly curled moustache, impeccable dress and exquisitely polished shoes, Wren Howard was every inch the second-in-command. His military bark and authoritarian manner concealed, his son tells us, an unaggressive temperament. Yet the mask became the man, and his reticence eventually sealed up whatever lay beneath.

The interest of the book flags a little after these two extraordinary and very English characters fade from the scene. In recent years the firm of Jonathan Cape has become one of a diminishing number of publishers which has resisted the process of what, without intended irony, is called rationalization: with the result that it does not belong to a bus company, paint firm or even television group. Nor, at the other end of the scale, has it any affinity with those tiny quixotic publishers, one-man bands, that still somehow go on springing up, still keep on whistling hopefully in the dark. Instead it has taken the middle course and avoided seduction by American companies by entering a sort of *mariage blanc* with Chatto and Windus, a very similar publishing house.

Mr Howard's handsome book has been produced with the greatest care and stands as the very model of a model Cape biography. Some of its pages may be of too specialized interest for the general reader, but it must surely be required reading for all publishers for many years to come, while even authors may distil much enjoyment from it of a more wry flavour.

*   *   *

This slim, handsome, highly expensive volume* comes from a good stable. Sired by Allen and Unwin, which in Anthony Blond's up-to-date form book *The Publishing Game* is rated as an 'illustrious, academic and institutional' stallion, out of that lusty dam Heinemann (dubiously noted by Mr Blond for its 'smart operations'), it follows hard on the heels of several publishing books, the favourite among which must still be Michael Howard's *Jonathan Cape, Publisher*, served somewhat incestuously by Cape last year.

These days the name of Allen and Unwin is used as a whip by disconsolate authors to urge on their own flagging publishers during the important Christmas season: for their distribution is second to none. Wisely, therefore, the trainers of *The Publishing Unwins*, Mr Dwye Evans and Mr Roland Gant, have entered it for the more modest January stakes. It should do reasonably well. It has a prancing air of confidence, as when Philip Unwin declares three thousand copies to be the minimum printing order for any book – a piece of information that may surprise some authors and possibly his own publishers too.

There is an extraordinary insensitivity that authors and publishers, otherwise men of the most exquisite refinement, exclusively reserve for each other. Any author who dares interfere with the production of his own work risks encountering this; any publisher who takes up his pen positively invites it. With this in mind let me first urge the attention of all authors to the index of this book, which is appalling. Otherwise, I must record it to be in many ways a charming volume, the tone being one of humour,

---

* *The Publishing Unwins* by Philip Unwin.

affection and, above all, enjoyment. Part family history, part publishing saga, it comprises a success story. There are few real incidents of failure, no regrets, no farragos of incompetence: the mood is one of congratulation – I would not say complacency. Chronicling with loving care their strengths and eccentricities, Mr Unwin brings marvellously to life his two publishing uncles T. Fisher Unwin and Stanley Unwin to whose autobiography this work acts as a valuable appendix.

It is an endearing narrative. But raise the binoculars of authors' paranoia, read between the lines, and a startlingly different picture emerges. Mr Unwin likens his family to Galsworthy's Forsytes, but it is a shock to discover that, despite his full, happy, well-regulated life, he too is something of a Forsyte. His charm, like that in his ungenerous description of the 'ladies of Soho', is spurious. Sales, of course, have been his real meat and drink, with prestige a piquant sauce. Yet although best-sellers are what he calls the 'important' books, he has, like any Victorian, a moral purpose and sees Allen and Unwin as having led the social revolution towards 'a fairer distribution of the country's wealth, a better regulated economy, wider educational opportunity'. While T. Fisher Unwin relied on the *oeuvre* of Ethel M. Dell, Stanley Unwin published *The Hobbit*, *Queen Mary*, *Kon-Tiki* and a funny book on lavatories.

The ideal author, Mr Unwin believes, is one who, like Bertrand Russell, is too busy to give his publisher any trouble and who 'repays' publication by being both a big seller and a big name. The ideal publisher tends to be a different animal: dictatorial, long-lived and so 'careful' about money that he will rinse out old tennis balls to forgo buying new.

There is therefore a kick to this book which may be felt less keenly by publishers on top than by authors struggling round the nag's hindquarters.

Out of Print

———◆——

About every nine months some British publisher celebrates a happy event. He will announce a new series. The books in question are to be cheaply priced and well produced; they will be of interest chiefly to students of English literature, but should appeal to all serious readers: and the first six titles are to be critical studies of the work of Conrad, George Eliot, Henry James, Joyce, D. H. Lawrence and Virginia Woolf. The next six titles are equally impressive, equally predictable. They get off to a well-publicized start, and are reviewed everywhere. But after the first two dozen volumes have appeared, nothing more is heard of the venture. Then it is time for someone else to have the same idea, and the whole process starts again.

Such publishers, of course, are tempted by the education market, and their series are built around those novelists and poets who have been declared by our teachers of English to be 'required reading'. The result is that there exists a plethora of books about Conrad, Lawrence and the rest, but almost none about the many excellent writers (never reached by these series) whose work has failed to become a canonical part of English literature at the universities.

It is easy to understand the appeal of a generally accepted great tradition of literature. As a means of simplifying the vast jungle of the printed word, it has obvious practical uses. The sight of all those novels, plays, poems and biographies is tiring, and the prospect of plunging into them unaided, terrifying. To spare us this exertion, the don has undertaken to attend to all our literary luggage and act as a kind of valet who will pack up what is needed for a journey around the world. What he recommends is read, and what is read must be published. No wonder we rely on him so greatly.

The objection to this system is not necessarily an objection to the writers officially selected, but to the vicariously dismissive attitude it promotes. Unlike their continental counterparts, British and American publishers do not often maintain large backlists, with the result that the work of many fine authors all too soon goes out of print and becomes almost unobtainable. In this way the choice is taken out of our hands.

All of us, probably, have some favourite unfashionable author. Occasionally a minority taste can be powerful enough to make for some isolated masterpiece a small niche in literary history – Henry Green's *Loving* and Sylvia Townsend Warner's *Mr Fortune's Maggot* have both deservedly achieved this status through the persistence of a small band of admirers. Sometimes, too, a novelist will, as it were, return from the dead. The recent resurrection of Jean Rhys, whose novels were rescued almost singlehanded by Francis Wyndham and have now been reissued, is a remarkable case in point. But it is also an exceptional case. The majority of forgotten writers are sunk without trace. For if we hold strictly to the well-worn routes mapped out by the Professors of English Literature, we will miss much that is remarkable – the poetry of Charlotte Mew, for example, and of Martyn Skinner. Has anyone considered bringing out some of Gilbert Cannan's novels? Praised by Henry James, dismissed by D. H. Lawrence, Cannan spent the last half of his life in a lunatic asylum (without, according unreliably to Richard Aldington, any justification), and is certainly a controversial enough figure to warrant some publisher looking again at *Round the Corner* or *Mendel*.

The taste of the don and the whim of the film-maker are the two ill-matched steeds to which a publisher's list of reprints is harnessed – and they draw it into some strangely paradoxical country. There can be no more striking example of this state of affairs than the plight of Patrick Hamilton. As a thriller writer, Patrick Hamilton is still well known, because his *Rope*, *Gaslight* and *Hangover Square* have all been filmed. But his finest work – the novels *Twenty Thousand Streets under the Sky* and *The Slaves of Solitude*, and his play *The Duke in Darkness* – is unknown because it does not appear on any English literature syllabus and has not attracted Alfred Hitchcock. There have been several attempts to revive interest in his novels, notably by Clancy Sigal, John Russell Taylor and J. B. Priestley, who described him as one of the 'very few genuine original novelists'. But when, more recently, Doris Lessing wanted to write a piece on him, she was told there was no curiosity about his books, and so her piece was never published.

Yet what she had to say was of vital significance to the whole condition of English literature to-day. For, in her opinion, Patrick Hamilton was:

> a marvellous novelist who's grossly neglected. And I can't think of any reason for it unless he's not a member of one of the cliques, one of the invisible brotherhoods that exist in England and especially in English literary life. I'm continually amazed that there's a kind of roll call of OK names from the 1930s, sort of Auden and Isherwood, etc. But Hamilton is never on them and he's a much better writer than any of them ... [He] was very much outside the tradition of an upper-class or middle-class writer of that time. He wrote novels about ordinary people. He wrote more sense about England, what was going on in England in the 1930s, than anybody else I can think of, and his novels are true now. You can go into any pub and see it going on. .... If somebody asked me today to give him some novels that show what Britain is like now, I'd give him Patrick Hamilton's.

The position for writers of non-fiction is even more anomalous. Expensive volumes of history and biography are eagerly commissioned by publishers because quick money may be made from them. They are reviewed, on the whole, at far greater length than novels or volumes of poetry. For three months they continue to sell, are overtaken by even newer history and biography, then die. Yet it is palpably ridiculous for, let us say, Robert Gathorne-Hardy's memoir of Logan Pearsall Smith to be permanently not in print because of a system that prints too much.

The trouble would seem to be that the wrong standards are employed. Biographies, in particular, are valued not for their intrinsic literary merit, but for their 'importance'; not for their originality of method, style or attitude, but for the new documents they quote. 'Apparently original information goes better with publishers,' Hugh Kingsmill ruefully commented when his *After Puritanism* had been turned down by an American publisher. '. . . A packet of unpublished letters dealing with the views on manure found by Samuel Butler in New Zealand would have helped.'

Non-fiction is regarded by many critics as non-creative. They confuse invention with creation, and thereby relegate to the regions of the uncreative such writers as Boswell, Carlyle, Gibbon, Macaulay, Ruskin and, to all intents and purposes, Johnson. This is about as sensible as saying that a portrait or landscape painter must be non-creative, and an abstract painter creative – as if it were the subject that conferred creativity on an artist.

Left high and dry by this climate of opinion is the delicate art of autobiography to which, ironically, the English bring a particular talent. The autobiography of the late J. R. Ackerley, published recently, has been hailed by several leading critics as a minor masterpiece. Yet there is no guarantee that it will be allowed to pass Cyril Connolly's ten-year test and still be available in 1979. After all, Arthur Calder-Marshall's *The Magic of My Youth* is now available neither in hardback nor in paperback. Autobiographies disappear because their authors are not celebrated enough in non-literary circles, and because the medium itself is overlooked by teachers and students of literature.

For this reason only the reminiscences of the famous are remembered. We all know, for instance that Augustus John wrote *Chiaroscuro*; but how many people have read his son Romilly John's delightful reminiscences, *The Seventh Child*, a book that certainly deserves to be remembered? Most people have heard of Sir Arnold Lunn's autobiographical novel, *The Harrovians*; but who knows of his brother Brian Lunn's marvellous autobiography, *Switchback*? It should be known, and it could be, if only publishers would realize their potential power; if only, instead of following various fads and fashions in the hope of making a quick commercial killing, they tried to influence taste, to create demand. In place of all those repetitious series of critical studies of great names, why doesn't someone start a library of autobiographies, from Benjamin Haydon to Edwin Muir and Gerald Brenan's *A Life of One's Own*? A country that neglects such books doesn't deserve to have them.

In the stock market of unread books and lost reputations, there is a perpetual turmoil of activity, fascinating for literary speculators to observe. Whose head will break the surface? Who will sink? Who swim? Since fashion, especially educational fashion, plays such a large part in success of this kind, individual quality is not enough. And where common sense is blocked, eccentricity must find a way. The late John Holms, for example, a self-confessed genius and author of one short story in the *Calendar of Modern Letters*, still has an impressive band of admirers. Holms's technique, a rather silent one, was to insist on potential. His promise was almost infinite. He would do such things – what they were no one knew yet – but they would be the wonders of the earth.

More recently the novelist William Gerhardie has made claims to be the best known unknown author in modern times. He has always, he points out, been especially well known to himself. But John Stewart Collis, whose unique series of books on natural phenomena has been compared to the work of Ruskin, finds Gerhardie's tactics at fault. Collis, with none of his volumes in print, refuses to admit that his name is not a household word, and his books international best-sellers. 'Tell them you are unjustly neglected,' he maintains, 'and they'll say: "Come, let's neglect him a little more."'

In spite of keen competition, Gerhardie now leads the table of concealed celebrities. A few years ago, at the age of seventy-one, he changed his name from Gerhardi to Gerhardie, reverting to an ancestral spelling that he had accidentally come across. This was an event. Numbers of reporters from the leading newspapers rang up to inquire why he had decided to do such a thing. Gerhardie had his answer ready. Shakespeare, he explained, had a final *e*. So did Dante, Blake and Goethe. Who was he to do otherwise? Such modesty was impressive, and was widely reported in the press.

Gerhardie sat back and waited. For a novelist whose splendid gifts have been praised by Arnold Bennett, Desmond MacCarthy, Katherine Mansfield, Edith Wharton and many others, it was ludicrous that not a single one of his novels should be in print. Quite lately he has been the subject of appreciative articles by Walter Allen, Michael Ivens, Olivia Manning, C. P. Snow and Philip Toynbee – all to no avail. He was an important influence on the work of, among others, William Cooper, Anthony Powell and Evelyn Waugh – but his own books are nearly impossible to get hold of. 'Why was there no shouting?' demanded H. G. Wells after *Futility*, Gerhardie's first novel, was published. Since orthodox methods had failed, perhaps this announcement, Gerhardie reasoned, might remind publishers of his existence. Who would be the first to put his new name on a title page? So he waited for the shouting to begin. Eventually he received one letter about his change of name. It was from his bank manager asking for a specimen of his new signature – an incident worthy, perhaps, of a Gerhardie novel.

Behind the big names of contemporary writing there stands a shadow cabinet of writers waiting to take over once the Wind of Change has blown. My own vote goes to Hugh Kingsmill as Leader of this opposition. Kingsmill is remembered by the reading public more as an ebullient personality, a man of abounding wit and vitality, than as a serious critic and biographer, so that now, nearly twenty years after his death, his writing is in danger of being forgotten altogether. In a moving and unusual memoir comprising an exchange of letters, two of Kingsmill's friends, Malcolm Muggeridge and Hesketh Pearson, brilliantly succeeded in re-creating him as one of the most stimulating of companions. But they made little attempt to establish him as a clearly recognizable literary figure.

*   *   *

Hugh Kingsmill Lunn, the second son of Sir Henry Lunn, was born at 46 Torrington Square, in London, on 21 November 1889. Not long after his birth the family moved to 5 Endsleigh Gardens on the northern boundary of Bloomsbury. But the happiest times of his childhood were spent in Switzerland, where the Lunns frequently went in connection with their travel business and the various religious organizations linked with it – the Church Travellers' Club and the Free Church Touring Guild.

At home, the Nonconformist-Evangelical atmosphere was less congenial to him. 'We were an earnest and upright body of men in those parts,' he afterwards acknowledged. Apart from his father, whose expanding business and religious industry were driving the rest of the family into the narrow upper regions of the house, there was his godfather, the Reverend Hugh Price Hughes, round the corner – a fiery Welsh orator whose ardour in promoting Social Purity was whipped by the Parnell case to a pitch of frenzy that makes W. T. Stead's utterances appear those of a veritable libertine. A little farther down the road lived Sir Percy Bunting, editor of the *Contemporary Review*, a monthly journal dealing exclusively with the problem of social evil, in a manner that might not have seemed very real to the prostitutes wandering along the far side of the gardens. His sister, Mrs Sheldon Amos, was more realistic, and on one notable occasion at a railway station was moved to strike a Guards officer who had been found guilty of seduction, crying out as she delivered the blow: 'You cad!' Besides such public-spirited friends as these, there also lived close at hand a Mr Algernon Coote, the founder and secretary of the National Vigilance Association, who saw to it that 'girls coming from the provinces for employment in London should be met on arrival, steered through the multitudinous perils of the street, and penned in a fold where liberty of action was restricted to attending church on Sundays'.

Fully conscious of their tremendous responsibilities to the community, when matters of especially grave importance arose, such as the purification of the Music Halls, or the Suppression of Nude Paintings, a number of this company would act in collaboration, calling on the Bishop of London to support them. And in national emergencies, under the zealous leadership of Sir Henry Lunn himself, the whole neighbourhood would rise up like a well-trained and formidable army of salvation.

This was the background in which Kingsmill's early years were spent, and against which much of his subsequent life and work was dedicated. 'The trouble with reformers,' he once wrote, 'is that they seldom have any happiness in their natures, and so they can only see what is harmful in a pleasure, never what is beneficial.'

From his parents, and especially perhaps from his mother, Kingsmill had inherited a vein of conventional religion. But he reacted strongly against his early Puritan environment, and at the age of twelve rejected orthodox Christianity, remarking that life would be far more pleasant if his mother made as many excuses for him as some clergymen did for God. Establishment religions had no place in his life, partly because such systems, he believed, 'whatever the philosophy out of which they have grown, necessarily value truth less than victory over rival systems'. Throughout his life he felt the weight of the millions who, by simplifying their emotional experiences, had narrowed themselves in Christ's name. His own inherited Puritanism was largely eclipsed by a deep strain of mysticism that, like all genuine mysticism, was in no way incompatible with humour or common sense. Something of his personal philosophy is summed up in the words of Polmont, the hero of his story *The End of the World*: 'Personal salvation! That was the clue to life. Each man to perfect himself unobtrusively, without forcing on others a technique that was perhaps suitable only to himself. . . . Shakespeare says that the world itself is a dream, and we shall wake out of life into nothingness. But I say we shall wake into life. The world is real – houses and trees, men and women, motor-buses and the moaning sea. But we have fallen asleep, and all these things, these simple and reasonable things, have been confused for us. But now the dream draws to its close, and we shall awake and smile at the perplexity and confusion that sleep has shed upon the world. Once more we shall see life as, even in this dream, I saw it a few minutes ago, the cab-horse and the stars, the chestnut trees and eternity, the great and the little, all parts of a self-explained and satisfying whole. My friends, be patient.'

Kingsmill's stoical optimism was like a great river in flood which, stopped in its course by practical experience, rose and reached out over unknown territory. The normal sights of this world, of nature, he treated as symbols of some other life, and behind the ordinary events of everyday existence he saw the workings of an extraordinary power. He could never have conformed to any religion that is unsympathetic to the love of men and women, whether that love is purely sensual or, at the other extreme, the attempt to fuse two desires in a single happiness divined beyond this life. Love, he believed, while having its roots in earthly passion, could expand beyond this and exist without passion, while passion was meaningless and even unhappy without love.

In the summer of 1903, Kingsmill was awarded a scholarship to Harrow, going there as a day boy. He seems to have been almost wholly inept at the various sports that formed so large a part of public school life, and later on could only recall one pleasant memory there. This was his first collision, at the age of sixteen, with the opposite sex. He had met the lady, who was his senior by several years, by accident on a strip of waste land after dark while he was returning home after school. Since he had only fourpence on him at the time and felt that payment on such an occasion should be made on a more generous scale or not at all, no money changed hands.

From Harrow, at the age of eighteen, Kingsmill won an exhibition to New College, Oxford. To his dismay he found that he was expected to devote two years of his life 'to a course of study grouped round Stubbs's investigations into the local government of our Anglo-Saxon ancestors'. But he was proof against the obscure fascination of Stubbs, and with Oxford in general was greatly disappointed. As the most famous seat of culture in the world, it would hold, he thought, 'the key to a poetic impassioned enjoyment of life'. It did not take him long to discover his error – 'about as long as it would take a man who went into a hen-house looking for birds of paradise'.

It was while he was at Oxford that Kingsmill read Frank Harris's *The Man Shakespeare*. Harris's dissimilarity to all stereotyped Victorians, dons and Methodists alike was in itself ample recommendation, and 'his praise of sensuality', Kingsmill later wrote, 'special pleading in one who has long since lost his illusions, sounded melodiously in the ear of youth, and I hastened to sit at the feet of a master whose message agreed so well with what I desired from life'. His adventures with Harris, in particular as his assistant on *Hearth and Home*, 'a blameless ladies' journal which did not long survive the ordeal of being edited by Harris', may be read in his extraordinarily witty and percipient biography of Harris.

His veneration for the master, much confused by these experiences, did not long survive, and by the outbreak of war had altogether vanished. In August 1914 he enlisted in a regiment of cyclists, and three months later he received a commission in the Royal Naval Volunteer Reserve (for service in the Royal Naval Division). He was an eccentric officer, and used to issue his orders of the day from his bed. These were taken by the sergeant-major, leaning through the window. On one occasion when he was supposed to inspect the guard but didn't like the idea of going through the mud, he sent for the guard and inspected them through the doorway, in slippers, with a newspaper under his arm. Such informalities somehow failed to prevent him from commanding a Company, as he recounts in his amusing war memoirs, *Behind Both Lines.*

'As acting Company commander, I was provided, against my will and better judgment, with a horse. Sterndale Bennett had returned to England for a few weeks, and our new C.O. was a cavalry colonel. My horse, fortunately a very phlegmatic animal, had this disadvantage, that when he resolved to be recalcitrant he was far too insensitive to bother about my hauling on his bit. There was a violent downpour at the first parade presided over by the new C.O. The rain drove slantingly into our eyes as we faced the colonel and after a moment's reflection my horse began to pivot slowly round. I struggled to keep him head on, but uselessly, and he ceased to rotate only when he and I were facing my company. The colonel did not refer to this obscene incident.'

After some two years of parades such as this, and various mock attacks practised 'with as close an approximation to the real thing as was consistent with the absence of an enemy and the presence of a general', Kingsmill reached the Western Front, where he was promptly captured, being led off behind the German lines quoting Heine.

The next fourteen months he spent at a prisoner-of-war camp at Karlsruhe, and it was here he wrote his first novel, *The Will to Love.* Another prisoner, Lance Sieveking, has given a description

of him at work there. He used to write 'in the Appel hut at
Karlsruhe. There he sat, crouched over the rickety table working
with happy concentration, slowly covering the sheet with his
small neat handwriting while all about him a cheerful hubbub
filled the air; four men just behind him playing ping-pong;
two men wrestling; a man with a very loud unmusical voice
singing . . .

'More than once I saw Hughie look up with a pained expression
during a lull in the din.

'"Don't stop, old man!" he would shout to the pair at the
piano, and then reproachfully to the resting ping-pong players:
"I say! You're not giving up, are you?" And then to me, or
anyone standing near, in a semi-confidential tone: "I find it helps
me to concentrate, y'know, old man."'

The Will to Love was the only one of his books to be published
under the name of Hugh Lunn. For the rest of his career, he wrote
as Hugh Kingsmill – his mother's maiden name. This was partly
to differentiate himself from his elder brother, Sir Arnold Lunn,
author of *The Harrovians*, and also his younger brother, Brian
Lunn, who was to write an outstanding autobiography. But it
was also a sign of his growing estrangement from the Lunn
family, and from his father in particular. For some years after the
war, Kingsmill worked in his father's tourist agency but in 1927,
when his first marriage (by which he had one daughter, Kathleen)
broke down, he left the family business, and relations between
him and his parents remained cool. 'Friends,' he bitterly remarked,
'are God's apology for relations.'

This was the turning-point in his career. He married again, a
Miss Dorothy Vernon, by whom he had one son, Brooke, who
became an Anglican priest, and two daughters, Edmée, now a nun
in an Anglican Order, and Dorothy who married Willis Hall, the
playwright. After this second marriage he devoted the rest of his
life to writing. He produced a number of highly original biographies, many essays, some novels, and a volume of parodies.
He also compiled several anthologies, and was literary editor of
Punch and of the *New English Review*. He died at Brighton on
15 May 1949.

*   *   *

During his life only one of his books was very widely known – the celebrated anthology *Invective and Abuse*. Of this, Kingsmill ruefully commented: 'No author has much tenderness for his most popular book, and his feeling that it is being favoured at the expense of his real masterpieces is particularly strong when, as in the present instance, it consists of extracts from other men's work.' Because of this 'collection of insults', he figured in the public mind as 'a sort of literary Jack the Ripper, red-eyed and sabre-toothed, scrabbling, year in, year out, among old folios for lost jewels of vilification'. Even at the end of his life Kingsmill would encounter persons who said that of course they knew of his work – 'that thing of yours on abuse'.

Rather more gratifying was the popularity of his parodies. These days the art of parody has become a much-underrated form of literary criticism. Kingsmill saw in parody potentially the perfect method of criticism, since it involved not an assertion of the will but an exercise of the imagination. His own parodies are less malicious than, for example, those of Max Beerbohm. They are penetrating rather than elaborate; that is to say they do not merely exaggerate some pronounced verbal characteristics, but seek to reveal, through the compression of caricature, the manner in which an author's outlook becomes fused with his literary style.

The conflict of will versus imagination obsessed Kingsmill, who made it the theme of several of his books. In his biography of Matthew Arnold this conflict is presented quite simply. His aim was to illustrate how the triumph of will over imagination led to the collapse of a poet into a prophet. He interpreted Arnold's occasional bursts of gaiety as little more than youthful indications of half-hearted revolt against the pious and sober training of his father; while his diluted Byronism was a mere gesture of filial impiety directed against the man who could never bring himself to read *Don Juan*. But the depression that took a deeper hold over him as the years advanced was produced, Kingsmill believed, by a disharmony arising from the unresolved struggle between his own naturally poetic temperament and the puritanical influence of his father's stronger personality.

Critics of Kingsmill's *Matthew Arnold* were particularly

incensed by his assertion that Marguerite of the poems was a real person in Arnold's life. Five years later, in 1933, the publication of Arnold's letters made it impossible for anyone to deny her existence. Kingsmill maintained that Arnold sacrificed his love for her to ostensibly moral, though intrinsically worldly, considerations. His renunciation of her symbolized the victory of Dr Arnold's will over his own more sympathetic nature.

'The reward for renunciation,' Kingsmill wrote, 'is some good greater than the thing renounced. To renounce with no vision of such good, from fear or in automatic obedience to some formula, is to weaken the springs of life, and to diminish the soul's resistance to this world.'

Kingsmill believed that the romantic fables and sentimental misconceptions that develop around a writer's reputation, and that masquerade as the truth, spring from the collective frustrations of people who come afterwards. By means of his criticism he sought to pare back the cuticle of lies, self-deceit and the habit and illusion that daily threaten to grow further over reality.

The four biographies that he published during the 1930s all illustrate this tendency. Each of them seeks to demolish some particular myth that had risen to a height of popularity where it was looked up to as being unchallengeable. The first of these, his life of Frank Harris, is a minor classic that has for ever shattered a never entirely secure legend. In place of a figure of vast creative power superior (as George Meredith asserted) to Balzac, and a spiritual equal (as Middleton Murry proclaimed) of Shakespeare himself, Kingsmill shows us a man of prodigious energy and a compendium of every form of charlatanism rampant in the complicated civilization of 1880 to 1914. A masterpiece of acute compression, of unsentimental yet sympathetic candour, the prose blends shrewdness, wit and humour in a way that discloses, yet at the same time seems to excuse, the weaknesses of human nature.

Kingsmill's next biography dealt with his favourite figure in English literary history, Samuel Johnson. His intention in this book was to qualify, by implication, the unstinted praise given by Macaulay and Carlyle to Boswell's *Johnson*. Certainly the penetrating character analysis he makes uncovers a deeper humanity than is readily discernible in Boswell's life. Boswell's insistence on Johnson's verbal ascendancy tended to promote the impression that he was the bigoted champion of social conventions and the established order, and to obscure his genuine individuality. Kingsmill supplanted the old John Bull conception with the portrait 'of an essentially imaginative nature clogged by melancholia, a profound thinker limited by inborn and irrational fears, and an intensely loving and compassionate soul hampered in its expression by lifelong disabilities of mind and body'.

An analytical rather than an impressionistic critic, Kingsmill liked to associate a literary work with the character of its author, with whom he partly identified himself. It was this relationship with his subject that accounts for the contrasting tone between his life of Samuel Johnson and his next biography, a life of Charles Dickens, which he called *The Sentimental Journey*. He found his own likeness to Johnson rather gratifying and extended to him a warm personal sympathy. But his points of similarity to Dickens irritated him so that he was at pains to distinguish himself from his subject and to stress his shortcomings.

Kingsmill's innate fairness of mind forbade him from expressing anything he felt to be of doubtful truth. He endeavoured to praise what he sincerely admired in Dickens – the humour of his minor characters and his wonderful descriptive powers – starting the paragraph with a few words of approbation, but then continuing with reservations which soon far exceed the opening eulogy. His own powers of imagination were free to expand only when the fate of his subject did not release in him pangs of personal envy. The hard struggle of Johnson brought out all his compassion. But Dickens's enormous early success exasperated him so much that his will was provoked to a pitch where, intermittently, it obliterated his sense of detachment.

Kingsmill's adversary in *The Sentimental Journey* was G. K. Chesterton, whose formulation of Dickens as a philanthropic and selfless social worker considerably vexed him. During his lifetime Dickens was considered vulgar, but after his death he became a great favourite with the refined and sophisticated classes of society, who felt that by reading him they were flirting with the newly fashionable spirit of democracy. Chesterton, the spokesman for this modern attitude, saw Dickens as 'a great-hearted lover of his kind, a laughing democrat blowing away all pretensions, social or intellectual, in the hurricane of his mirth'. For Kingsmill, on the other hand, 'his fascination lay in the immense gulf between his sentiments and his practice, in the fantastic, almost unbelievable extent to which he was not what Chesterton has painted him'.

In 1938, four years after publishing *The Sentimental Journey*, Kingsmill brought out *D. H. Lawrence*, his last full-length biography. His purpose in this book was to dispel the fable that Lawrence himself had erected and which enthusiastic disciples were proclaiming to the world. In *Sons and Lovers* Lawrence had portrayed himself as the son of a good-for-nothing father and an earnest Congregationalist mother. Kingsmill felt that this version of the truth rested on only a flimsy foundation. He attempted to show that Lawrence's father loved his wife and children, while his mother was a savage egotist who despised her ineffectual, softhearted husband and focused her thwarted ambitions on her son.

The conflict between his parents was never resolved in Lawrence, and hindered the fruitful development of his genius. His marriage Kingsmill also saw as harmful to the poetic element in him, which he had come nearest to disentangling from his desire for a life of action during his youthful friendship with Jessie Chambers – Miriam in *Sons and Lovers*.

The theme that recurs in all these biographies is also present in several of Kingsmill's novels and critical essays, and illustrates the way in which remarkable men are simplified into myths by popular fancy acting through suggestible minds. The legends that enhaloed men as dissimilar as Cromwell and Casanova were, he maintained, bubbles blown up by unsatisfied desires for power and pleasure. Some of Kingsmill's literary essays were collected towards the end of his life in a brilliant volume entitled *The Progress of a Biographer*, which shows that his criticism was essentially classical in its approach. 'He insisted', wrote Douglas Jerrold, 'that a man's values must only be influenced by his good or ill fortune, his prejudices or his sentiments in so far as these influences had been formed by reason, illuminated by imagination and disciplined by an act of will directed to the search for truth.'

For Kingsmill the pursuit of the imagination was love and

truth; that of the will, lust and power. Through the imagination that yearned for union with another life, he believed we might apprehend a harmony that envelops though it does not penetrate our present existence. The will, with its passion to dominate and possess, destroyed this unity, leaving chaos and division.

*   *   *

Although a few percipient critics have testified eloquently to the individual nature of Kingsmill's talent, most have found themselves at a loss as to where to place him on the literary stage. Their task has been made no easier by Kingsmill's steadfast refusal to engage his own will in the cultural and political factions of the day. He did not inhabit Bloomsbury or visit Garsington; he did not belong to a Left or Right Book Club, or fight in the Spanish Civil War; he did not immure himself behind the fortifications of a university.

His three meetings with T. S. Eliot he likened to audiences given by the Pope to some obscure Nonconformist minister on a visit to Rome; and on the single occasion he met Wyndham Lewis, then in the trough of paranoia, he was suspected of poisoning the food and asked to leave. In the end he has been put down by some as a product of the Strachey school of biography, and by others as a Freudian critic. It is particularly ironic that this type of inept labelling, against which he continuously fought so hard, should have become the chief cause of his own obscurity.

His admirers seldom agree as to what is his finest book. Malcolm Muggeridge, I fancy, prefers his *Frank Harris*; Hesketh Pearson liked his *The Return of William Shakespeare*; and my own favourite is *The Progress of a Biographer*. In his recently published letters, George Orwell pronounced Kingsmill's *The Sentimental Journey* to be the best biography of Dickens – it has now been out of print for over thirty years. He also reveals that, hoping Kingsmill's *After Puritanism* might be reprinted, he had written about it in a review, but that this passage had been omitted by the editor, for, as with Patrick Hamilton, there was no curiosity about his books.

But curiosity will not come of itself, it must be stimulated. Far more might be achieved, by making Kingsmill's writings available, than justice to a single author. For twenty years the literary standards that he championed in the *New English Review* have been eclipsed by educationist critical systems whose control on what we read, and therefore on what we publish, has been paramount. But Kingsmill belonged to no school of critics. He judged literature by its truthfulness, and by its power to reveal individual truths through humour, pathos, tenderness. No one had a sharper eye than he for detecting humbug. The truth he sought for is the truth we live, not speak, so that were we to give currency to his uncompromising values, there might well be a revolution in our present tastes and literary attitudes. At the very least there would be fewer series of books about Henry James, D. H. Lawrence and Conrad.

Perhaps Kingsmill's isolated position during his career, his independent tone and lucid style are best conveyed in the final passage to his essay 'The Genealogy of Hitler', a passage that may be read as an epitaph to his own life. 'What is divine in man is elusive and impalpable,' he wrote, 'and he is easily tempted to embody it in a concrete form – a church, a country, a social system, a leader – so that he may realize it with less effort and serve it with more profit. Yet, as even Lincoln proved, the attempt to externalize the kingdom of heaven in a temporal shape must end in disaster. It cannot be created by charters and constitutions nor established by arms. Those who set out for it alone will reach it together, and those who seek it in company will perish by themselves.'

William Gerhardie

————◆▶————

The career of William Gerhardie, who celebrated his seventy-sixth birthday last year [1971], presents an extraordinary example of how, in the ever more densely-grown jungle of the printed word, a writer of rare gifts can become lost to view.

His first novel, *Futility*, was written mainly at Oxford. Another undergraduate, John Rothenstein, who first shared a set of rooms with Gerhardie in Worcester College, has given a vivid impression of what he was like: 'Few people I have ever known have an acuter sense of the absurd, of the difference between the realities of life and the obscuring cant.' Yet there were times, Rothenstein concedes, when he resented the midday emergence into their common sitting-room of this tall, nervously-pacing being with the high-veined forehead, the sensual mouth (red, in the memory of the late Lord Sackville, like a begonia):

> 'whom sleep had charged with the desire for aggressive argument, about politics or literature, but more often about sex or religion, which I regarded as private matters. This view of them he ridiculed, forced me to declare myself, assailed any conclusions I had reached, and in general . . . compelled me, as no one had before, to think clearly and independently. . . . Association with Gerhardie was a rigorous discipline, for he talked almost continuously and scarcely ever went out.'

Owing to this hibernation, Gerhardie's career at Oxford was socially and athletically unobtrusive. He took his degrees quietly, he remembers, 'without exciting the university'. Shunning all forms of out-door exercise except lawn tennis, he spent most of the time in talk, in particular about his military intervention in Siberia, where he had served as a captain on the staff of the British

Military Mission. The tragi-comic aspects of this episode were a constant source of inventive reminiscence to be distilled into *Futility*. He neglected to win prizes, and his chief work in the English school (as his tutor Nichol Smith pointed out) was the completion of this novel.

Gerhardie sent it successively to thirteen publishers who persisted in returning it to him 'as if it were some kind of tennis ball sent over to them for that purpose'. Thinking that a passionate recommendation from some leading writer might do the trick, he eventually forwarded the typescript to Katherine Mansfield, whom he had never met but whose stories he admired. Unknown to him, she was in the mountains of Switzerland, dying of consumption. But she replied by return of post, read it within a week, and at the end of a fortnight had found a publisher, Cobden-Sanderson. 'It is a living book,' she wrote to him (14 November 1921). 'What I mean by that is, it is warm; one can put it down and it goes on breathing.'

It was published in 1922, very well reviewed and, in the eyes of the world, made its author an instant success – but of esteem rather than coveted circulation. Everyone had read the book, but no one seemed to have bought it. Cobden-Sanderson euphemistically reported it to be selling 'steadily' – that was about a couple of copies every couple of weeks. *Futility*, which stunned the world of letters, had left it silent with admiration.

In a letter to a friend the following year Gerhardie wrote: 'I haven't abandoned all hope. . . . As for Wells – Ah! I don't expect he will ever read it now.' His publisher had sent copies to Shaw, Arnold Bennett and H. G. Wells. Bennett, who was to become one of Gerhardie's staunchest admirers, greatly enjoyed the book; and Shaw told him: 'If you're English, you're a genius, but if you're Russian. . . .' at which point Gerhardie quickly broke in to expatiate upon his undoubted English parentage and ancestry. But it was Wells who made the novel famous. 'Why was there no shouting about Gerhardie's *Futility* – shouting to reach the suburbs and country towns?' he asked in *The Adelphi*; '. . . true, devastating. A wonderful book.'

Gerhardie uses his war-time experiences in *Futility* to throw into relief his main theme. It is perhaps the first English work to strike the 'waiting' motif that was to become fashionable many years later with Beckett's *Godot*. The father who gathers about him an army of wrangling dependants as his hopes of a fortune rise while his actual fortune diminishes, when asked at a crucial stage what he will do, decides: 'I think I'll wait. It can't be long now.' Against this tragically unchanging background is set the story of an Englishman brought up in Russia, and the pathos of his grow- ing love for Nina, the second of three bewitching daughters. 'One wonders at the firmness of the hand which has held together all the fun, pathos and irony of the thronged sprawling tale,' wrote Edith Wharton in her preface to the American edition, 'and guided it so resolutely to an inevitable conclusion.'

*   *   *

'There is a book,' wrote Desmond MacCarthy in the *New States- man*, 'no one interested in Chekhov's work should miss reading. It has been out some time, and it is by Mr William Gerhardie who wrote that admirable novel about Russian life, *Futility*. The critical study is one of the best I have read. I do not feel that it is too late to recommend this book, because it is one that will find a per- manent place in any library of critical literature.'

Written, for the most part, while Gerhardie was still at Oxford, *Anton Chekhov* was published in 1923, the year after *Futility* had appeared. It was the first critical study of Chekhov in any lan- guage, not excluding Russian. In America, where its publication coincided with the appearance there of the Moscow Art Theatre, it met, as in England, with general acclaim, the *New York Times* in a mammoth review hailing it as 'one of the ablest critical studies of recent years', and adding: 'It is certainly the most delightful.' Today, in Soviet Russia, it is spoken of as a standard work; while to English readers it has remained one of the most authoritative studies available.

Gerhardie was uniquely placed to write this book. As both *Futility* and *The Polyglots*, his next novel on Russian themes, show, his own writing, though it sparkles with more comic absurdity, is deeply influenced by Chekhov. Born in old St Peters- burg of English parents, Gerhardie had attended a preparatory and two secondary Russian schools before going to Oxford and had been brought up bilingual. By the 1920s certain British critics, such as Middleton Murry, had, without owning a word of Russian, made a corner for themselves in the Constance Garnett translations. Murry, in fact, reviewed this book at length in the *Times Literary Supplement* in a manner suggesting that the author was in a stage of development from which he, Murry, had just emerged, and that he was watching Gerhardie's progress with hope from a point farther along the road. But Gerhardie had already sailed up-wind of his reviewer by demonstrating that the humour and lyricism which suffuse Chekhov's original have a trick of evaporating in translation and that the Garnett rendering was essentially an approximation, echoing a certain melodious tone at some expense of good English, and letting the humour go. It was thus that Gerhardie became, in the words of C. P. Snow, 'the first person in England actively to interpret Chekhov to his fellow writers'.

Although it had earned him a B.Litt. Oxon. – the most respected degree in the Faculty of Mediaeval and Modern Languages and Literature – this book is in no sense a dry dissertation: it is a work of love. Gerhardie's love of Chekhov is part of his love of life, for what he singles out above all else in Chekhov's stories and plays is their complex feel of life as opposed to that neatness by which we usually recognize fiction. Most writers, he argues, produce either introspective fiction at the expense of the visible world; or romantic fiction expressing the smooth dreamy side of life divorced from material reality; or again they produce 'realistic' fiction, employing real material facts with the smooth directness only possible in a romance. But 'it is the balance of these three elements that gives his [Chekhov's] work a lifelike touch, removes him altogether from the musty flavour of tradition which attaches to the sedate profession of letters. When we read Chekhov we somehow forget all literary associations. It is as if, forsaking our various professions, we stepped aside to get a better view of life.'

Such enlightened enthusiasm makes for the best kind of criticism, full of extraordinary subtleties, of knowledge and mystery joined in a way that only love can divine. 'It is an excitement and a warmth in the mind that linger for months after reading,' wrote Christopher Morley describing his feelings for this book in *The*

Romany Stain. 'It fulfils that beautiful truth that Mr Gerhardie (in his Chekhov book) laid down – "A work of art whose aim and meaning were quite clear to the writer in the act of writing it would perish as the universe would perish if its aim were clearly known to it".'

Anton Chekhov deals with the whole of Chekhov's work, and that part of it concerned with the dramatist should be read by everyone interested in modern drama. In a crucial passage, Gerhardie explains how Chekhov resurrects the complete illusion of life 'by using a totally different kind of plot, the tissues of which, as in life, lie below the surface of events, and, unobtrusive, shape our destiny . . . [and] by choosing for his themes stories which were not of the unlikely kind (because taken from real life and developed into "stories"), but just as they would probably have happened if allowed to run their natural course in real life.'

Stanislavsky's much-vaunted 'Method' was, in Gerhardie's view, far too artificial a contrivance for Chekhov's plays and achieved little more than stultifying the acting through the regimentation of a ringmaster over-rehearsing his cast to the point of lifeless insensibility. In this it had a result directly opposed to the spirit of Chekhov: that of forcing the life out of the plays. Chekhov himself was convinced that Stanislavsky never really read his plays, his chief concern being how he could alter them. But it was Gerhardie who first identified Stanislavsky as Chekhov's prime enemy. In *The Times* and elsewhere, he exposed him for his gross emotional impropriety in cutting out the most telling, the most shattering conclusion of the *Three Sisters*, when Tusenbach is carried in on a stretcher, killed; and deplored his tacking on of all sorts of ludicrous and unnecessary scenes, such as candelabra falling off the ceiling while people are dancing overhead in *The Cherry Orchard*.

The only way to judge a poet, Wordsworth has said, is to love him. It is this love, this deep understanding by one imaginative writer of another, that finally gives Gerhardie's *Chekhov* its endearing and enduring quality. The book is an interpretation and a celebration of Chekhov's genius, communicating all his miraculous naturalness without that sorry echo of the consumptive's cough. Not often are scholarship and entertainment, argument and illustration so happily combined. To some extent, Gerhardie writes, 'literature like his may take the place of actual experience, without the physical exertion, sacrifices, inconvenience, and pain that is inseparable from the business of living; and when they die [readers of Chekhov] they may congratulate themselves on having lived a hundred lives – but paid for one!'

It is here that Gerhardie repays his debt to Chekhov in life with a small gem of literature.

*   *   *

Like *Futility*, Gerhardie's second novel, *The Polyglots*, published in 1925 when the author was twenty-nine, draws largely on personal experiences. The son of a successful British industrialist living in St Petersburg and his Yorkshire wife, Gerhardie had been considered the dunce of the family and sent to England in his late teens to be trained for what was loosely called 'a commercial career' – that is, to acquire some financial acumen or, in default, marry a rich bride. But he detested commerce, and dreamed only of the dramatic triumphs with which he hoped to take the London theatres by storm. To improve his English style he was studying Wilde, and an elegant cane, long locks and a languid expression were parts of his literary make-up at this time.

During the War he was posted to the staff of the British Military Attaché at Petrograd and, arriving there with an enormous sword bought second-hand in the Charing Cross Road, was welcomed as an old campaigner. The Russian Revolution (which ruined Gerhardie's father who owed his life to being identified as 'the British Socialist *Keir Hardie*') sent Gerhardie back to England. But in 1918 he set out again, and after crossing America and Japan reached Vladivostock, where the British Military Mission had established itself. After two years in Siberia, mostly in the company of generals, he sailed home by way of Singapore, Colombo and Port Said – a journey that forms the closing chapters of *The Polyglots*.

The Polyglots is the narrative of a high-spirited young officer who comes across a Belgian family, rich in eccentrics, to whom he is related and with whom he lives while on a military mission to the Far East. There are obvious parallels with Gerhardie's own

life. His impressions of the First and Second Revolution in Petrograd and the Allied intervention in Russia of 1918–20, of the
whole business of interfering on an international scale in other
people's affairs, are recorded here and in *Futility*. His characters
are never comic 'Russian' stereotypes, they are ourselves, and the
people we meet every day whose full humour we do not appreciate
until our eyes have been opened by a great writer. 'In both novels',
Walter Allen writes,

> 'the nature of the comedy is defined by the tone of the prose in
> which they are written. It is highly personal, light and glancing,
> often lyrical but always self-deflating. . . . It pins down unerr-
> ingly absurdity and contradiction – of characters and aspirations
> and situations – but does so without malice; the narrator is as
> conscious of his own absurdity as of the other characters';
> the comic, we are made to feel, is the other face of the tragic,
> and absurdity is at the heart of things.'

Much of *The Polyglots* was written at Innsbruck. Gerhardie
completed it under difficult conditions, while his father was
dying. His mother would read out pages from the manuscript
to the old man 'to kill time', and for the most part he listened
without comment, though occasionally pronouncing some passage
to be 'instructive'. But when she came to the sea-burial of Natasha
– a scene of exquisite verbal simplicity – she began to cry, and this
bothered him. 'Don't cry,' he urged her. 'It's not real. It's only a
book. Willy has invented it.'

On *The Polyglots* were pinned all their hopes of re-making the
family fortune, but Gerhardie's father died a few months before
publication. The book did make Gerhardie's name as a novelist;
but as to the fortune he later calculated that, contrary to expectation, it had brought in 'something equivalent, in terms of royalties,
to nothing'.

*   *   *

The short novel, two short stories and one long-short story that
together comprise *Pretty Creatures* were all written between the
years 1925 and 1927, and they show Gerhardie's particular gifts
in their purest form. The prose is highly compressed, stripped of

all inessentials. It relies on verbs and adverbs rather than on adjectives – a cleaner, more wholesome style. In a review of *Pretty Creatures*, Arnold Bennett claimed that here was the prose style of the future: '*Car le mot c'est le Verbe et le Verbe c'est Dieu*'. Not a word is wasted; not a word that does not fit with its neighbours to contribute to a peculiar and insistent rhythm. From 'Tristan und Isolde', a most exquisite *aperçu* of Wagner's opera running correlatively with the mounting ecstasy and agony of 'der ode Tag', to 'The Big Drum', a record that every dog has his day; from 'The Vanity Bag', a truthful piece of *genre* centred on Innsbruck with its provincial setting of the Austrian parochial aristocracy, to his étude on black notes 'A Bad End', the musical significance of these pretty creatures is everywhere manifest. For however accurately you write, however carefully you define, however logically and clearly you communicate your meaning, there is always some part of the truth that cannot be articulated, and it is this part that must be conveyed by the musical quality of the writing: the tone. In Gerhardie's tone we can catch that fluid undercurrent by which we recognize our life, because we see that he refuses to simplify existence in order to round off a story.

This musical significance also tells us what not to look for in Gerhardie's writing. Would you seek moral instruction in a symphony? If not, then do not look for it here. The implications of such things may exist, but not the things themselves. From all those fashionable and transitory concerns that enable the literary historian neatly to 'place' an author in the ranks of literature Gerhardie seems remarkably free – temporarily, perhaps, to his loss. For his aim is to combine, not segregate. Therefore we must not look in his writing for one aspect of life divorced from another, we must not seek, in isolation, some specialist grain of undissolved information – on unemployment, for example, in the 1920s, or the machinery of the Spanish Civil War. About hunger and war we may read in Gerhardie's books, but not for their own sake, not treated as if they represented the whole of life. His purpose is to create works of beauty, and he sets out to achieve this by the tone of his writing, by keeping in equilibrium many feelings and attitudes that we tend to think of as incompatible –

in particular what is actual with what we conceive to be ideal. He blends realism with romanticism, romanticism with irony. The skill lies in doing this in such a way that the romantic element does not make the story less real but more so, that the irony does not obliterate romance, for reality is all these things and even a lie is an aspect of the truth. It is in the orchestration of these diverse elements that Gerhardie excels. As with music, the delight derives not from guessing what is to come next, but from our memory of its design, from our delighted recognition of the cunning of its parts, our concurrence in the cumulative fitness of the whole.

Since explanation is death in fiction, we should not seek a 'message' in Gerhardie's books. He does not tell us what to think or how to be better citizens, nor does he instruct us who is wrong and who right in these stories. As with life itself we must come to our own conclusions, and enjoy them for the pleasure which they contain. Look, for example, at his story 'In the Wood'. We do not know for certain whether Lieutenant Barahmeiev will make love to the landlord's wife. We do not know whether he is what he seems to be, an empty bluffer, or whether she is in part deceitful. We can read it several ways. The story carries within it another miniature Gerhardie short story in the Lieutenant's recollection of his inconclusive first love affair, and in his audience's response to this story we may hear a parody of the obtuse critic's reaction to Gerhardie's work, a warning of how not to read him:

'The Lieutenant ceased.
'"Well?" we said. "Go on."
'"That's all," said the Lieutenant.
'"But what happened afterwards?" asked Vera Solomonovna.
'"Nothing happened."
'"But *how*?" she said in a tone as though she had been wronged.
'"Well, that's all there is to tell."
'"But – it's no proper story even."
'"I can't help that," he answered, almost angrily. "This is what happened, and this is where it ended. I can't falsify the facts to suit your taste. We don't, my dear Vera Solomonovna, live our lives to provide plots for stories."'

Nor, conversely, should novelists write stories for those who simply want to escape from life. This is not to say that Gerhardie's stories are, as the Lieutenant's was thought to be, pointless or without a moral. 'A Bad End', the story of an unintentional act of manslaughter, the trial for murder, conviction and execution of Mr Proudfoot – accorded the seal of authenticity by Lord Birkenhead, a former Lord Chancellor – was used as propaganda against capital punishment by Victor Gollancz. 'The Vanity Bag', too, is susceptible to moral interpretation. The American who falls in love with a girl in Salzburg, whose vanity bag must needs convince him in the end that he has nothing more to hope from her, is rewarded by the unsought heavy companionship of her literary father – a bag of vanity. But none of these stories are intended to provide us with answers to particular questions. They do not show us how life should be lived – they do not exhort us in this way. Instead they show us our ideals and illusions plus what is, in the material sense, reality. For life, as depicted by Gerhardie, is neither horrible nor happy, but strange and unique, transitory yet static, funny, beautiful and awful. 'But when one listens to music,' Chekhov wrote, 'all this is – that some people lie in their graves and sleep, and that one woman is alive and, grey-haired, is now sitting in a box in the theatre, seems quiet and majestic, and the avalanche [romantic love] no longer meaningless, since in nature everything has a meaning. And everything is forgiven, and it would be strange not to forgive.'

This simultaneous effect of life's diversity is the impression which Gerhardie's work creates, and when we read him we discover with delight that our half-realized thoughts concerning the fluidness, complexity and elusiveness of life have been articulately confirmed.

*   *   *

Pretty Creatures was dedicated, 'in the absence of Napoleon Buonaparte', to Lord Beaverbrook whom Gerhardie first met in 1925. 'Dear Sir, – If it would be convenient for you to call on me here [23 St Bride Street] I should like to see you.' Gerhardie had been in Vienna when this urgent summons from Beaverbrook arrived, and, in other circumstances, he might have remained there several years. However, stopping only to collect his father's urn (which he deposited on his way back at the station cloakroom in Paris), he hastened to London to hear Beaverbrook extol the excellence of *The Polyglots*. 'He had,' remembers Gerhardie, 'very fine judgment.' From this meeting in 1925 there grew a warm friendship, and from this friendship came *Doom*.

Over the next months Beaverbrook entertained Gerhardie very grandly, introducing him to all the smart set in London, the great and the beautiful. 'You must meet him. He's nice,' D. H. Lawrence wrote to Middleton Murry – elsewhere adding: '[He] came to see me for an hour, and stayed seven hours.' Such heady attentions are unusual for a writer, and Gerhardie confesses that he felt flattered. If only, he sometimes reflected, he had had less genius, how Lord Beaverbrook might have helped him! After all, he seemed prepared to do almost anything for him as a journalist: he had even promised him, as a wedding present, the *Evening Standard*. Only Gerhardie, who never married, was not a journalist. 'I am,' he insisted, 'an artist. Probably a great artist. It pleases me when you treat me as an artist.' So that was how Beaverbrook did treat him, tenderly, with affection, but without commercial profit. In vain he had attempted to convert *The Polyglots* into a best-seller (though not, Gerhardie noted, with quite the zeal he put into his Empire Campaign); but his real gift lay in the material he was giving Gerhardie for his next novel.

The whirl of Beaverbrook's hospitality – the yachts, the week-ends, the night clubs – grew so absorbing that it precluded any actual work and before the end of 1925 Gerhardie fled abroad. By New Year's Day 1926 he had set up temporary headquarters in the South of France where, he assured Beaverbrook, 'the Muse is visiting me every morning'. Like Dickens with *Household Words*, he had agreed to write a serialised novel for the *Daily Express* and, in a burst of optimism, was soon confiding that 'I am getting lots of fun, and a fair amount of happiness, out of writing this serial, now that I am free from interruption, and I do not think you will be disappointed. Ah, if I could perhaps persuade you to become a novelist! To experience that rare feeling of walking a little outside and beside life ... on the roof of No 23 St Bride Street.'

Gerhardie's correspondence with Beaverbrook at this time gives a fascinating account of the novel's development, the author's personality and his friendship with the chief character in the book. Already, by February 1926, he is admitting that his serial 'is in a bad way'. His imagination was not that of a science fiction writer, and by placing the narrative in the future he felt that he risked giving it an air of unreality. He wanted, for example, a handful of people left on a mountain top with the rest of the world disintegrated to nothing. The problem had defeated the trained scientific mind of H. G. Wells (who suggested it would have to be a dream) and it was D. H. Lawrence who, breaking out into ripples of girlish laughter at the ingenuity of his solution, gave him the metaphor of a laddered stocking, so that the world disintegrated piecemeal. It is not every day that a world vanishes so plausibly, or with so much delicacy and charm.

But the reality which at first seemed so elusive on paper was presenting itself elsewhere in the most inconvenient ways. His house in the South of France, on which he had spent much time and whitewash, had let him down. 'The hens won't lay, the doors won't lock, the stoves won't heat,' he complained to Beaverbrook; and the maid, 'a slender girl of sixteen summers', had become, in place of his novel, the centre of all his thoughts and actions – though mainly because she suffered from constant toothache and 'wants attending to'. However, he promised, 'I will see to it that literature does not suffer.'

A further threat to the book was, he believed, supplied by Rebecca West whom Gerhardie met at Antibes and who 'curiously enough is also writing a book about you', he accused Beaverbrook (14 September 1926). His dismay was shortlived. 'My sense of dissatisfaction with myself,' he explained, 'completely left me when I learnt that she had been at it for three years.' He himself had been at work now a mere year or so and was returning to the task 'with renewed interest. The fact of the matter was that when I started writing I was too close to the experiences (in London) which inspired it. I can only write in retrospect, when the irrelevant has filtered through and the essential remains in my memory; and I am now approaching this condition of mind and soul.'

During this period he received almost obtrusive encouragement from Beaverbrook. 'Will you go on with your novel now?' he asked; '... why don't you come and see me again? You should settle in this country here for a few months. I will pay your expenses.' Wisely Gerhardie resisted the temptation. 'As for my settling down in England, your offer to pay my expenses is characteristically generous,' he replied, 'but I'd hate to come empty-handed. I think if I stay here I will produce the novel.' His confidence seemed justified, and by October he was reporting that 'the old plot has been reinforced by a new one and the newspaper proprietor is involved in a *story*, for which you won't thank me. I am really glad that I postponed it, for it is stronger and better and madder than before.'

If *Doom* is Gerhardie's maddest novel, this was partly due to the element of comic fantasy that he had by now successfully introduced into his relationship with Beaverbrook. Connoisseurs of Gerhardie have always admired the manner in which he eclipses what is actual with what is fantastic to produce his own subtle light of reality. The newspaper world was an ideal arena in which to practise this art. It was not long before he was promising, indeed threatening, with 'a flourish of the pen', to take over all policy decisions on behalf of the Beaverbrook press. For a start, on the literary side, why should they not publish plays – he happened to have just completed one himself. Then there was the question of foreign policy. Luckily Gerhardie had a brother domiciled in Helsingfors, so there was no difficulty there. 'He is not a journalist,' Gerhardie reassured Beaverbrook, adding by way of endorsement, 'Helsingfors is not Rome'. On artistic matters generally, Gerhardie entertained far-ranging plans. 'What I really meant to ask you,' he explained to Beaverbrook (27 December 1926), 'was whether you would care to collaborate with me in writing a musical comedy ... I have a good plot, and a number of unexpectedly promising melodies have occurred to me. I have a certain difficulty in writing them down as my musical education is sadly inadequate. But I could overcome this by humming them into a recording phonograph; and no doubt you could produce others, and we could get some old hack to set them down in writing and to orchestrate the thing in accordance with our wishes. You once told me that you had a great gift for jazz music, and having received could no doubt emit a fair supply of it! And you are full of stimulating ideas as I remember when discussing my novel with you.'

Under the continuous pressure of such advice, Lord Beaverbrook absconded for some time to the Upper Nile, but a stream of fantasy pursued him even to the seat of his holiday. Gerhardie himself had descended into Algeria where 'a beautiful new mistress ... comes to see me three times a week and costs me 50 francs a time, and so I can't afford to neglect a chance of selling my article ...' These Algerian adventures, which were eventually to enrich his novel *Resurrection*, could, so Gerhardie judged, be put to immediate use in the columns of the *Daily Express* for the moral benefit of its readers. 'I've been round to a number of houses of ill-fame for which Algiers is ill-famed,' he explained, 'but my instinct for self-preservation causes me, in this place, to multiply precautions so that I feel I might be in a padded overcoat. There is more comedy than lust about these places. Sex *is* a problem – for the *Daily Express* to solve. Very simple. Birth control, on the one hand; the elimination of disease on the other; and free love after that. There is no danger of overstepping the mark as some Puritans imagine; for when people have had enough they stop.'

Such commonsense fantasies were parried by Beaverbrook (the son of a rector) unsatisfactorily, until Gerhardie felt obliged to inform him (16 January 1927): 'I am very disappointed in you. I think newspaper proprietors ought to be altogether abolished and all control seized by the authors!!'

That summer, the sun slowly drove Gerhardie north – but he was no longer empty-handed. From Paris he announced (21 June 1927) the conditions for his invasion of London. 'I should like to come and show you my serial. But if you are cruising in the Mediterranean or shooting birds in remote corners of the country or otherwise not in the mood to attend to my particular literature I will stay in Paris, which city, but for your absence from it, appeals to me more than London, which, conversely, appeals to me mainly on account of your presence there.' A few days later Beaverbrook (who had just written an *Express* article about

Gerhardie as a 'Splendid Failure') picked him up at Ostend in a yacht full of girls. So the extraordinary friendship continued to prosper and to fertilize Gerhardie's *Doom*.

Gerhardie was now at the height of his literary fame and this new novel, like the accouchement of a political Duchess, was awaited with considerable speculation. When it appeared in April 1928 it sold better than any of the previous books and he was acknowledged, almost everywhere, to be a master of the ridiculous. The looseness of the book's structure enabled Gerhardie to combine an extravagant fantasia with a Fleet Street satire, fusing them together with poetry and wit. Yet amid the potpourri of comedy and manners, there is an underlying melancholy which culminates in the atomic disintegration of all but a few refugees in a hotel on a rounded mountain top isolated from the earth and now circling the sun – a token world for the vanished planet.

It is a confusing book. Evelyn Waugh, whose favourite Gerhardie novel it always remained, compared the writing to that of Ivy Compton Burnett, and elsewhere critics likened it to, among others, Beerbohm, Giraudoux, Huxley and 'the cool irresponsible dexterity of Paul Morand'. Re-reading it today, *Doom* seems like nothing else in the language, and the best contemporary critic was probably Arnold Bennett who wrote of its 'wild and brilliant originality'.

In his autobiography, Gerhardie portrayed Beaverbrook as 'a potential great man without a mission'. It was, in the judgment of Beaverbrook's biographer A. J. P. Taylor, 'the only book known to me which gives anything like a convincing picture of Beaverbrook in middle age'. *Doom*, in many ways, is a vehicle for exploring the sensations felt within the orbit of Beaverbrook who, as Lord Ottercove the newspaper Napoleon, is described as 'the big drum in the jazz band of our civilization' whose saving grace was that he 'suffered from an inferiority complex in the presence of Lord Beaverbrook'. Before getting to know him, Gerhardie had regarded Beaverbrook as 'less of a personality than a power', though he soon found his force and charm to be 'quite irresistible'. Yet in *Doom* Ottercove retains his power, even in dishabille. In his vest and pants he is 'still looking the part, still the unchallenged proprietor of the *Daily Runner*'. Gerhardie handles him with great subtlety, and with a ruthlessness which yet somehow shows both appreciation and affection. Whenever Ottercove appears on the scene the other characters take their lead from him. At one point someone suggests a celebration. 'Lord Ottercove did not reply. Lord Ottercove hated to act on other people's suggestions ... If he approved of a suggestion he said nothing; then, a few moments later, made it himself. "I'm taking you out tonight, all of you."'

For all its absurdities the book works and is largely held together by Ottercove's power which does not dominate the other characters but draws reactions from them. His immense energy carries along a huge entourage that includes several people Gerhardie had met through Beaverbrook – Lord Castlerosse who appears as Lord de Jones, and Arnold Bennett who, in the guise of Vernon Sprott, is described as 'a writer of talent but a merchant of genius'. Then, in the young novelist Frank Dickin, we catch an amusing glimpse of the William Gerhardie of that time, in turn anxious, elated, dismayed but always observant with a quiet authority.

Some extra confusion has been shed on this confusing novel by the multiplicity of its titles. Gerhardie had originally wanted to call it *Doom*, but his British publishers vetoed this on the ground that such reverberations of gloom would at once kill all sales. In America, even his second choice *Jazz and Jasper* (a title which hinted at the two values, social and spiritual, that in collision provide the theme of the novel) was also unacceptable. The Jazz Age, which according to Scott Fitzgerald had begun with the May Day riots of 1919, was already almost over, and Gerhardie was obliged to rename his book *Eva's Apples*. When, in 1947, the novel was republished its title was improved to *My Sinful Earth* and the title page bore an explanatory epigraph from Shakespeare's sonnet CXLVI:

> 'Poor soul, the centre of my sinful earth,
> Fool'd by these rebel powers that thee array,
> Why dost thou pine within and suffer dearth,
> Painting thy outward walls so costly gay?'

Only now, some forty-five years after its first appearance, has this novel of the twenties, that foreshadows the coming of our own era, reverted to its original title *Doom* which seems, the author ventures to think, an understatement.

*   *   *

Gerhardie's novels 'on Russian themes' attracted a considerable following in the 1920s. He toured America delivering lectures; and was described by Arnold Bennett as 'the pet of the intelligentsia and the darling of Mayfair'. No writer, as Neville Braybrooke has reminded us, could 'have been more lionised'. But a number of writers were suspicious of the fuss made over him at this time.

Far from being one of those cynical and sophisticated good-time-in-a-bad-world stereotypes, so rampant in the gay twenties, Gerhardie believed neither in the good time nor the bad world. Despite a title that suggests embittered disillusionment, *Futility* had questioned why man was having such a bad time in a good world; and in *The Polyglots* and *Doom* the author had further explored this theme. By 1930 the period of popular post-war discouragement was at an end, but the mislabelling attached to Gerhardie's ironical tragedies stuck. 'Sophistication, cynicism and the like, which still cling to me, I don't know why, have not endeared me to anyone,' he wrote to his publisher in May 1931. 'Sobriety, a dogged dullness, goodness and honest stupidity should be stressed as features characteristic of me. Then England will begin to read my books.'

England had ceased to read his books once he had begun to write about Englishmen. It was all very well for Russians and other foreigners with unpronounceable names to behave in a 'Chekhovian' manner; but Englishmen, living just round the corner in Kennington, simply did not do so. They were too sensible.

In this peculiar way Gerhardie's work began to lose favour. The novels he wrote in the thirties are in no sense inferior to those of the twenties. But the swing in fashion to sociological literature and politically 'committed' verse and fiction did not produce a climate in which Gerhardie's individual gifts could be readily appreciated. *Pending Heaven* (1930) was the first to suffer although, as the critic Gorley Putt has pointed out in his book *Scholars of the Heart*, this novel contains within it the same beat of life as its predecessors:

> 'It recaptures the impudent tenderness of *Futility* and *The Polyglots* and with it the authentic Gerhardie note. There are a couple of enchanting, exasperating Gerhardie children. And in this gay pavilion there are those clear panes through which can be seen the white radiance, when not of eternity, then of the inescapable human predicament.'

Pending Heaven is the story of two men treading the donkey-round of paradise deferred, their literary friendship strained to breaking point by rivalry in love. The opening chapter is consecrated to Gerhardie's meeting with that sensitive and ebullient character Hugh Kingsmill, with whom he was to form a long, precarious friendship. 'Kingsmill's habit, I regret to say,' he wrote in *Memoirs of a Polyglot*, 'is to abscond and set up house with someone in whom I have invested a good deal of emotion, and then to defend the purity of their hearth against my visits, though indulgent enough to consent to meet me outside his new home.' Kingsmill's remarkable personality helped to provide Gerhardie with the character of Max Fisher – 'a great, sensitive, witty being, boisterous, tender, and refreshing as a sea breeze'.

Max Fisher's search for love – 'a state of well-being native and near to him from which he has been sundered' – is the theme of *Pending Heaven*. 'But as each woman who attracts him figures for a time as the custodian of the happiness he is seeking,' Kingsmill wrote in *The Progress of a Biographer*, 'he becomes more and more involved in the world from which he is trying to escape, until death suddenly sets him free.'

The particular excellence of *Pending Heaven* is that through the imaginative use of symbol and metaphor it expresses complicated things very simply. The tone is one of freshness, of warmth and suppleness. We are spared that glaze of intellectuality which can come between the writer and his subject, making simple things seem complicated. Gerhardie does not set out to invent 'psychologically convincing characters' since he believes (as Philip Toynbee has explained) that 'this involves a superfluous artifice which cuts across the grain of his natural material'. He also believes that the construction of artful and well-balanced plots – in the manner of Henry James – is a mistaken ambition for the novelist, because elaborate artifice only strangles the plots that exist in life itself. His own ultimate aim as a novelist has been to reveal the beauty of the world, in however strange, wry or distinctive a form. 'Candour and tenderness are the guardian angels of this novelist,' wrote Gorley Putt, '– and frivolity his attendant imp.' But since the comic and the tragic attitudes are deeply intermingled in Gerhardie, *Pending Heaven* is neither farce nor satire. Its humorous, lyrical pages, which give one continual small shocks of delight as one reads them, are intimations of a genuine poetic sensibility responding to the underlying mystery of life.

Pending Heaven marks a watershed in Gerhardie's literary career. His next novel, *Resurrection*, which was published four years later in 1934, seems very different from his first books. If *The Polyglots* was conceived by the Evelyn Waugh generation at Oxford to be the young man's bible, *Resurrection* became the mature reader's *via ad poesem*. Already, in *The Polyglots*, he had touched the nerve of faith. 'If,' he asks, 'the whole world be unreal, by what standard, what undying reality is it so? If we are to be dead for all time, by what living truth is it to be?' Elsewhere in the novel, when the narrator is asked whether we survive after death, he answers in the affirmative. But the next life, he adds, is disconnected from our world: it is a release from memory, a perpetuation of the immortal I.

Another possibility involving the shedding, like dirty linen, both of the memory and of the self, is put forward in *Pending Heaven*. Mr Jones, in this life, is Mr Jones by virtue of his constant anxiety to be helpful to Mr Jones, to go out of his way to serve Mr Jones. When death comes, all that is left of Mr Jones is a soul-liberating feeling that cares not two hoots for the late Mr Jones. Yet it is possible to argue, Gerhardie says, that this impersonal feeling represents, like the butterfly concealed within the grub, the real, the integral Mr Jones who, having got rid of his bodily shackles, is at last able to be his unrestricted self.

Gerhardie who, as I think his short story 'A Bad End' shows, had once been afraid of death, nourished a poetic yearning for immortality which was in no way supported by sentimentality.

> 'The immortality I desire [he confessed in *Memoirs of a Polyglot*], I cannot imagine, for the immortality I can imagine I am wise enough not to desire. My hope is that, if there cannot, must not, be a heaven according to my present liking, there will be one according to a view of things to which I shall be won over.'

As a natural optimist he was 'fully confident' in his survival after death; as a natural realist 'I would not care to stake £5 on it, if it came to the point'. That, in 1931, was the extent to which he was inclined to take belief on trust.

Three years later his beliefs had completely altered. In *Memoirs of a Polyglot* he had first suggested the possibility of an alternative state of immortality – a Mr Jones 'suffused with memories mellowed by this distance of time into poetry, rightly defined as "emotion recollected in tranquillity"'. It is this view of a Mr Jones *in excelsis* to which he was won over while writing *Resurrection*, and it is this conception which he explored in his novel.

Resurrection is an adventure story – a 'thought-adventure' as Walter Allen calls it – of a novelist who, in the book, is writing a novel to be called *Resurrection*. Early on, while resting before a London ball, the hero wakes to find himself detached from the gross envelope of his body, an astral projection unconfined by the prison of time and space. Following this occult experience, he goes that night to the ball at which, against a background of social comedy, this theme is taken up and developed into a passionate argument for the immortality of the soul, illustrated by the recollections of a year rich in travel and having the power to evoke a vanished lifetime in a day.

When I first read William Gerhardie's books some fifteen years ago, I was under the impression that he had already achieved, in a permanent form, the state of immortality about which he wrote with such eloquence. *Resurrection*, it seemed to me, was his masterpiece. Re-reading his books now, I am still of that opinion. It is, as Toynbee has written, 'an astonishing Proustian master-

piece ... which embraces more of Gerhardie, more of his attitudes, personality and literary achievement than any other'. But
it is also, as Hugh Kingsmill warned readers in his Preface to the
1948 edition, 'a bewilderingly rich book in which it is easy to lose
the way'. Many have done just this. To Aleister Crowley, the
Great Beast 666, Gerhardie figured as a dangerous rival in the
world of coloured magic. 'You are right to brush aside Gerhardie's
vague experiments and half-baked metaphysics,' Crowley urged
James Agate (4 October 1934). 'Why not listen to those who have
given a life's work to the subject?' But Agate would not listen,
and the Great Beast continued to shake his head in wonder at the
attention Gerhardie's single astral projection had attracted: 'Why,
I've 'ad 'undreds!' he complained.

Resurrection is not a volume of hocuspocus. Some critics, it is
true, have questioned whether it is a novel in the accepted sense;
but such classifications are beside the point. It is perhaps what
Tristram Shandy was supposed to be, Kingsmill once observed,
but wasn't. The form which it takes, in its originality, may appear
strange at first, but this is no arid literary experiment. The shape
and style, even the highly self-absorbed tone which Graham
Greene described as 'an impudence if we did not feel it as a charm',
are all dictated by the unusual material and what Gerhardie
needed to structure out of it. As one grows familiar with the
book one begins to appreciate that it is so comprehensive in
plan, to use the words of Edwin Muir, 'that no better form could
have been devised for the writer's purpose of describing an
experience of his in which his soul leaves his body, and from this
experience setting out to demonstrate the immortality of the
soul'.

Resurrection is a philosophical not a scientific work. Its significance is not simply that it convinced Gerhardie that we do not
die, but that it has revealed to him a poetically invaluable illumina-
tion of reality. As witty as *Futility* or *The Polyglots*, it displays a
dialectical genius and a power of poetic invention that many
would not have suspected in these earlier novels.

'In the present I am held in a vice by the future,' Gerhardie
reflects. 'But if I strive to live in the future I am held in a vice by
images of the past. However much I twist and turn, I am doomed

to live in the past. Only in death can I redeem the present – be free to roam in it at will.' This underlying theme he subsequently formulated in the phrase 'Nothing is until it is over.' To the future, to immortality itself, he looks forward with a sense of nostalgia. 'A man's real life,' Hugh Kingsmill explained in his lucid critique of *Resurrection*,

'... is not in his desires, so engrossing till they are realized, nor in his projects, so clear in anticipation, so vague in recollection, but in the feelings and images, irrelevant to his purposes, which float above him as he presses forward, the hound Habit and the bitch Anxiety at his heels, what is left of him by the one being torn to rags by the other. Only in the realm of memory is he safe: "From here he can retrace his steps in their world and the two dogs cannot touch him; so he lives his life over again, lingering in the roads and lanes through which he has fled with the two angry hounds at his heels, and this time it is good."

'To illustrate his meaning, Gerhardie narrates the story of a certain year in his life. In this narrative, a masterpiece of imaginative humour, the humour is rooted in a perception not of what is socially incongruous, humour's usual subject matter, but of what is spiritually incongruous. The habit, which still lingers on, of regarding humour and religious insight as incompatible derives from the Old Testament conception of the divine. In the presence of an angry God, as of an angry employer, schoolmaster or drill-sergeant, the range of humour is necessarily a narrow one. Humour and the universe have enlarged their boundaries together, and the subject matter of humour in its highest development is the other side of ecstasy, the soul looking back at its strange movements when it was tethered to the tree of Time, as ecstasy is the soul untethered and content. So after the narrative comes the vision – "Dream on, tall elms in windy sunshine. Grow green and young. Oaks, send up your sap through lusty hollows! Trees, stretch out your branches, drink with your leafy lungs the ocean air! And I'll live on. . . ."'

Quite different in mood, though still unmistakably Gerhardiesque, was his next novel, *Of Mortal Love*, which I suspect to be his own favourite. It is a simple love story, its narrative extending like a chain of tiny trigger movements releasing enormous emotional forces. The characters, especially the enchanting and wayward Dinah, may behave superficially or appear rootless: but the theme of the novel is a profound and ambitious one – a charting of the development of human love, through succeeding stages, from the erotic to the imaginative – the very theme, in reverse, of Donne's poem 'The Ecstasy'.

Few things are more difficult to achieve than unsentimentalized simplicity. The book was first published in 1936, but there is evidence to show that Gerhardie had been engaged on it as early as 1920. A love story, pure and simple, was always one of his most cherished literary ambitions, but from year to year he would postpone it for writing less fragile and elusive. Urged by Katherine Mansfield in 1922 not to abandon it, he continued steadily, if intermittently, to bring it to fulfilment. Even after the first publication he considerably reshaped its structure for a new edition that was brought out thirteen years later.

Of Mortal Love is remarkable for its carefully-pitched tone – a deft blending of humour, pathos, and tenderness that is exactly appropriate for revealing the mystery of the love it chronicles. Its form is most skilfully and deliberately wrought, yet the mood is one of complete naturalness, and it achieves a miraculous mixture of candour and sophistication. 'Nothing in the world comes between Mr Gerhardie and the true expression of his feelings,' C. P. Snow has written of this novel, '– without the slightest trace of moral vanity, without any preconception of what one is expected to feel, he just sets down what his emotions truly are, in simplicity of heart, in a spirit free from shame, both innocent and penitential.'

*   *   *

Gerhardie's last novel, *My Wife's the Least of It*, represents his only foray into the hilarious Pickwickian tradition of novel writing. Its structure is episodic, for it's an offshoot of the picaresque novel and relies on a high proportion of dialogue. Since people do not behave logically in life, neither should they do so in fiction. But in Gerhardie's books they *attempt* to do so. What he shows us is the lunacy of logic, and the illogical quagmires into which the straight and narrow path of logic unerringly leads us. His dialogue catches this illogical paradox, or paradox of logic, marvellously well, and his meticulously odd speech rhythms, repetitive yet with intricate variations, are like a musical refrain serving to orchestrate the idiosyncratic behaviour of his characters.

Like much of Gerhardie's fiction, the literary value of *My Wife's the Least of It* does not depend upon suspense or dense plot construction. It is a sane study of general insanity, and the technique which Gerhardie employs to heighten this insanity is one that he had first put to use sixteen years earlier in *Futility*: perpetual deferment. Ostensibly this novel is the expanded version of an original manuscript written by Mr Baldridge, a one-time novelist who, following his marriage to a mad millionairess, rises to a position of unprecedented public esteem in the administration of charities. This device enables Gerhardie to portray Mr Baldridge's inside history, as the Swedish critic Bo Gunnarsson has pointed out, without identifying himself with his central character.

When Mr Baldridge succeeds in welcoming without any sense of shock the fact of his sixty-first birthday, he feels able to congratulate himself on having reached a philosophical condition of life, a period of discreet maturity where greed, lust, even vanity itself, have finally been conquered. Calm might not be life's crown but calm was best. But then a young man, Harold Burke, recognizes the likelihood of a film in Baldridge's one-time success, a pre-war novel called *Dixie*; and in the endless peregrinations and vicissitudes of this film script we see how Baldridge, a man no better and no worse than any other man, is tempted into losing his new-found power of renunciation. Not *why* but *why not* becomes his motivating question. What weakens the springs of his soul's resistance to this life is nothing more nor less than the pressure of epic idiocy. For how can a man compose his soul in patience within such a lunatic climate? And how can he fail to get the better of such stupidity? This is a seductive question for those who have forgotten Goethe's warning that against stupidity the gods themselves struggle in vain.

'Five hundred pages of uninterrupted laughter' – this was how, quoting a review, Faber and Faber (the book's original publisher) advertised it. Yet, in truth, this is a sad book – not depressing, for it is wonderfully fertilized by humour, but remorseless, like a Chinese torture. The unfortunate Baldridge is never the pessimist: it is his continual optimism that exhausts him. As the lost opportunities multiply and the absurdity rises almost to a screaming pitch, we may protest, 'Surely this is enough.' But we are not to be spared. The pointless unavailing activity spins us round faster and faster; the switchback of anticipation and disappointment jolts us ever more mercilessly up and down until we cry out in desperation – and still we are not heeded, but ingeniously carried, without regard to our feelings, on and on.

Gerhardie does not tell us that all hope is vain. He shows us that hope, if harnessed exclusively to the external world, must take us nowhere in the end. The intimations in *My Wife's the Least of It* are of money, not immortality; and the paradise that is so tantalisingly deferred is of this world alone. He has not written a social satire, still less a critique of the film industry (though what better book, in the circumstances, to be filmed?): he has given us an illustration, detail by dire detail, minute by minute, of our life in time. The film world symbolises the visible surface of things divorced from all poetic implications. It is actual, but unreal. It is nightmare. Everyone is tremendously excited about *Dixie* and no one ever rejects it. But nobody really cares about it, only about what they might get out of it, and at the conclusion, after all the harrowing misadventures, it is doubtful whether anyone has read a single word of it. Here surely, was a prophetic glimpse into the age of McLuhan. In such a world everything is there for man to abuse. Through *My Wife's the Least of It*, hidden to closed hearts, there runs the whole gamut of the Word from the Garden of Eden to the Garden of Gethsemane.

My Wife's the Least of It is remarkable for the number of characters from Gerhardie's other novels who, as in some final curtain call, reappear. From *The Polyglots* there is Aunt Teresa, much the same but more subdued; Uncle Emanuel, now the skilled inventor of totally useless devices; and Major Beastly, as honest and insensitive, as stupid and straightforward as ever. Mary Brandon who once, because incapable of understanding its vital importance, lost her chance to love, is the same Mary Brandon of Gerhardie's play *Donna Quixote*. Lord Cornet, an ever-absent film magnate of whom there is much discussion, comes from *Pending Heaven*, where he plays a similarly elusive role. This trick of reintroducing his own characters in slightly altered connotations was one subsequently employed by Evelyn Waugh. But Waugh's tone is less gentle than Gerhardie's and in its component parts (as opposed to its cumulative effect) more exaggerated. During the Coronation of George VI, Gerhardie's Aunt Minnie, who originally appeared in *Of Mortal Love* and whose enthusiasm for the ceremony is second to no one's, drops off to sleep on the balcony where, hours later, having dreamt of the procession but not actually seen it passing below her, she is found in the drizzling rain, happily waving a miniature Union Jack. The way Evelyn Waugh would have treated this scene, as Gorley Putt suggested, is to send her toppling over the rails or place a parrot on her shoulder, while School of Waugh, seeking to raise the hilarity even further, would have caused the parrot to *push* her off the balcony.

Among the new characters Captain Job Devonshire is perhaps the best drawn, but my own favourite is Marigold, small, slight, with her elaborate coiffure of unrolling curls, her talent for petty troubles, her grudging tone of generosity. In the chapter where she leaves Baldridge's employment, 'Good-Bye Mr Baldridge', Gerhardie has combined comedy and pathos more poignantly perhaps than anywhere else in his work.

Among his novels of the 1930s *My Wife's the Least of It* occupies a place similar to that of *Doom* in the previous decade. Both are prophetic, concerned with the future, but the limited future. Of the possibilities beyond time, which Gerhardie revealed in *Resurrection*, there is no hint – unless it is in Gerhardie's clairvoyant humour which implies another dimension and provides a detached, but not unfeeling, appraisal of Baldridge's predicament. For Baldridge himself, such clairvoyance is more difficult to achieve, for indignation threatens him with loss of humour.

After the desolation in *Of Mortal Love*, 'the rain of tears falling through the shadows of the world' as Desmond MacCarthy wrote, the hilarity of *My Wife's the Least of It* was welcome, and the book was generously received by almost the entire London press when it was first published in 1938. It was, as John Davenport commented, 'a tardy tribute'. But at last nothing (barring a war) seemed able to prevent Gerhardie's novels receiving the general acclaim they had for so long been on the very point of receiving. His theme of protracted patience, however, had developed the habit of spilling over into his own life. For twenty years he had been extraordinarily prolific. Besides his novels and short stories, his *Anton Chekhov*, he had written a brilliant autobiography, *Memoirs of a Polyglot* (1931), collaborated with Hugh Kingsmill on a book about Casanova, with Prince Leopold Loewenstein-Wertheim on a manual of detailed character studies through self-analysis, and with Brian Lunn on a fantastic history of mankind presented through the imaginary experiences of Satan. In 1940 came his final work to date, a massive study of the Romanov dynasty which is substantially a history of Russia. Then silence.

In the thirty-four years since *My Wife's the Least of It* first appeared, Gerhardie has published no new novel, so one is entitled to ask whether, like Baldridge, he has decided against publishing more fiction. That he has been converted from literature to philanthropy there is no sign. For almost a quarter of a century he has been at work on a tetralogy *This Present Breath*, now nearly completed, 'At the fag-end of your life you don't care much what you say or what is said to you,' he has written in a recent essay in *Encounter*:

'One has shot one's bolt, and it is too late, one's loving parents who might have taken some pride in commendation, long since departed, to take much pleasure in praise or hurt at blame.'

Here is a mood of renunciation very similar to that which Baldridge enjoyed at the beginning of *My Wife's the Least of It*. So it is understandable if, with Baldridge's example before him even though his own zeal for writing is unchecked, Gerhardie does not wish to expose himself to what Coleridge called 'the head-dimming, heart-damping principle of judging a work by its defects, not its beauties'.

*   *   *

There have been a number of attempts to revive serious interest in his work during the last thirty years, but by far the most ambitious of these is represented in the revised definitive edition of his works that Macdonald is now preparing. Gerhardie has never lacked admirers. 'He is one of the immortals,' Olivia Manning wrote of him. 'He is our Gogol's overcoat. We all come out of him.' One possible reason for his unjust neglect is suggested by comparing his career with that of E. M. Forster. Forster's six novels were written over a period of nineteen years; Gerhardie's seven over sixteen years. In addition, each produced a volume of short stories, *The Celestial Omnibus* and *Pretty Creatures*, and published several non-fiction titles. Forster's reputation subsequently swelled with every year he failed to write a novel. But while, with nervous modesty, he backed further and further into the limelight, Gerhardie, 'a novelist of at least equivalent stature and achievement' in Philip Toynbee's estimation, seemed to be swaggering off the literary stage altogether. Forster's disciples have always, almost unanimously, agreed that his masterpiece was *A Passage to India*, followed by *Howard's End*. But among Gerhardie's followers there has been no such consensus. Robert Nye has singled out *Of Mortal Love* – 'a sort of prolonged and infinitely complicated orgasm of the imagination' – as his finest novel; but Anthony Powell wrote that the material in *Of Mortal Love* sometimes seems to be not quite sufficiently assimilated by the author: 'that is by the high standards set by *The Polyglots*.' It would not be going too far, he added, to say that *The Polyglots* was 'a classic' – whatever Edith Wharton, who much preferred *Futility*, 'may have thought to the contrary'. On the other hand, Arnold Bennett's favourite was *Doom* (a novel for which Edith Wharton had not a good word) until it was displaced in his affections by *Pending Heaven* (described by Edith Wharton as 'a peach'). To this I should perhaps add that *Resurrection*, my own first choice, is dismissed by C. P. Snow, one of Gerhardie's most appreciative critics, as 'not my favourite'.

This critical disagreement has created a confusing situation, and readers approaching Gerhardie's work for the first time might well do worse than start with *Memoirs of a Polyglot*. From this autobiography they will learn, of course, many facts about the author. His life has been full of 'odd and incredible events', as the poet Michael Ivens has written:

'In 1930, for example, he had set out for Africa to buy himself a harem and found himself, by accident, sharing a cabin with Himmler. The then unknown Nazi official was captivated by Gerhardie's project which, after an excellent start in which Himmler politely carried William's case ashore and, as an apothecary's son-in-law, obligingly sniffed at the anti-flea powder Gerhardie was prudently buying at a French chemist's, ended in a series of Gerhardiean mishaps ... Then there was the unfortunate affair of the collapse of the entire plumbing system in Edith Wharton's château because of half a loaf jettisoned by him down a lavatory, and the story of the prolonged deposit of an urn containing his father's ashes in the left-luggage of a Paris railway station.'

But it is not primarily for its information, nor even simply for its marvellous spirit of comedy that *Memoirs of a Polyglot* is a permanently valuable book. This value comes from its self-revelation, in particular from its revelation of Gerhardie's literary personality, and his technique of making life a vocation and distilling it in fiction.

'It is the book of a man who has found his way through the world by the light of his own lamp [wrote Desmond Mac-Carthy]. Like Mr George Moore he was born candid, and his subtlety springs from a kind of childishness ... Valuing himself for having preserved – without the smallest effort, by the by – his integrity of vision through life, he naturally takes a detached view of his general behaviour, and can record his faults, follies and failures with amusement or unblushing curiosity.'

The new reissue of his works in what he calls an 'as good as posthumous definitive edition' comes not a moment too soon and it is difficult to see how, despite all his passion for postponement, Gerhardie can forestall his proper literary recognition much longer.

The last thirty years, though silent, have not been uneventful. Gerhardie has lived the life of a London hermit, locked and bolted in his flat without newspapers or television or sometimes even radio and heating, his only link with the outside world an endless telephone line, and the remembrance of things past. But in room after room of this flat, stacked in innumerable cardboard boxes, *This Present Breath* has been gradually and with meticulous care evolving. And the answer to those who may have felt anxiety over Gerhardie's creative future must lie with this tetralogy in one volume, over which he has been working for almost a quarter of a century, and which bears its epigraph from Dante's *Paradiso: Legato con amore in un volume.*

Patrick Hamilton

'Behold my income!' Patrick Hamilton apologized to Angus Hall, opening a sombre chest of unread press cuttings. They were, he explained, all reviews of his two stage thrillers *Rope* and *Gaslight*; and it is chiefly for these, and possibly his other thriller, the novel *Hangover Square* (which was twice filmed), that he is best remembered today. Bruce Hamilton, in this slight but charming memoir,* will have done his brother's literary reputation great service if he redirects at least part of the public's attention to the lesser-known work.

The story of Patrick Hamilton's life is strange and sad. His father, the son of a rector, married a prostitute whom he happened to meet in the promenade of the Empire Theatre. From his quixotic exertions to reclaim her she eventually escaped at Wimbledon by throwing herself under a train. He then married a lady, expert in the copying of oil paintings, who sang light songs from time to time, had contributed to the *Strand* magazine, and was to bear him three children of whom Patrick was the youngest. Both had a talent for unhappy marriages (this was her second marriage also) and it was not long before there were violent scenes, aggravated by his drinking.

If it is true that writers need eccentric parents, then Patrick was particularly fortunate in his father. Bernard Hamilton was a born comic, without any sense of humour. A one-time disciple of Madame Blavatsky, he liked to hold forth about religion, Arthur Conan Doyle recalled, 'at great length and very well'. One of these performances in the best Hamiltonian style earned him the congratulations of Henry Irving, who interrupted: '*What* a low comedian you would have made.'

* *The Light Went Out: The Life of Patrick Hamilton* by Bruce Hamilton.

To Patrick's relief, his father travelled widely – and always with great effect. From France he returned with an ineffable Gallic accent; from Italy he came back a conscript father with a dash of Mussolini; Spain gave him an air of grave courtesy and a grandee's dignity; alighting at Euston station, very Scotch and drunk after a trip up north, he declared: 'My boy, if ever it comes to war between England and Scotland, you and I will cross the border.' Shortly afterwards, when Patrick was sent to a commercial school in Holborn, Bernard wrote to instruct him:

'On Sabbath mornings you will sit, regularly, under the minister of the Scots Presbyterian Church near St Pancras. This is a *parade*. You will then proceed to Chiswick, reporting for Dinner at one-thirty, military time – i.e. five minutes early . . . You will bring with you a weekly report on conduct and progress from your tutors, endorsed by the Principal. If any difficulty should arise, you are to say that I, your father, the author and barrister, require this.

'You will make enquiries as to membership of the City Volunteer or Cadet Companies: I believe such bodies still exist. Understand this is an *order*; excuses will have no more avail with me than the preachments of Mormon missionaries.

'For exercise I recommend rowing. Ascertain the conditions of membership of London or Thames Boat Clubs – you cannot hope for Leander.'

The stress between father and son, which under this treatment grew increasingly bad, implanted within Patrick extreme anxiety which took the form of a neurotic fear of the dark and the passionate craving for certainty. Like Graham Greene, his favourite modern novelist with whom his work has many affinities, he needed some absolute faith. But the dogmatic communism he embraced never really suited his gentle personality and created more tension than support.

To get away from his father he went on the stage, playing small parts on tour and in repertory, and picking up the tricks of the trade. But he could never escape from Bernard's genetic influence and his life became a hideous parody of his father's. Extremely susceptible to beautiful girls, he fell desperately in love with a prostitute from whom only emotional exhaustion at last enabled him to release himself. Following his father's example, he also married twice, tearing his life apart between the two women and bringing suffering to all three of them.

As everything got more out of hand, so he began drinking prodigiously. He seemed to be in search of a substitute father from among his friends, who included Claud Cockburn, 'a *grand* drinking companion with a sense of humour' and that generous, irresponsible man-of-promise John Davenport: it was a question of the blind drunk leading the blind drunk. But with drink Patrick lost his humour, became aggressive, *was* his father. Drink paralysed his will, put a stop to his writing and eventually killed him.

It is a tragic story, but for lovers of his work it need not be depressing. For on the page he turned his defeats into advantages: the anxiety into suspense; the doubt into pathos; the monotony into a marvellous spirit of comedy; his drunkenness into a catalyst in the event-plot of *Hangover Square*; a dreadful car accident into the theme of his radio classic *To the Public Danger*. The reality he could not endure in life he used unsparingly in his best work.

His plays are more perfectly constructed and their suspense more ingeniously sustained: but they are on the whole less rich than the novels. The disciplines of playwriting did however force him to omit some of his characteristic faults of repetition and facetiousness. *Rope* is a *tour de force*; *Gaslight* a masterpiece technically and emotionally. But perhaps the best of all is *The Duke in Darkness* with its trembling balance of hope and despair rising at the end to unbearable pathos. This fictional story of the fifteen-year-old imprisonment of the 'Duke of Laterraine' during the French civil wars of the sixteenth century is his *King Lear*, though its epigraph should come from *Richard II*:

> 'I have been studying how I may compare
> This prison where I live unto the world.'

But the novels have more of his peculiar blend of comedy-and-pathos. *Twenty Thousand Streets Under the Sky*, his London trilogy, contains all of him – his sensitivity, suspense, tenderness and his invention of the monster-bore – that terrible mixture of the banal and the sinister who entertains the reader by driving the other characters in the book to distraction. But re-reading it now, his inflation (he uses far too many syllables) and over-deliberation spoil for me what was once his most moving novel. Bruce Hamilton selects as his masterpiece *The Slaves of Solitude* which, with *Hangover Square*, is now re-issued (both with the same introduction by J. B. Priestley). It is, like all his novels, about very ordinary people, about the homeless. 'He takes us into a kind of No-Man's-Land of shabby hotels, dingy boarding-houses and all those saloon bars where the homeless can meet,' writes Mr Priestley, '. . . he is the novelist of innocence, appallingly vulnerable, and of malevolence, coming out of some mysterious darkness of evil.'

It says much about the divorce between the in-bred world of literature and the actual world that Patrick Hamilton should be so neglected by the literary establishment. In the end it is the human anguish that remains with one, a yearning for happiness so passionate that it dissolves the Marxism he proclaims – 'God help us, God help all of us, every one, all of us.'

'Said to be a Writer'

*'However strong the emotion is, one ought to test it . . .
J'ai passé par là, and know how one is carried away
and at the same time, if one is to do good work one must
accept the discipline which can be got, while this emotion
is given to one and shouldn't be sacrificed to the lack
of it.'*

So wrote Charlotte Mew in 1913. The simplicity of this approach
to writing, at a time when the passion for categorization was
dividing poets into opposing camps, explains to some extent why
she herself remained so curiously unplaced in the ranks of her
contemporaries. She moved rarely, and with distaste, in literary
circles. Her apparent lack of intellectuality precluded her both
from the Bloomsbury milieu and from its pre-war satellite, the
Imagists, while her economy of language and avoidance of sentimentality in dealing with man's loneliness in isolation from God
and his fellow creatures, set her apart from the rural prettiness of
much Georgian poetry and second-rate patriotism of the Imperial
poets. Other reasons for her neglect are not difficult to surmise. A
Collected Edition of her poems appeared in 1953, with a valuable
biographical introduction by Mrs Harold Monro, wife of the
Georgian poet and publisher, and a personal friend of Charlotte
Mew during the last fourteen years of her life. Biographical investigations were hampered nevertheless by her own formidable
views on what she considered permissible to write about a dead
friend. 'I have never forgotten,' writes Mrs Monro, 'her tirade
to me about what she considered to be Violet Hunt's treatment of
W. H. Hudson in what she wrote about him after his death. . . .

It was my knowledge of her views on such matters that kept me
fifteen years producing the Memoir . . .'

Analytical appreciations of her work were similarly baulked by
her rage at any attempt to unearth psychological or physiological
phenomena in her poetry. A book on the Endocrine Glands,
which analysed 'I have been through the Gates' in a manner
popular in the heyday of Freudian psycho-analysis, provoked
terror among her friends, lest someone should inadvertently draw
her attention to it. Fortunately, none of her acquaintances were
interested in the subject, but the question remained: in the absence
of documentary material, how many, if any, biographical assump-
tions could reasonably be made from the work of this writer?

Born in 1869, the eldest of four children, into an upper-middle-
class Victorian family, Charlotte Mew gave the appearance of
being a product typical of her age and environment. Letters, personal documents and the testimonies of her contemporaries give
no indication that she deviated on any occasion from the rigid
moral code which she professed, and her poetry provides a
curiously moving example of a writer whose work bears no
apparent relation to the circumstances of her life or to the ethics
upon which her personal behaviour rested. The slightest breath of
scandal sufficed for her to break friendships completely and for
always, as happened in the case of May Sinclair, whose companionship and admiration she had valued over several years. On similar grounds she snubbed an invitation from Ottoline Morrell, at a
time when the patronage of that lady was coveted by writers and
artists considerably better placed than herself.

Such an uncompromising attitude formed a strange contrast to
the sympathy and reverence with which she handled human
frailties in her poetry, and to her indictments against a God she
saw as subjugator and antagonist, imposing His Will on a
passionate and recalcitrant humanity.

> 'If it is your will that we should be content
> with the tame, bloodless things.
> As pale as angels smirking by, with
> folded wings –
> Oh! I know Virtue, and the peace it brings!'

Her fierce resistance to overtures of friendship, and her apparent indifference to criticism, concealed only partially a very real solitude that became eventually an extension of her despair in isolation from God.

> 'But, up there, from Your still, star-lighted
> > tree
> What can You know, what can You really
> > see
> Of this dark ditch, the soul of me?'

Suspicious of praise, and amazed that anyone should want to read her work, she was nevertheless deeply moved when in 1923, at the instigation of Masefield and Hardy, she was accorded recognition in the form of a Civil List pension of £75 a year. A letter of the period, to Sydney Cockerell, revealed something of the self-eclipsing nature of her personality:

'... when you showed me Masefield's letter and said you'd spoken to Hardy, I felt I was in the water and couldn't get out without such ungraciousness to all you good and great people that there seemed nothing for it but to stay there and be as grateful as a (morally) "demn moist body" can be. Still it's the most unnatural thing I've ever done, and makes me feel a sort of suicide.'

When financial disaster struck her family in 1898, the Victorian in her had asserted itself. It was two years before the ignominy of the presence of lodgers on the top floor of their Gordon Street house became known even to close friends. The necessity for maintaining appearances perpetuated the mystery surrounding the two youngest children in the family, who, it was learnt after Charlotte's death, had both been committed to asylums in the Isle of Wight, when scarcely out of childhood. Tormented by their condition and its possible implications, she and her sister, Anne, had pledged themselves to celibacy. In their loneliness they drew closer to each other, Charlotte – reticent and inclined to melancholy – finding a perfect complement in her sister, an accomplished artist with a natural gaiety of spirit, who in appearance closely resembled Marie-Antoinette. 'They were,' said one acquaintance, 'like two Brontë sisters reincarnate.'

The presence, in Anne, of a confidante and companion now largely sufficed in the way of contact with the outside world, and Charlotte defiantly resisted attempts to draw her out of her retreat. From Dieppe she wrote in 1914:

'It makes all the difference to be in the right place ... one realizes the place much more alone I think – it's all there is and you don't feel it through another mind which mixes up things – I wonder if Art – as they say, is a rather inhuman thing ...'

In 1919 she sent the following, more spirited reply, to an invitation from Sydney Cockerell, then director of the Fitzwilliam Museum, to visit him in Cambridge:

'As to Cambridge, Dear and very kind Mr Cockerell, I am not going to Cambridge, or to Oxford, or to any other strange houses, or to see any other strange people, for the good of my soul or body, any more than your Sub-Prioress, for the good of hers, is going back into the world, which perhaps both of us know well enough. "In short", as Mary Stuart would say, "we are au contraire".'

Breaching the fortifications of the Mew stronghold was made considerably more hazardous by the presence of Willie – a nonagenarian, man-hating parrot, who swore at male intruders, and who had eventually to be chloroformed in his dotage by a woman friend, since his hatred of men precluded a vet. In masochistic defiance of this formidable trio (reinforced, until her death, by 'Ma'), Cockerell's visits persisted, accompanied by such mollifying gifts as maroon leather-bound copies of Keats from the library of the Fitzwilliam. Aware of a certain 'anxious indignation' on Cockerell's part as she preferred the book on loan to a friend who was present, Charlotte – in an interlude of merriment reminiscent of an occasion in her youth when she had danced in directoire knickers in the cabin of a Channel ferry – added: '*Yes and don't use a rasher of bacon for a bookmark*'.

In later years a factotum, Jane, was employed to help with the running of the house, and did much to maintain the sublunary atmosphere of Delancey Street, where the sisters now lived. In 1921 a letter to Mrs Monro revealed new discoveries of poetical talent:

'... If the Poetry Bookshop is looking for a new Keats, Jane picked up a Charlady (at her Friday Chapel Entertainment) who is wanting a publisher for her verses – literally done over the stair – some 150 I believe – the chef d'oeuvre are on the Cinegraft i.e. Cenotaph ... Jane thinks 158 is "a great quantity for a pare person" ...'

As for her own output, it fell rather short of this figure. After 1916 she in fact produced very little, and the books which she had formerly devoured with such voracity ceased to occupy so much of her time: 'Poor Dr Scott,' she wrote from France in 1914, 'says domesticities have stopped me writing "just as she'd started a new book" – the marvel is, she ever does start them.'

And in 1920, she confessed that her reading average was 'about two books per annum, and now declining'.

The gradual falling-off of intellectual and artistic activity was partly the result of a weakening of concentrative powers, exacerbated by constant interruptions from Jane, although she herself encouraged rumours that she used pages of her own manuscripts to make spills for Willie to chew, or to light the cigarettes which she hand-rolled and smoked continuously to offset her nervousness. More generally, her approach to subjects, by the side door of emotion, possibly rendered her inadequate to deal with the direct horrors of war, and the few poems of 1915–18 – 'Epitaph', 'May, 1915', and 'Cenotaph', perpetuate the unlocalized sadness of the prewar poems. It was this quality that separated her from the Georgian poets. Owen and Sassoon with whom the world of poetry again entered the world of public affairs.

Ironically, it was not until 1915, when she was well into middle-age and had already written her best poetry, that she made her first appearance in the Poetry Bookshop. 'She was', writes Mrs Monro, 'very small, only about four feet ten inches. She wore a long double-breasted top-coat of tweed with a velvet collar inset, and carried a horn-handled umbrella, unrolled, under her arm, as if it were psychologically necessary to her, a weapon against the world. The whole time she was speaking she kept her head cocked at a defiant angle. When she came into the shop she was asked, "Are you Charlotte Mew?" and her reply, delivered characteristically with a slight smile of amusement, was: "I am sorry to say I am."'

The self-deprecation which she felt in the company of other human beings sharpened considerably her sense of communion with the natural world. A poem which she particularly liked to read (and may have written) concerned a Breton shepherd who fell asleep one night under a roadside cross, and was discovered the following morning as a pile of leaves. Such a death, she implied, was what she herself would have wished for.

But her sensuous delight in the colours, lights and perfumes of the natural world was frequently more pagan than pantheistic; and her strong sense of sin, nourished by Victorian prejudice, doomed to failure any idea of using such phenomena – as Suger had done – in the service of a more direct communion with God. Death and salvation in her work come eventually to mean complete renunciation of the world – a sacrifice she felt herself incapable of making.

The expectation of friends during these years, that she might eventually commit herself to Catholicism, remained unfulfilled. The compound of pessimistic theism and defiant rejection of 'Madeleine in Church', which one Methodist printer refused because he considered it blasphemous, had replaced the earlier searching and supplication of 'At the Convent Gate' and 'She was a Sinner'. This mood alternated with attempts to reduce a God too remote and amorphous to worship, to physical terms which she was better able to grasp. Most frequently these took the form of visions of the Crucifixion, where the physical aspects of suffering were most immediate. Or they referred, under various guises, to a specific New Testament incident – the washing of Christ's feet with her hair by the adulteress, in Luke – which came to possess a significance far beyond itself –

> 'Only the hair of any woman can belong to
> God ...'

And:

> 'Death would spare the glory of your head
> In the long sweetness of the hair that does
>   not die ...'

In 1927, during a holiday in Chichester, Anne was found to be suffering from an incurable disease. When, a few months later, she died, it became a source of constant torment to Charlotte that because she had not had a vein opened in Anne's wrist, her sister might have been buried alive. Eventually, Charlotte was admitted to the nursing home in Beaumont Street, where the depressing outlook on to a grey wall, shut off from the colours and lights which had been the substance of so much of her poetry, finally overcame her. On 28 March 1928 she received a last visit from Alida Monro; taking from a drawer a much-treasured copy of her poem 'Fin de Fête', handwritten by Thomas Hardy on the back of a British Museum readingroom slip, she gave it into her friend's keeping, affectionately squeezing her shoulder as a gesture of farewell. It was perhaps the only time that she had ever made deliberate physical contact with anyone. The following morning, she took a bottle of lysol to her room and drank the contents. To doctors trying to revive her she murmured in a moment of consciousness, 'Don't keep me, let me go'.

The measure of her obscurity was touchingly demonstrated the following day, in a newspaper report which named her as

> 'Charlotte New – said to be a writer.'

'I know,' she had written to Cockerell, 'that you are going to be French in the next world, and so was I – but when it comes to the point – I wonder.'

At the time of her death, her isolation from spiritual and earthly consolations was very nearly complete. Her poetry, spread over nearly half a century, appears as a chronological record of the slow falling from Grace, which was the process, as she saw it, of life itself. If Hell, as total 'inscape', had a very real and terrifying meaning for her, as it did for Hopkins, Paradise had the flimsy reality of day-dreams:

'I too, would ask Him to remember me
If there were any Paradise beyond this
earth that I could see.'

But in 'Not for that City', we have a hint of the weariness of life
and longing for total oblivion which characterized the last deso-
late months of her life.

'We strain our eyes beyond this dusk to
see
What, from the threshold of eternity
We shall step into. No. I think we shun
The splendour of that everlasting glare,
The clamour of that never-ending song.
And if for anything we greatly long,
It is for some remote and quiet stair
Which winds to silence and a space of
sleep
Too sound for waking and for dreams
too deep.'

Autobiographies

There are fundamentally two types of autobiography, the public and the private. The book world, these days, is piled high with the former – those vast unmanageable tomes concocted by ex-Presidents or, worse still, by their wives, secretaries and personal assistants who regurgitate their lists of dinner-guests, spill out their shorthand notes on to the tapes for the nameless publisher-editors to package up for them in hard and soft covers. Such books lassoo the headlines of the year before last, and pull themselves weightily up the best-seller lists – that strange class of once-bought never-read volumes which are traditionally spoken about with hushed voices as 'documents of our time', which are seen in everyone's drawing-room, unopened, perhaps indeed unopenable.

In a modest way, almost in spite of himself, James Lees-Milne could be counted a public figure. A distinguished historian of architecture, 'an aristocrat in mind and culture' as Harold Nicolson in his diary described him, he devoted all his energies and abilities, as adviser to the National Trust of Great Britain, to preserving the country houses of England. But he has elected to write a private autobiography, and it is another self he portrays here.

The theme of his book* is presented in the first paragraph. 'My world was the only real world. Nothing about it seemed incongruous; and those events which happened in it were never inconsequential. Its relation with the great outside world was tenuous. By which I do not deny that a few of my notable fancies were sparked off by contacts with the unreal, outside world. For of course they often were.'

Another Self is a chain of these momentous contacts between the

* *Another Self* by James Lees-Milne.

real internal world and the actual objective world that surrounds it. No man is wholly self-sufficient; we must all collide from time to time with other private worlds. As a child, the author longed to be admired by his father. He was not born in a heroic mould, but his day-dreams were full of heroism. 'I would dream of stopping a runaway railway engine by throwing myself across the track,' he writes, 'of flashing past the winning post on Derby Day, of taking curtain after curtain call at the Stratford-on-Avon pantomime, or of advising the King over an intimate cup of tea at Buckingham Palace how to deal with obstreperous suffragettes.' In practice he cut a less dashing figure. His father, an honourable man, but aggressively shy and not gifted with imagination, was a deft and practised sportsman, never idle, an excellent amateur plumber, electrician, motor mechanic, carpenter, with a healthy contempt for art and literature. James was a great disappointment to him, dreamy, butter-fingered, dependably wrong, a secret reader and without any talent for sport. The two of them mixed like oil and water. But when their private worlds collided, when the son endeavoured to translate his secret fantasies into actuality by performing a miracle for the benefit of his father, the consequences were astonishing, dreadful, and very funny.

His mother's personality was naturally far more sympathetic to him. She was beautiful, romantic, amusing. But she was also deeply eccentric – a habit of disappearing into thin air with some unknown balloonist was only one of her odd ways. So extreme were her fantasies that when her son became caught up in them his very life would be in danger. A single fantastic journey that she arranged for him during which he completely lost his trousers, was nearly blown up by an exploding coffee machine on a train, and then run off with by a horse makes one wonder how he survived childhood.

Often his career has been a contest of preconceived fantasies versus plain facts. The ferocious Corsican bandit he met under the impression he was someone's harmless elderly uncle; the beautiful stranger with whom he swapped addresses late one night outside the Café Royal only to find that he had returned home with his own name and address, so that they never met again: in such episodes as these, his fantasies have cheated him by altogether eclipsing the ephemeral world, by acting as a defence against some aspects of life.

Several of the people who appear in this book are public figures, but all of them are glimpsed in private moments or seen from some esoteric angle: T. E. Lawrence at breakfast, 'a gnome-like creature with a gnome's chin and prominent boots'; Eddie Marsh, that 'prim and virginal man of letters sitting ... bolt upright on the end of my bed, half-undressed in a collarless starched shirt and a pair of thick woollen combinations down to his ankles', reciting interminable passages from *Paradise Lost*; Stanley Baldwin, the Prime Minister, resembling in his physical contours the 'wonderfully dim county' of Worcestershire, rugged, jagged and unspectacular. It was as a bottle-washer that the author got to know Oswald Mosley; as a stenographer he saw Lord Lloyd; from the post of third junior secretary, whose job was to wear an Old Etonian tie and hold out a towel to Very Important People emerging from the lavatory, that he viewed Sir Roderick Jones, chairman of Reuters. His pen portraits of these and others catch them, as it were, unawares and are extraordinarily vivid.

Each chapter in this book has been constructed as a sort of adventure story illustrating, with many subtle variations, the author's central theme and rising to a superb climax of pathos or unexpectedness, hilarity, even farce. Strung skilfully together, written in a beautifully controlled and sensitive style, fertilized by a vein of rich, wry humour, they coalesce to form what is undoubtedly a remarkable work of literature.

But the end is sad, almost unbearably so. The author's real world receives from without two direct hits. The first of these occurred when a bomb fell on a building he was passing, the result of which was that he contracted Jacksonian epilepsy. The second direct hit was to a girl he had never met but with whom he was in love, and who loved him. Their lines had accidentally crossed while telephoning, and their relationship had developed solely by means of the telephone. It was the perfect fantasy affair, incapable of disenchantment. But one day her house was bombed, and when he telephoned all he heard was the high-pitched piercing scream of a line out of order. The book ends abruptly with this scream, which echoes in one's imagination long after one has put it down.

Has the author's inner world survived the bombardment of such a hostile environment? He does not directly tell us. But from the buoyant tone of his book, its mystic glimpses of eternal truths, I feel confident that it has.

* * *

Authors' prefaces are written for grateful reviewers to paraphrase. Mr V. S. Pritchett, in this second volume of his autobiography,* has not written a formal preface, but his first two pages, in which he defines the subject of his book, effectively serve as one. He is the most professional of authors, allowing no discrepancy between purpose and performance, but, he tells us, 'the professional writer who spends his time becoming other people and places, real or imaginary, finds he has written his life away and has become almost nothing'. Life exists to be turned into literature and the subject-matter of this book is the raw material for his stories and novels, carefully selected and reworked to form a chain of episodes that, in their cumulative effect, gain from one another wonderfully well.

The narrative opens with Pritchett, aged twenty, travelling to Paris. It is a bid for liberty. Here he sees his first pepper mill, eats his first *omelette fines herbes*, drinks his second glass of wine, and in hot pursuit of the literary life, takes a job as photographer's assistant. But his adventures are almost all misadventures including a wretched attempt at selling ostrich feathers in the Faubourg St Honoré, a contest in which he is mercilessly outwitted by the priests of pharmacy while trying to buy contraceptives, and the humiliating experience (while employed in the glue trade) of having his trousers pulled off by a band of factory girls. He does, however, enjoy a first love-affair, and his description of this is written with a perfect blend of tenderness and high comedy. Finally he achieves his first piece of published writing: a joke in the Paris *New York Herald* with his full name and address printed beneath it. He was at the bottom rung.

* *Midnight Oil* by V. S. Pritchett.

The next stage up the ladder took him, as correspondent for *The Monitor*, to Ireland and then, in January 1924, he went to Spain, a country about which he was later to write two books and which brought about a fundamental change in his life. 'I was to get one of those moral shocks,' he writes 'that make one question everything one has taken for granted.' Finding himself among agnostics, he was liberated from the dry husk of Christian Science in which he had been brought up, and released, like a butterfly from its torpid chrysalis, into the clear light of scepticism. He became involved in the realities of Spanish politics, was converted to humanism: and then there was the landscape. In a revealing passage describing the Castilian scene, he writes

'The earth did not fade into the transcendental; rock was rock, trees were trees, mountains were mountains and wilderness was wilderness. There was nothing of the 'deeply interfused'; there was something that could be known and which it was necessary to know. There was a sense of the immediate and finite, so much more satisfying than the infinite, which had really starved me; a sense of the physical not of the spiritual. I felt I was human.'

After seven years of foreign travel he returned to London and, as part of his struggle to 'commence author' without benefit of Bloomsbury, attained the rank of librarian at the Bath Club. From its metropolitan lair Bloomsbury is represented as controlling English culture. Pritchett, who believed in a country life outside literary circles, felt entirely independent of it. But since he was helped by Raymond Mortimer and David Garnett and was a close friend of Gerald Brenan's, his independence seems incomplete. Soon he is publishing short stories, has metamorphosed (with an initial commission to review his own first book) into a *New Statesman* reviewer, and begins to receive what perhaps all authors need even more than royalties: praise.

It is a success story. But, as it proceeds, Pritchett himself – as he has warned us – fades from the narrative. The search for his vocation has led him back towards his childhood and to his obsessional subject. From *A Cab at the Door* one meets again his father, and with the same joy with which one greets the reappearance of

Widmerpool in an Anthony Powell novel. Pritchett's portrait of him, and in a more minor key of his mother, is full of the richest humour – not the loud cracking of jokes but an exploration of the living bond between them, felt with that mixture of sympathy and detachment for which all writers strive.

Every author, Pritchett claims, is two people; the valet and the master or writer whom he is hopefully pursuing. At twenty he was all valet; now, in his seventieth year, he is all master – yet with the uncomfortable suspicion that he has been totally translated into words and that, from the actual world he so acutely observes, he has almost vanished. But surely this feeling is parallel to the sense of 'life elsewhere' that Pritchett the agnostic finds so 'curious', and is the best transfiguration any writer can want. For what is all this striving after style, this 'search for the strange form', if it is not an index of our ache for lost perfection?

In describing Forrest Reid's autobiography *Apostate*, Pritchett writes: 'It is a minor classic, and it will stand beside Gosse's *Father and Son*.' These words may be applied with equal truth to his own two volumes *A Cab at the Door* and *Midnight Oil*.

*   *   *

Mr Collis's autobiography* is a unique success story. As a child he was cordially hated by his mother; during his entire education he failed to gain any 'school-cleverness' and was considered a dunce; in the army, though given the benefit of much 'sergeant-experience', he was at his best when most inconspicuous; his married life was marred by appalling 'money-anxiety'; even on the land, working happily as a farm labourer, he was not, he admits, 'quick on the uptake'. Finally, in the promoting of his literary career he has been thoroughly impractical. He is now in his seventies and still green.

How then is his story a success? What many people would regard as humiliating failures, Mr Collis feels sincerely grateful for. How fortunate that his mother absolved him from prolonged filial duty; how lucky his schoolmasters did not spoil Wordsworth. Of course there have been vulgar triumphs – at the Oxford Union (temporarily named 'the Colliseum'), or when he

* *Bound Upon a Course* by John Stewart Collis.

received the Royal Society of Literature award. But Mr Collis has not been discouraged by these successes; he has not succumbed to them. The course on which he is bound has been dictated by instinct, not reason. How else to avoid *mis*calculation? His gift is 'slowness'. Obstinately he has persisted in this slowness and become wise. From his very disappointments he has constructed a paradoxical philosophy of optimism and good sense. It is not common sense. He excels at showing us what we already know – or thought we knew until we discover we had simply taken it for granted. Under his treatment the obvious grows remarkable, even ludicrous. The incredulity with which he meets the humdrum is sometimes irresistible. He gazes open-eyed at what most of us overlook because to us it has grown stale. But not to Collis. He has the curiosity of a child and can rediscover miraculously the strangeness of the commonplace, the excitement of the ordinary. And he has the literary ability to make us share in this rediscovery.

It is no surprise to learn that, clothed in his divine absurdity, Mr Collis has been regarded as a bit of an eccentric. How else should one regard someone who swims naked at night in the Thames at Rotherhithe, or scales Mount Etna in gym shoes? For his own part he is a connoisseur of eccentrics – his heroic description of them, thesis-maddened in the Reading Room of the British Museum, is a high point of hilarity.

But this book also contains many vivid miniature pen portraits of less unconventional literary people – Yeats, T. S. Eliot, Sinclair Lewis, Rose Macaulay. More unusual is a fascinating interview with Count Keyserling in 1937, and an elaborate description of that peculiar man Middleton Murry. The evocation of his friendship with Stephen Potter is a most moving blend of poignancy and laughter; the pages on Bernard Shaw form a brilliant miniature biography.

But this autobiography is far from being a 'bookish' volume. For intimations of the truth, Collis turned to Nature which gave him a sense of brotherhood, of *belonging* he found nowhere else. He writes of the country with knowledge and feeling, without any trace of false pastoralism.

Above all Mr Collis is a stylist, a master of lyrical rhetoric, of rhetoric with restraint. His prose is rhythmic yet precise, for there are always solid foundations supporting the lyric element. He has a sensitive delight in beauty and his writing at its best is rare oratory, a speaking language that tells not just of literature but life. He achieves a synthesis between fact and idea, people and places, poetry and science. It is the unity of such things he seeks and conveys.

Why is it that Mr Collis is not 'required reading'? It must be admitted he is a fearfully ignorant fellow. He is ignorant of politics and especially ignorant of literary politics. Of fashion he is disastrously ignorant – why else would he write of the two cultures before anyone else had heard of them, and of pollution before anyone would listen? He is ignorant of generation gaps, of class consciousness, and of who is important. Such ignorance is often repaid for a time by being ignored. But with every book he writes it is becoming harder to ignore Mr Collis.

*   *   *

The late J. R. Ackerley seemed a man of formidable shyness. With his defensive dead-pan expression, his piercing stare, his occasional dark frown, he had the equipment to provoke great timidity in others. As an editor he was held in considerable awe; as a writer he was highly respected by a number of fellow writers including E. M. Forster and Christopher Isherwood; but for the reading public in general he remained almost an unknown figure.

In these memoirs,* on which he worked intermittently for thirty years, he records his birth in an opening sentence that has already become famous: 'I was born in 1896 and my parents were married in 1919.' His career was outwardly orthodox, quietly distinguished. He was educated at Rossall, a standard English public school; was wounded twice in World War I, and taken prisoner; went up to Cambridge; travelled, and at the age of thirty-nine was appointed editor of *The Listener*, a post he held for nearly twenty-five years.

During his life he wrote a three-act play based on his experiences as a prisoner of war, and three good small books, *Hindoo Holi-*

* *My Father and Myself* by J. R. Ackerley.

day and *My Dog Tulip*, both memoirs, and a novel *We Think the World of You*.

So much for what might be called his public career. It finds little place in this autobiographical volume, which is primarily a reconstruction of his private life. Like Edmund Gosse's *Father and Son*, it is a study of two temperaments; and in the pursuit of his father's elusive character, it resembles A. J. A. Symons's *The Quest for Corvo*. It should certainly join these books as a classic of autobiographical literature.

His father, Alfred Ackerley, was a kind, easy-going man, and to all appearances a person of imposing respectability. Massive and commanding in stature, he nevertheless exerted little autho-rity at home where, for the first seven years of his son's life, he was only an infrequent visitor. To protect himself, he shied away from all emotional situations, and puffed up around himself a conventional smokescreen, aided by the paraphernalia of his Gentlemen's cigars, his speeches in praise of the 'stiff upper lip', and his dirty stories that are popularly supposed to be substitutes for direct action.

It was only after his death that, for his son, this established image of the paterfamilias was shattered, and the respectable, dull householder was replaced by a mysterious figure who had led a concealed double life.

If the father was a secretly promiscuous heterosexual, the son was a blatant homosexual, prowling the streets and bars in search of an Ideal Friend, all the time growing more anxious and sexually incontinent, until, in his long pursuit of love through sex, he reached, not happiness, but the nightmare of neurotic impotence.

Finally, peace and contentment came to him in the shape of an Alsatian bitch, Tulip, to whom this book is dedicated. The anxieties, the frustrations, the wastage of time and spirit were ended. 'She offered me what I had never found in my sexual life, constant, single-hearted, incorruptible, uncritical devotion, which is in the nature of dogs to offer. She placed herself entirely under my control. From the moment she established herself in my heart and home, my obsession with sex fell wholly away from me.'

But essentially this book is the story of noncommunication between father and son, and its effect on the son. He wanted to confide, but his father preferred not to know or to be known, and could neither offer nor invite confidences. So the years of deception rolled by in amiable incomprehension. It is, the author wrote, 'a stupid story, shamefully stupid that two intelligent people, even though parent and son between whom special difficulties of communication are said to lie, should have gone along together, perfectly friendly, for so many years, without ever reaching the closeness of an intimate conversation, almost totally ignorant of each other's hearts and minds.'

The tone in which the author explores this theme is detached, sometimes to the point of bleakness. But there is much pathos, unmarred by recrimination, self-pity or sentimentality. Written in lucid, exact prose, the book has been constructed with the greatest skill, planned like an elaborate mystery story in that it discards chronology in order to space out the revelations and heighten the suspense. First one area is shaded in, then another, until suddenly the whole picture is before us. It is a remarkable achievement.

For many years now the art of autobiography has been stranded on a no-man's land between history and biography, which are thought of as more 'important', and novels and poetry, which are considered more 'creative'. Some of the finest autobiographies of our time are consequently out of print. It is to be hoped that *My Father and Myself*, besides making for itself a permanent place in literature, will help to remedy this state of affairs by turning the attention of readers and publishers back to this neglected art form.

The Carlyles

Carlyle, to a large extent, is the nineteenth-century counterpart of Dr Johnson. Both were aware of great powers lying within themselves, yet both suffered from a melancholia that prevented their developing these powers easily. Such a brake on their progress tended to produce in them some uncertainty of aim, so that they began as moralists, finding a steadying influence on themselves through the instruction of others. But once the cataract of morality had formed they could never peel it off, and in each case it has obscured the real, clear-sighted nature of their genius. Courage, wit, eloquence, humour: all these were theirs. Yet by a perversion of taste such accomplishments were valued only as means to a wholly serious end. For both became celebrated, not as human beings but as oracles. Carlyle, indeed, by his *carte blanche* approval of Boswell's *Johnson*, assisted in this process, suggesting that all Johnson lay within Boswell's pages despite the fact that the fifty-three years of Johnson's life before he met Boswell occupy only about one-fifth of the biography.

The oversimplified view of Johnson as a brilliantly disgruntled John Bull is matched by that of Carlyle as a dyspeptic Jeremiah. The objection to these reputations is not that they contain no truth, but that they exalt what was weakest in each of them. Carlyle's chief defect sprang from his thwarted desire for a life of action, the frustration of which was at the root of his prophetic literature and which produced, according to his mood, bouts of irritable contempt or hysterical hero-worship of some exponent of force. But his delight in Boswell points the way to his real genius. For what he admired in Boswell, he possessed himself in a high degree: a fascination with humanity and a passionate observation of life. Both were artists in autobiography.

Carlyle's reputation as a philosopher has ebbed lately, but for many years it impeded a proper evaluation of his achievement. Havelock Ellis was one of the first to challenge the standards by which he was measured. 'The popular judgment is hopelessly wrong,' he wrote. 'We can never understand Carlyle until we get rid of the "great prophet" notion. Carlyle is not a "great moral teacher" but, in the high sense, a great *comedian*.' Like Johnson once again, Carlyle writes best when his writing most resembles talk. It is largely for this reason that the poet and humourist in him can best be seen not in his formal works written for the public good, but in his private correspondence written off duty.

The present edition* of this correspondence, now being prepared by Professor Charles Sanders and his team at the universities of Duke and Edinburgh, will be by far the fullest we have had. It is a model of what such a work should be. The scholarship is helpful but unobtrusive, the volumes handsome and unpretentious – though I could have wished for some more illustrations – the good taste so fine that the price is nowhere discoverable. The editors have been at pains to make it as complete a collection as possible. After debating what might reasonably be omitted they were 'forced to conclude that in a critical edition of the complete letters everything should be retained'. Surely this was the proper decision and, perhaps even more important, come to in the proper spirit.

When finished this edition will number something over thirty volumes. The project was begun in 1952, and lo! already, within twenty years, the first four are in front of us. If the work continues to be pressed forward at this rate, it will be completed well in time for our great-grandchildren – and those of the editors – to enjoy. For those who wish to make their editions definitive there must always be a race to see who can be last, for the last lasts longest. This is the only way to defeat those journalists of scholarship who, in order to be first with unpublished material, will not assist their colleagues. It is a short-term policy, and they are merely the hares in the race for editorial immortality. Pro-

* *The Collected Letters of Thomas and Jane Welsh Carlyle, 1812–28*, edited by Professor Charles Richard Sanders, Kenneth J. Fielding and others.

fessor Sanders has entered a positively invincible team of tortoises, and their work, which is impeccably done, should last for ever: if completed by then.

The difficulties they have encountered and which, in varying degrees, must confront all scholars, are set forth with eloquent restraint in Professor Sanders' Introduction. Though half the Carlyle letters are in the National Library of Scotland, the rest are scattered through libraries and private collections throughout the world, and there is no way of tracing them except by systematic trial and error. No other branch of learning, certainly no scientist, would accept such a time-wasting and amateur state of affairs. Surely it is high time for some computer-index of manuscripts to be set up, financed by an enlightened foundation and with tentacles switched into the large sale-rooms so as to give as up-to-date information as possible. What historian, except those who confuse money and stamina with originality, would deny the value of this? What Keeper of Manuscripts, now plagued every day for letters he does not have, would not breathe a sigh of relief?

Professor Sanders' original plan was to collect only the letters of Thomas Carlyle, but it soon became apparent that Jane Carlyle's correspondence was indispensable to the work. The wisdom of this conclusion is manifest on almost every page. It is not simply that their letters belong together for the sake of the event-plot; it is that they marvellously complement each other. She is the more natural letter-writer of the two, more fluent, more intimate, more modern. She matches his force with her charm; his learning with her playfulness; his philosophy with her satire. She brings the best out in him – much tenderness and fun and passages of inspired exaggeration clothed in the half-poetic, half-humorous fascination of his own quaint idiom. One of his specialities (rather tut-tutted at by his academic editors) is a lyrical vituperation, as when he denounces his dyspepsia as 'the ugly ragged trull', calls Bronson Alcott with his vegetarianism a 'Potato Quixote', describes D'Israeli as 'this great blubbering numscull!' or castigates Heine as 'a filthy foetid sausage of boiled victuals'.

Carlyle first met Jane Welsh in the summer of 1821, and four days later he was writing to her of 'those Elysian hours we spent together' and testifying: 'Positively I must see you soon – or I shall get into a very absurd state.' His early letters to her are effusive, but in a conventional-romantic way. Hers to him begin politely cool, partly because of her mother's disapproval of their friendship, and then grow delightfully mocking. She parodies his attempts at the Byronic style, returns in caricature his very phrases to him, teases him mercilessly, forces him, almost in spite of himself, to laugh. And since laughter is always the best medicine for morality, so she helps to release the poet and humourist in him. 'I must cease to preach,' he concedes.

He was not a romantic figure. 'He scratched the fenders dreadful[l]y,' Jane wrote to Eliza Stoddart after one of his visits, '– I must have a pair of carpet-shoes and hand-cuffs prepared for him the next time – His tongue only should be left at liberty, his other members are most fantastically awkward.' Jane was highly susceptible to good looks in men, but none of her good-looking admirers could stimulate her imagination as Carlyle could by his conversation – the 'language of talent and genius' as she called it.

Between the lines of their correspondence there is much pathos. Early on she defines the limits of their relationship, which she tactfully attributes to her own shortcomings: 'I will be to you a true, a constant, a devoted *friend* – but not a Mistress – a Sister – but not a Wife – *Falling in love* and marrying like other Misses is quite out of the question – I have too *little* romance in my disposition ever to be in love with you or any other man; and too *much* ever to marry without love.' Yet later she suddenly exclaims: 'I wish to be loved as well as admired', and this makes him nervous. Their destinies are intermingled, he replies, but 'what a pitiful conclusion to all this would a vulgar wedding make!' And later he again tells her: 'Think on me as of one that will live and die to do you service; whose good will, if his good deeds cannot, may perhaps deserve some gratitude; but whom it is dangerous and useless to love.' Each is mightily relieved by the other's absolute determination never to marry. 'Were you my brother I would love you the same,' she writes; and he answers: 'you have put over our concerns *on the very footing where I wished them to stand* . . . You love me as a sister, and will not wed: I love you in all possible senses of the word, and will not wed, any more than you.'

What could have persuaded them to change their minds? To some extent, as she came to realize, their friendship was a barrier against her marrying anyone else. Though physically unattractive to her yet, after a time, he was 'almost necessary to my existence'. He represented her only escape from the fearful narrowness and inanity of her mother's world. 'You are encircled with drivelling and folly,' Carlyle wrote to her; 'nothing that your mind can relish or care for; companionless, tho' your heart is full of warm affections.' From passionate romantic love she was sealed off by the frozen rules of her class – 'Oh this everlasting etiquette!' she fulminates, 'how many, and how ungrateful are the sacrifices it requires.'

He changed his mind partly on account of his worsening health which had become an obstacle to his happiness and his ambition. If they were married, he argues, he would 'look upon the recovery of my health and equanimity, and with these, of regular profitable and natural habits of activity, as things which are no longer doubtful. I have lost them, by departing from Nature; I must find them by returning to her.' And so, although she refused her immediate positive assent to his proposal, she agreed to 'abate something of my romantic ideal'.

Seldom has a love-match been entered into with such misgivings, so many backward glances. While he 'heartily recoiled' from the wedding, she confessed 'this marriage, I find, is like death'. They were married, eventually, in October 1826 after five years of exhaustive courtship correspondence. How sensible they were, how level-headed, how cautious-romantic. Never can a marriage have been so thoroughly reconnoitred, so anxiously surveyed, so *paper-prepared*. Both were absolutely candid in presenting and weighing up their disadvantages. Yet in the end they were still very wonderfully in the dark and had entered a maze of unhappiness from which there was to be no escape.

Notes on Ruskin

———◄◆►———

'Ruskin was what Spinoza has been called, a God-intoxicated man; he had a gift of divine rhapsody, which reached at times to inspiration. But it is not enough to be God-intoxicated, for into him whose mind is disorderly and ignorant and ill-disciplined the gods pour their wines in vain.' This judgment of Havelock Ellis, delivered in 1923, still seems just and discriminating. From the start Ruskin was cursed with advantages. By his father, a wealthy wine-merchant, and his mother, a possessive puritan who indoctrinated him with the Bible, he was much pampered. And to these easy circumstances was added a further affliction: he was an early success. Whatever he wrote was instantly printed, instantly praised.

Despite such set-backs he grew into a generous man, with a keen appreciation of nature and a love of beauty in art. He was the first to recognize the genius of Turner; it was he who rescued the Pre-Raphaelites from the derision of other critics. But about the year 1860 the course of his life changed. There were two chief causes. First the influence of Carlyle, whose 'lovely moral sense' helped to warp Ruskin's natural delight in beauty, leading him to an intense exasperation masked as moral indignation; and secondly the gradual advance of his manic-depressive illness, in the grip of which he alternated between excessive self-confidence and morbid despair. His inherent weaknesses, which were vanity, self-indulgence and ill-discipline as a writer, were not caused by this illness, but accentuated. Sometimes he is capricious, parochial or just plain silly; and at other times profound and imaginative: and these variations in quality often jostle one another on the same page. Like our own Mr Geoffrey Grigson, he is pretty good on grass and trees – it is human beings who unsettle him. Instead of criticizing life or art from a standpoint reached by steady reflection, he threw out as final judgments whatever the mood of the moment suggested. In his youth, for example, he had announced that chastity and great art were indissolubly connected. But at the age of forty, overcome by sensations he does not seem to have experienced before, he decided that magnificent animality distinguished the best poets and artists. That his own life was not marked by such animality troubled him and, from England, he appears to have contemplated orgies on the Continent. What actually happened was curiouser: he fell in love with a girl of eleven, Rose La Touche. But in 1875 Rose died. It is in the following year, when Ruskin was aged fifty-seven, that his Brantwood Diary,* now published for the first time, opens.

It would be too much to claim that this diary conveys nothing at all. For wind and water, for sunsets and cloud formations scrupulously annotated, it could hardly be improved on. On those who are anxious over the weather that prevailed between 1876 and 1884 along the border of Lancashire and Westmorland, the volume may be pressed with confidence. The weather, of course, affects us all. But the weather of about a hundred years ago is a more specialist concern to which not all of us can eagerly respond. To Ruskin himself weather was partly a means of self-escape, partly, in less balanced moods, a reflection of himself. Fine skies purified him; but a rainy day could be a personal insult, a slap in the face from God.

For the most part this diary is laconic and without any literary value whatever. It was not intended for publication and since Ruskin's vanity was not stimulated we get none of his divine rhapsody or even his extreme silliness: we get the dead centre. The tone is one of vacuity, scrupulously charted. He takes an inventory of nature, but this is not poetry, it is description: accurate, meticulous, unforgettably dull.

Other subjects which Ruskin touches upon include his overwork, loss of sleep, the minute fluctuations in the barometer of his moods, his dreams and the deliriums from which he began to suffer about this ime. But so far from these telling us much new

* The Brantwood Diary of John Ruskin together with Selected Related Letters and Sketches of Persons Mentioned. Edited and annotated by Helen Gill Viljoen.

information about him, we need, evidently, more information to tell us about the entries. For every word of Ruskin's in this diary you will read five or six by his enthusiastic editor Mrs Viljoen. Nothing is too trivial to escape her attention. Indeed, triviality is her forte. Anyone can spot the important, the obvious; it takes a scholar of Mrs Viljoen's class to disinter the useless. The less significant a fact, the more eagerly she seizes upon it and presses it upon her readers. The book is consequently swamped by what she calls the 'underflow' – some would call it overflow – of her microscopic notes. The logical end to this kind of scholarship must surely be to elevate the editor's contribution so that it occupies the main narrative, reducing the diary itself to the foot of the page. It is a pity that Mrs Viljoen, who has done so much in this direction, will not be credited with such a breakthrough in scholarship.

To the lay reader, as Mrs Viljoen recognizes, the 'mere text of the entries cannot be particularly meaningful'. They are like 'a great heap of bare bones', she writes, '– bones which need to be clothed with flesh and blood'. And so to animate what she elegantly refers to as Ruskin's 'annual units' she has added her notes: footnotes and supplementary notes; reference notes and notes in the form of sketches, prefaces and introductions innumerable. If notes like these provide flesh, this is corpulent, this is gross.

It is possible to say that Mrs Viljoen knows more of Ruskin than Ruskin ever knew about himself because she has struggled to learn what he did not trouble to remember. Yet even with the most extended treatment she has not been able to prolong these few scraps of diary much beyond three hundred and fifty pages. As a makeweight she has tacked on some two hundred pages of letters, and these, requiring fewer notes, are very properly considered to be less important. Only a quarter of the letters are actually by Ruskin, though these, admittedly, are among the least interesting. Others are written to him, but a good number are neither to nor from him. Nor, for good measure, are they written, very many of them, in the years when Ruskin was keeping his Brantwood Diary. Is Mrs Viljoen a Mistress of Inconsequence? Or has she been seeking after some new aesthetic unity?

The clue is noted in a preface. The manuscript of the Brant-wood Diary, which should have been included years ago in the three-volume edition of Ruskin's diaries prepared by W. H. Whitehouse and Joan Evans, belonged to a Mr F. J. Sharpe, who sat on it immovably, unwilling to let anyone use it. But not being able to take it with him when he died he expressed a wish, just before his death, that his collection of Ruskiniana be handed over to the redoubtable Mrs Viljoen. Among this collection was much miscellaneous correspondence which gave her the notion that 'it can also seem particularly appropriate to include these letters in a book conceived as a monument to Mr Sharpe'.

It is a pretty thought, but one not productive of a volume that has any coherence. For this is a white elephant of a book, and Mrs Viljoen in preparing it has shown scholarship without any sense of proportion, without style, without wit, without point. Let no one underrate the energy and labour she has put into her task. It is gigantic. But it is work for the sake of work, where the means themselves become the ends. As such it has a kind of purity, for of any ulterior motive it is quite innocent. With the facts of Ruskin's life that are valuable or entertaining she is not primarily concerned. Her speciality is those other facts that are neither. She is a rare connoisseur of the tedious. In contemplating this monument she has raised, one is reminded of Carlyle's description of Coleridge: 'Never did I see such apparatus got ready for thinking, and so little thought. He mounts scaffolding, pulleys, and tackle, gathers all the tools in the neighbourhood with labour, with noise, demonstration, precept, abuse, and sets – three bricks.'

It is particularly regrettable when, as in this case, the bricks are set in a space reserved for a window.

Edwardians

———◆———

The Edwardian Age continues to fascinate us because in the context of modern English history it is unique. It was a time of great turbulence and crisis, of the formal garden party versus the unrespectable Labour party, of vast wealth and leisure contrasted with anxiety and dire poverty. Today it forms our authentic link to the solid traditions of Victorianism. But at the time it was a battlefield for the outmoded ideas of the mid-nineteenth century, still kept alive by artificial stimulants, and the new ideas that make up the basis of modern society.

For these and other reasons, the Edwardian Age has persistently attracted social historians. One of the most recent of these, Samuel Hynes, professor of English at Swarthmore College, for the sake of convenience begins his panorama* at the turn of the century and extends it to the outbreak of World War I. The weakness of all such panoramas is that they widen the gulf between appearance and reality. For the world of the average social historian is very far from being the world in which ordinary people live. The routine business of earning a living leaves little time for the majority of human beings in any age to indulge in the class, sex and intellectual antagonisms of which we so frequently read.

Miraculously, however, Mr Hynes has written a study of Edwardianism that retains much of the glow of real life. He has done this by refusing, so far as possible, to simplify the issues. Throughout his book, he preserves an excellent balance between sentiment and shrewd common sense. Most important of all, he has come to this period as a student of literature; and although his book is not literary history, it is very largely literary biography.

* *The Edwardian Turn of Mind* by Samuel Hynes.

He approaches reality, therefore, not through statistics, but through the individual. His method of recapturing the intellectual climate of the times is to explore those areas of Edwardian conflict that seem to him most crucial – 'politics, science, the arts, the relations between men and women'.

Politically, it was an era of great change and disillusionment. For many, the death of Queen Victoria symbolized the end of England's greatness. People were demoralized by the Boer War; and one man, R. S. S. Baden-Powell, took the threat of imperial decline so seriously as to found, in defence of the Empire, the Boy Scout movement. So popular were these Scouts that in next to no time they had been joined by six thousand girls, thereby making Baden-Powell the embarrassed and unwilling sponsor of military co-education.

Mr Hynes's narrative is full of such diverting details. With his biographer's temperament, he is always seeking examples of general tendencies in the careers of individuals. He finds, for instance, a parallel to the fall of Tory England in the disintegration of Kipling; and his chapter on the failure of Edwardian Liberalism turns out to be a study of two Liberal imaginations that failed – those of C. F. G. Masterman and John Galsworthy. As Liberalism grew less capable of action, so socialism assumed the progressive role in Edwardian life. It was, he argues, the variousness of socialism that gave it flexibility and momentum, and he illustrates this variousness with descriptions of two leading but incompatible Fabians – Beatrice Webb and H. G. Wells.

Mr Hynes devotes two interesting chapters to censorship in the arts, and one to the complicated topic of emancipation. He is especially entertaining on aspects of the sex war, which he treats largely through the writings of Havelock Ellis and Edward Carpenter, both of whom tried to liberate the human spirit by helping 'to create an informed public that would accept and support reforms in the laws governing sexual behaviour and in time modify the general social attitudes towards sex'.

Edward Carpenter is placed by Mr Hynes 'among the ancestors of Bloomsbury' and it is the Bloomsbury Group – in particular Roger Fry – that he believes was responsible for forcing 'upon the English consciousness ideas that were at once modern and foreign'. This achievement was crucial. Victorian conservatism had depended for its strength upon complete insularity. Fry's Post-Impressionist exhibition of 1910 'marked a point at which English attitudes towards Englishness, the Continent, and tradition changed radically'.

On non-literary matters, Mr Hynes is sometimes rather biased, and he occasionally forgets that the job of all artists is not to fix the destiny of kingdoms, but to practise their art to the best of their ability. It is a pity, too, that his book contains no bibliography and that the Biographical Sketches, which appear as one of the appendices, should be so perfunctory. The book, therefore, is not intended as a definitive work of reference. Since the past is always changing, according to the angle at which we look back on it, there will be many more studies of the age. But few of them are likely to be so well-constructed and compulsively readable as *The Edwardian Turn of Mind*.

*   *   *

Mr J. B. Priestley, in his book on the Edwardians,* refers to Professor Hynes's 'careful American account' with qualified enthusiasm. His own enthusiastic English account is a far more personal study. He reveals, for example, that the Edwardian Age actually dawned one day in 1901, at the very moment when J. B. Priestley, though 'only a child', testified to the extraordinary popularity of the new King. Until now this King has always been familiarly known as Bertie, but 'I shall call him Edward', Mr Priestley announces in his chapter mysteriously entitled 'Young Bertie' – and he adds that 'it would be cheating' to write of the age 'while attempting to keep out' the person who happened to give it his name.

The temptation to do so must have been considerable, for it appears that the most important personage of these times, far from being King Edward, was none other than J. B. Priestley. Curiously absent from the book's companion volume, *The Prince of Pleasure and his Regency*, Mr Priestley here comes into his own. 'As I have said before,' he repeats, 'we are all in history.' But some of us, of course, are more in than others; some of us, almost in spite of ourselves, have history thrust upon us.

* *The Edwardians* by J. B. Priestley.

Mr Priestley is an extreme example of this thrusting process. Again and again history has overtaken him unawares. It was he who, one day on the Isle of Wight, made the historic discovery of just how thick Princess Beatrice's German accent was; and it was he who, while in the country near a railway station, received the historic news of Edward's appendicitis. The book is crowded with many other such momentous scenes, pregnant with personal history. There are descriptions of J. B. Priestley lunching and dining, playing the piano and playing tennis: of Lord Kitchener being inspected at Aldershot by Mr J. B. Priestley, and of J. B. Priestley inspecting the dockers at Copenhagen. Such is the force of this man's presence that even his absence becomes, somehow, a positive accomplishment. Several times, for example, we are informed in italics of his remoteness from Edwardian high society; and elsewhere he frankly admits he is no ballet dancer. On the other hand he is a writer who knows the literature of the period exceptionally well, and he gives us a number of interesting quotations from such works as *Literature and Western Man* and *Margin Released*, as well as significant references to *Bright Day* and *Trumpets Over the Sea*.

In an introductory note the author remarks on the curious fact that 'I keep popping up in this chronicle'. And he gives us his explanation: 'the publishers ... insisted that I should'. We are invited to see Mr George Rainbird, Mr Charles Pick of Heinemann and, from Harper and Row, Mr Cass Canfield converging upon Mr Priestley's home, and during lunch persuading him with difficulty to overcome his natural modesty. In their efforts, these publishers have been remarkably successful, but for the sake of the book it would have been better had they failed. For what has gone wrong with this panorama of Edwardianism is its tone.

None of this would matter much were there not so many excellent things scattered through these pages. The rich variety of Edwardian life suits Mr Priestley's prodigal talents. He is a marvellously good guide to the Edwardian music halls; his analysis of the class system, with all its strange anomalies, is percipient and well-balanced; his accounts of the Crippen case, of the Titanic disaster, and of the Suffragette movement are absorbing. He cannot write a dull page if he tries. At its best this book has been written by J. B. Priestley the novelist, who evokes so wittily the famous week-end house-parties of Edwardian high society:

'... there were processions of food and drink from eight in the morning until late at night. Not since Imperial Rome can there have been so many signposts to gluttony ...

'... The talk throughout most of these long luncheons and dinners was vapid, the women prattling, the men uttering pompous nothings. Any subject worth discussing was generally barred. How tempting then to start an illicit affair, to let eyes meet across the dining table for a dangerous second or two, to feel for a fleeting but meaningful moment the pressure of a hand, to play, late on Saturday, the only exciting game the day had offered on tiptoe from bedroom to bedroom! The very keeping up of appearances made it all the more enticing.

'... These Edwardian garden-party ladies, with their elaborate and ridiculous hats and padded coiffures, with their tight-lacing and tiny waists and well-covered prominences in front and behind (so they always seem as if they are about to bow), with all their hidden petticoats and long trailing skirts, with nothing of them clearly seen except eyes and mouths and help-less-looking dimpled hands ... [were] temptresses. ... And their lusty males, crammed with all that Edwardian food and inflamed by all its drink, were constantly tempted, were avidly longing to discover what the women were really like once the frippery and finery and social disguise were removed. So the illicit affair, however dangerous, the little tap on the bedroom door behind which the delicious creature, with heroic bared bosom and great marmoreal thighs, was waiting – oh it was all irresistible!'

In spite of there being two Mr Priestleys at work on this volume, neither has had the time to deal with such topics as architecture, decoration, fashion or sport. So another collaborator, Mary Anne Norbury, was called in to cover these by means of some of the two hundred and fifty illustrations. These illustrations she has selected well, though as with everything in this book, there are some oddities. For example, there are no portraits of J. B. Priestley, though Miss Norbury has secured a photograph of his home in Bradford. Sometimes, too, the pictures are very curiously placed in the narrative. The chapter called 'Nineteen-fourteen' is illustrated by Duncan Grant's painting 'The Tub' dated 1912, and by Wilson Steer's 'Girl in Blue' dated 1910. In the section on writers appears 'The Cloud' by Arthur Hacker, presumably to show where authors' heads are; Henry Lamb's portrait of Lytton Strachey, mentioned on page 111 as a picture never owned by J. B. Priestley, is reproduced on page 63 in the chapter called 'A Time of Tension'.

On the surface *The Edwardians* is a very resplendent piece of book-making. But for those of us who think of Mr Priestley as an accomplished writer rather than a coffee-table maker of books, it must come as a disappointment.

A. E. Housman

To judge from his letters* A. E. Housman was a caricature of a
don, incapable of hope, cocooned in the comforts of esoteric
scholarship, unwearyingly pursuing a life of monotonous correct-
ness. Despite his wit he was not – would not even have wished
to be – a great letter writer. His correspondence must be read in
conjunction with his poems and with some knowledge of his early
life in order to show, behind the iron reticence, the poignancy
that makes him recognizably human.

He was born on 26 March 1859 and spent most of his childhood
and adolescence in Worcestershire within sight, on the western
horizon, of Shropshire, 'which made me feel romantic about it'.
He took care later on not to get to know the county well, and
many of the topographical details in *A Shropshire Lad* are, he was
able to boast, 'quite wrong'. It was for him a never-never land –
'a land I have not known' – romantic and unrequited, where
troubled lads turn their backs on the half-life that Housman
himself endured and recklessly pour down their throats the
bitter-sweet draught of death.

The eldest of a family of seven, Housman's background
was conventionally middle-class – High Church, High Tory
and somewhat puritanical. But shortly after the birth of her
seventh child his mother fell ill, probably with cancer, and
died on Alfred's twelfth birthday. Two years later his father,
a solicitor, married Lucy Housman, a cousin of almost fifty,
who relied on Alfred's assistance in bringing up the large
family.

By the time he went up to St John's College, Oxford, he had
become a most studious, proper young man, very well-behaved

* *The Letters of A. E. Housman* edited by Henry Maas.

and armed with a strong sense of duty. His letters to his step-mother are mostly obedient sight-seeing documents containing observations on architecture, sunsets and the peculiarities of foreign weather; those to his father are recitals of Union matters and the tittle-tattle of local politics.

There is one exception, a marvellous description of Ruskin, that is unique in his correspondence then or later:

'This afternoon Ruskin gave us a great outburst against modern times. He had got a picture of Turner's, framed and glassed, representing Leicester and the Abbey in the distance at sunset, over a river. He read the account of Wolsey's death out of *Henry VIII*. Then he pointed to the picture as representing Leicester when Turner had drawn it. Then he said, "You, if you like, may go to Leicester to see what it is like now. I never shall. But I can make a pretty good guess." Then he caught up a paintbrush. "These stepping-stones of course have been done away with, and are replaced by a be-au-ti-ful iron bridge." Then he dashed in the iron bridge on the glass of the picture. "The colour of the stream is supplied on one side by the indigo factory." Forthwith one side of the stream became indigo. "On the other side by the soap factory." Soap dashed in. "They mix in the middle – like curds," he said, working them together with a sort of malicious deliberation. "This field, over which you see the sun setting behind the abbey, is now occupied in a *proper* manner." Then there went a flame of scarlet across the picture, which developed itself into windows and roofs and red brick, and rushed up into a chimney. "The atmosphere is supplied – thus!" A puff and cloud of smoke all over Turner's sky: and then the brush thrown down, and Ruskin confronting modern civilization amidst a tempest of applause, which he always elicits now, as he has this term become immensely popular, his lectures being crowded, whereas of old he used to prophesy to empty benches.

'How he confuted the geological survey, and science in general, by the help of the college cook, I have no time to tell you, but remain, with love to father and all, your affectionate son.

                                        ALFRED E. HOUSMAN'

'Oxford had not much effect on me,' he wrote to a correspondent many years later, 'except that there I met my greatest friend.' This was a fellow scholar at St John's, Moses Jackson, tall, handsome and self-confident, a brilliant scientist 'who,' he confided to his brother Laurence, 'had more influence on my life than anyone else.' During their last year at Oxford they shared rooms in St Giles' and Housman fell deeply in love with him.

It was this year that the first mystery enters Housman's career. In his examinations he barely attempted to answer the questions and had to leave Oxford without a degree. A few months before his father, who had sacrificed much for Alfred's education, suffered a stroke. But it was less the depression resulting from this that accounted for his failure than his long-drawn-out passion for Jackson. This 'unhappy love' altered his whole life. 'I abandoned Christianity at thirteen but went on believing in God till I was twenty-one,' he afterwards told his sister Katharine, 'and towards the end of that time I did a good deal of praying for certain persons and for myself.' But prayer gave him no salvation, and that pagan pessimism, in which so much of his poetry is steeped, began to engulf him.

A year later he followed Jackson to London, taking a job at the Patent Office where his friend was working and sharing lodgings with him and his brother Adalbert, a young man 'greatly resembling his elder brother in attractive qualities'. This arrangement lasted some three years, but they cannot have been happy years for Housman. 'The troubles of my early manhood,' he said, 'were real and great.' A crisis came late in 1885. What exactly happened is not known but, following something in the nature of a quarrel, Housman disappeared. Jackson, fearing suicide, wrote to his father. But after a week Housman returned, and shortly afterwards moved to a new address to live alone.

The implication behind this break is that, despite a mutual attraction, Moses Jackson could not respond to Housman's love for him and, as Laurence Housman has explained, '*shied away* from the full implication, knowing that he could not share it *in kind*'. Housman, who did admit the full implication of their relationship, was mortified, and all further intimacy became shameful to him. This shame which swept over him was not simply a moral self-disgust, but a vanity permanently wounded that, in spite of his craving to be liked, made it impossible for him to open himself up to anyone else – except perhaps Moses' brother. The rest of his life was spent repairing this vanity.

'I did not begin to write poetry in earnest till the really emotional part of my life was over,' Housman told a correspondent. By the time he actually came to write *A Shropshire Lad* many of its poems had already been completed in the brilliantly-lit chambers of his subconscious, so that all he had to do was to take them down, like dictation. The Open Sesame releasing this flow of poetry was the death of his father in November 1894 which resulted in five months' 'continuous excitement' during which most of the book was written. In later years Housman liked to attribute the 'morbid secretion' of poetry to illness, but it seems to have been a state of guilt that brought his poems into existence. His father's death revived long-suppressed conflicts between parental duty and the annihilating force of his 'nameless and abominable' love. A catalyst in this process, as Henry Maas suggests, may well have been the Oscar Wilde trial, which must have demonstrated to Housman's painfully conformist mind just how ruthlessly 'the laws of God, the laws of man' were interpreted and enforced in Victorian England.

With Moses married and abroad, and Adalbert dead, Housman resolved to expect no more happiness. Indeed, he did everything to guard against it. As Professor of Latin at Cambridge he immersed himself in the study of obscure classical texts with a ferocious single-mindedness that made him the terror of other scholars. Total oblivion was his creed and his consolation; it was a revenge for lack of love, a denial of everything that might make the heart beat a little quicker. He took pleasure in refusing as many honours as possible, in avoiding payment for his work and in the suppression of any feeling that might be construed a weakness. He insisted upon his own barrenness, attributing his poetry to sciatica and sore throats, and (to the fury of Dr Leavis) proclaiming that all poetry was better for containing no meaning. His chief pleasure, perhaps, was sleep; his chief ambition to be invited to the Colchester oyster feast – an invitation which, when it eventually came, he turned down. He was a skilled epicure in the High Table style, cultivated a fastidious taste in pornography and carried on a mild flirtation with aeroplanes. Beyond the university, in the world where he felt 'a stranger and afraid', he looked, so Max Beerbohm observed, like 'an absconding cashier'.

The 'essential business' of Housman's poetry was to harmonize the sadness of the universe – 'it is somehow more sustaining than prose'; that of his letters was to chart the long white road, bleached of all emotions, 'that leads me from my love'. It is a dry dictionary world this correspondence reveals. The smaller the subject, the more pointed and succinct his wit. If they are boring, these letters, it is with the sustained boredom of the connoisseur, always vaguely enjoyable like a slow anaesthetic. It is a restful book.

Of the 1,500 letters traced, about one half have been published in this volume. The chief omission is the entire correspondence to Moses Jackson. From the five years of Housman's association with Jackson, the editor has been allowed to publish nothing. Nor is there any example of his pornographic letters, all those to his friend Arthur Platt having been destroyed by Mrs Platt as being 'too Rabelaisian'. Mr Maas, who is the headmaster of a girls' school in Shropshire, has edited the book very competently, but sometimes rather curiously. He does not tell us whether the one specimen of Housman's correspondence to Moses Jackson he has seen comes from the collection so nervously guarded by the Jackson family, or is the isolated one which many years later accompanied a gift of *Last Poems* and is now in America. In any event, it seems a little sweeping to suggest that these letters 'will not seriously affect what is already known of Housman's relations with Jackson'. About the relationship with Adalbert, which Laurence Housman believed was reciprocated, he is totally reticent. On the other hand he is very forthcoming about Thomas Hardy who, a footnote informs us, was a 'novelist and poet', about T. S. Eliot, an 'American-born poet and critic', and many others no less obscure. Such contrapuntal reticence and exactitude would have sounded sweetly in Housman's ears.

J. M. Barrie

'Barrie, as I read him, is part mother, part hero-worshipping maiden, part grandfather, and part pixie with no man in him at all,' Desmond MacCarthy wrote to Lady Cynthia Asquith. 'His genius is a coquettish thing, with just a drop of benevolent acid in it sometimes.' Whatever else he might be, James Barrie was not a weak man. Photographs of him show a hard calculating face, 'the face of someone,' a critic observed, 'whose sympathy and tenderness are turned in on himself, and for whom other people exist only as ministers to his own self-love and self-pity.'

Though far from being attractive, Barrie will continue to attract critics and biographers because of the strange complexity of his character, the interweaving of fact and fantasy which threaded the pattern of his literary career. He is a tempting, but dangerous subject. Over the past forty years, at least half-a-dozen biographies have been written about him. But Janet Dunbar's latest book* makes use of three valuable new sources of information: the Walter J. Beinecke archive of Barrie's letters, manuscripts and notebooks at Yale; the full diaries of Lady Cynthia Asquith, a part of which were published last year; and the hitherto totally unpublished correspondence Barrie wrote to the Davies brothers who inspired what Peter Llewelyn Davies called 'that terrible masterpiece', *Peter Pan*.

The biography Miss Dunbar has written with the aid of this fresh material is a reconstruction of Barrie's life chiefly in terms of his relationships with four women. The first and most influential of these was his mother, Margaret Ogilvy. A possessive, puritanical, Presbyterian woman of a type that flourishes so uncompromisingly well amid the kirks of Scotland, she exerted on her family a far

* *J. M. Barrie: The Man Behind the Image* by Janet Dunbar.

stronger grip than her burly but taciturn husband. Of the ten children, her favourite was not James but an elder brother, David. When David died at the age of fourteen, James determined to woo his mother from her overwhelming grief by becoming so like David that she would not notice the difference. He pursued this substitute role with such enterprise that he almost ceased to enjoy any separate existence of his own. But impersonation can go so far and no further, and he later found that a more satisfactory method of pleasing Margaret Ogilvy almost in spite of herself was to steep himself in her memories, to become the ideal listener to stories of her past life. These stories he wrote down and got published – a collaboration between mother and son that launched Barrie on his career.

This career soon took him to London. The wish to delight his mother had become the chief spur to his ambition, and he worked with extraordinary industry to achieve this aim. By now he needed someone to take Margaret Ogilvy's place – a substitute, to some extent, as he had once been. It was a need, and a revenge for lack of love. An actress would be ideally gifted for the part. Pretty actresses always stimulated Barrie's romantic imagination, and they had the additional advantage of ceasing to be real people for him as soon as they stepped off the stage.

Mary Ansell, who played the second lead in his play *Walker, London*, seemed a perfect choice. Besides being ravishingly pretty, she was a superb listener. Their courtship, which appears to have taken place largely in restaurants, was a contest of silences in which hers, pregnant with unstinted praise, grew to be the more obstinate. She out-listened him and, in 1894, at the age of thirty-four, he married her. They had a dog, but no children. Their marriage lasted some fifteen years, was never consummated, and, for her, was unhappy from the start. Barrie refused to take medical advice about his impotence, refused even to discuss it, and his silences now considerably outdistanced hers. This neglect was made all the more ironic by his continual ecstasies on the wonder of motherhood, and by the extraordinary fantasies in which he indulged for the worship of beautiful women and their children.

The chief of these was for Sylvia Davies, the daughter of George du Maurier. He insinuated himself into her affections with a ruthless dog-like devotion. His remorseless financial generosity to her five sons put her husband, much to his irritation, under a heavy debt of obligation from which he was unable to extricate himself.

Lady Cynthia Asquith's husband was outmanoeuvred in much the same fashion. She needed money, Barrie bought admiration. For nineteen years she acted as his personal secretary, looking after him almost as his nurse and mother. It was an added satisfaction to him that she should be titled.

'Desperate attempt to grow up but can't' – this was the true pathos of Barrie's life. In an adult world he had only surrogates for love to offer – emotional bribery, sexless sentimentality. He was a formidably kind man, but vain and unhappy, dominating women in much the same way as babies can dominate them, feeding on their time and devotion. But women, unlike most men, could sense the pathos of the man who wanted to love, but was unable to. Boys, he wrote, 'cannot love. Oh, is it not cruel to ask a boy to love?'

It is fitting that his latest biographer should be a woman. In Miss Dunbar's pages Barrie is never presented as a case; he is always a human being. She does not conceal his weaknesses, but succeeds in making him remarkably sympathetic. Only in her use of the Peter Davies material is she disappointing, leaving off her excellent narrative in favour of an extraordinarily dull compilation of unedited letters and notes.

Though her book largely supersedes Denis Mackail's biography, it will not establish itself as the definitive Life. Miss Dunbar is no literary critic. She makes no mention of Barrie's delightful and little-known comedy, *My Lady Nicotine*; she draws no conclusions about the most revealing of his works, that bitter satirical fantasy *Better Dead*; she does not connect *The Admirable Crichton* with his growing snobbery; no one could guess from her treatment of Barrie's famous rectorial address on 'Courage' that it was one of the least courageous speeches ever made.

But Miss Dunbar knows her limitations. She is not over-ambitious and has produced a very good book that anyone interested in the literature of the early twentieth century will enjoy.

Bertrand Russell

————◄◆►————

Bertrand Russell is one of the most extraordinary phenomena of this century. A mathematician of genius, a man of passionate and impulsive emotions, a humanist, wit and crusader, he is the least logical of logicians, the most unphilosophical of philosophers. His career comprises an astonishing series of paradoxes. How is it that someone so perspicacious can be so full of contradictions, that someone so sincere in his search for truth can be so erratic in its service, that someone so sensitive can on occasions be so unfeeling?

This second volume of his autobiography,* which covers the years from the beginning of World War I almost to the end of World War II, opens with a passage that is highly characteristic:

'The period from 1910 to 1914 was a time of transition. My life before 1910 and my life after 1914 were as sharply separated as Faust's life before and after he met Mephistopheles. I underwent a process of rejuvenation, inaugurated by Ottoline Morrell and continued by the war. It may seem curious that the war should rejuvenate anybody, but in fact it shook me out of my prejudices and made me think afresh on a number of fundamental questions. It also provided me with a new kind of activity, for which I did not feel the staleness that beset me whenever I tried to return to mathematical logic. I have therefore got into the habit of thinking of myself as a non-supernatural Faust for whom Mephistopheles was represented by the Great War.'

Readers of Lord Russell's first volume will recall that such moments of transition have come thick and fast in his life. He was always changing into 'a completely different person', as he des-

* *The Autobiography of Bertrand Russell 1914–44.*

cribed it – the most remarkable conversion of these early years being the break-up of his first marriage: 'I went out bicycling one afternoon, and suddenly, as I was riding along a country road, I realized that I no longer loved Alys.'

These turning-points, for all their frequency, seldom fail to take him by complete surprise. Despite his undeniable brilliance, he remains a strangely unpsychological thinker, possessing little self-knowledge or insight into the motives of other people. His thought hardly ever rises from formulated emotion, but is made up of abstract, unconnected general theories. For although his feelings are strong, they seem less quick to develop than the processes of his intellect – a discrepancy in timing that can make his attitude at times appear curiously naïve.

Obliquely, Lord Russell acknowledges this discrepancy. 'I have never since 1940,' he writes, 'recovered the same degree of unity between opinion and emotion as I had possessed from 1914 to 1918.' These war years form the longest and most fascinating section of his book. Everything was altered for him. He metamorphosed from a don to a Don Quixote, and, predictably, 'changed my whole conception of human nature'. Now that opinion and emotion were uniquely matched, he grew deeply pessimistic. The propaganda of the belligerent nations disgusted him. 'I hate the planet and the human race – I am ashamed to belong to such a species,' he confessed to Lady Constance Malleson.

His courage and energy in helping conscientious objectors is already well-known. But what, until now, has not perhaps been fully appreciated is the depth of Lord Russell's loneliness over those years. 'Cambridge has ceased to be a home and a refuge to me since the war began,' he told Lady Ottoline Morrell. Because of his unfashionable opinions he was removed from his lectureship at Trinity, Cambridge, shunned by many of his old friends, and finally imprisoned. The letters he wrote at this time are full of moving admissions of his isolation. He felt himself to be a ghost, unable to make contact with other people.

Yet this loneliness, though aggravated by the unnatural conditions of war, was part of the intrinsic temperament from which he was always trying to escape. The solitude of his early years had made him long to feel that oneness with large bodies of human beings that was being experienced by the crowds of patriots. He joined the No Conscription Fellowship, gave a series of highly successful pacifist lectures, but felt that all his efforts were trivial and useless.

His most satisfactory escape came through a love affair with Lady Constance Malleson. His account of this is an odd mixture of candour and reticence. 'We did not go to bed the first time we were lovers,' he tells us, 'as there was too much to say.' In this autobiography, however, he says very little. He is not really interested in human relationships, and his descriptions of them are often perfunctory. We are given his own powerful reactions, but not very much idea of the other person involved, and little sense of the untidy complexity of life. His admirably pellucid style conveys a world that is essentially simple – a clear-cut world of right versus wrong. This love affair seems to have ended in failure partly because the ultimate thing he has always lived for is not personal happiness but 'some kind of struggling emergence of mind'.

Men, rather than women, stimulated his mind. He gives us brief, vivid sketches of such friends as Wittgenstein, T. S. Eliot and Clifford Allen. But on the whole these profiles are disappointing. The best is that of D. H. Lawrence. They had been introduced in 1915 by Ottoline Morrell under the impression that each would admire the other. But their relationship, as depicted by Lord Russell, was a hilarious comedy of mutual incomprehension. Although in these war years, they appeared to hold much in common, their natures were fundamentally dissimilar.

Lawrence was like some Old Testament prophet, fulminating against the sins of his contemporaries; Russell, far more cerebral and precise, resembles a dogmatic but ingenious prelate who is losing his faith. At first Russell was inexplicably impressed by all Lawrence's sound and fury. But when Lawrence advised him to 'start at the very beginning and be a perfect baby', admiration gave way to bewilderment, and finally the endless Lawrentian insistence upon 'blood-consciousness' and denunciations of Russell's 'perverted blood-lust' enraged him. Each filled the other with a sort of mouthing despair. And when Lawrence appealed: 'Let's become strangers again,' Russell was only too happy to comply.

After the war Russell travelled to Russia and China, trying to discover some secret of wisdom that he might proclaim to the muddled nations. He married again, had children – the desire for which had become a consuming passion with him – wrote innumerable books and lectured widely. But still he could not eradicate the despair in his soul. 'I know the great loneliness,' he wrote, 'as I wander through the world like a ghost, speaking in tones that are not heard, lost as if I had fallen from some other planet.'

Then came another of his turning-points. His prophetic ardour cooled, and social questions ceased to hold the centre of his emotions in quite the same way. With his wife he started an experimental school. But even here he could not discover any attainable ideals to replace those which he had lately come to think of as unattainable. Several of his principles of education he later came to believe were mistaken, and he was surprised to find that his capacity for forgiveness was not equal to the demands that his pupils made on it. He grew into something of a disciplinarian, damaged the happiness that had existed between himself and his own children, and in 1931 he left both his wife and the school.

The last stage in this abandonment of beliefs was his renounce-ment of the doctrine of non-resistance. The ardent-eyed pacifist of World War I found himself in 1939 in America, rather critical of American neutrality.

Much was previously known about Lord Russell's career from his own books, from the biographical studies by Alan Wood and Herbert Gottschalk, from G. H. Hardy's *Bertrand Russell and Trinity*, and from the countless biographies and memoirs of his friends. There were therefore two reasonable alternatives open to him: to write either a single volume, based fairly exclusively on unpublished information, or a three-decker definitive 'Life' of him-self. Unfortunately he has done neither. As with the first volume, he fixes on to the end of each chapter a fairly haphazard selection of letters to, from and about himself. This is a lamentable method, inartistic, and displaying an almost infinite capacity for taking no pains. Very many of the letters are extremely interesting, and almost all the narrative is good. But stacked together in this way, each section diminishes the interest of the other, since the reader must traverse every period of Lord Russell's life, from beginning to end, twice.

Up to the year 1931 Lord Russell has relied upon an account of his life he dictated to his secretary some 37 years ago. After that date his narrative grows increasingly sketchy, and he covers the last 13 years of this volume (up to 1944) in less than 20 pages. Yet out of this uneven work there is a marvellous essay in autobiography struggling to emerge, so that, for all the enjoyment of this book, one puts it down at the end with a feeling of disappointment, a sense of some great opportunity lost.

Lytton Strachey by Himself

'I never travel without my diary,' says Gwendolen in *The Importance of Being Earnest.* 'One should always have something sensational to read in the train.'

Intermittently throughout his life Lytton Strachey kept a diary, but by today's standards none of them are very sensational. They were written, on the whole, in a lower key than his letters. 'No good letter,' he tells us in an essay on Horace Walpole, 'was ever written to convey information or to please the recipient: it may achieve both these results incidentally; but its fundamental purpose is to express the personality of the writer.' Strachey himself was a copious letter-writer, and his correspondence certainly does convey many aspects of his strange personality very vividly. But many of his letters *were* written, at least in part, to please their recipients. The Strachey we see in these letters is among friends: his diaries reveal him by himself.

The first two diaries he kept, at the ages of ten and eleven, were obedient documents, composed almost in automatic response to the literary atmosphere in which he grew up. Spurred on by Lady Strachey, he and his brothers and sisters were perpetually producing magazines, turning out quantities of verse, filling notebooks with playlets, grappling with literary puzzles, dutifully copying down passages from Shakespeare. Lytton's own contributions, to judge from these first short diaries, were nothing exceptional. They are amusing, as many children's pieces are, for their combination of directness and inconsequence. What was more unusual for a boy of this age was the absence of tiresome boasting, the honesty and odd self-deflationary humour: 'I had some shots at buoys passing with a smaller gun and hit once and missed five times!'

But perhaps the most interesting aspect of these pieces is their revelation of the literary pressure against which all the Strachey children lived. 'Mama read the Iliad' sounds like some chorus almost sinister in its repetition.

The journal Strachey kept of his travels between December 1892 and May 1893 was also started as something of a duty. To a limited extent it was not a private diary at all: it was almost certain to be read by his family once he got home. Yet there is no sense of constriction or self-consciousness in the writing of it, little feeling of anyone reading over his shoulder.

The voyages he describes acted as a temporary severing of the umbilical cord attaching him to Lancaster Gate, that dark architectural monstrosity which so shadowed his spirit. The atmosphere is one of blue sea-skies and blue hills in the distance, of the 'heavenly music' of military bands, of 'wondrous sights' – mirages and octopuses and powdered horses – which so intoxicated him that 'Oh! it is like some beautiful dream'. From this enchantment he awoke only after he was back in Lancaster Gate, and, like Caliban, 'cried to dream again'.

Perhaps because he had escaped some distance from the petticoat circle of his family, he was able to set down his individual personality in these pages with great clarity. He seems to have been a curious mixture of precociousness and conservatism. His precociousness was partly the result of a rapidly developing mind that gave him the ability to express himself very lucidly, partly a sensitivity to other people which told him what to say, and when to say nothing. He had a natural gift for treating, without incivility, all grown-ups as his equals, and this spared him the embarrassment of adults behaving towards him like children. Quite self-sufficient in his manner, he gave little trouble and was seen by many as being extraordinarily mature. But this 'maturity' was really a camouflage, a means of concealing his natural shyness. He did not break up his social timidity or his obsessive self-awareness; he skated successfully round them. So they remained intact to block later on the direct expression of his emotions. Passion, tragedy, outrage, boredom – such things he would convey by humour, often a defensive irony, for this was his 'criticism of life'.

In one sense, Strachey was 'older' at this time than at any other stage of his career. His conservatism was pretty well absolute. It was a romantic quality, and largely visual. He was alive to all the nice distinctions of what rank might inspect the guard on what occasions, of differences in uniform and the rivalries of regiments. He even rose from his bed at 6 a.m. to catch sight of some soldiers disembarking.

'The Cape Highlander (volunteers) played the pipes as they were marching away. They did look so lovely especially after their sea kit which consists of blue trousers and coats and Neapolitan fisherman's hats, only blue. As they marched off there seemed to be a great many of them, although there was only half a regiment. The Cape Highlanders think themselves far superior to the Black Watch!!!'

A few months later, he became highly indignant on learning that his uncle was resigning his commission and returning to the drabness of civilian life. 'I am most disgusted with Uncle Charlie for leaving the army,' he told his mother.

Like many semi-invalids, Strachey loved travelling, and his life-long appetite for travel was almost certainly whetted by this first journey. It was, as he explains, 'a unique experience', and the pages in which he describes it form a unique journal. Its virtues are many. The mood throughout is light and delicious. He does not weigh it down, as so many boys of twelve or thirteen would have been tempted to do, with chunks of 'important' geographical and historical information. His descriptions are brief and vivid, and he conveys his personal response to all he can see, 'with the aid of spectacles', about him. The world was a mysterious but uncomplicated place, full of magical beauty and thrilling adventures – donkey rides, pyramids and marvellous carnivals. Above all he communicates his bubbling sense of enjoyment. It is an infectious happy diary.

It also displays distinct literary ability, especially a natural talent for narrative. Strachey was a keenly observant boy, already slightly cynical about such human frailties as vanity and pride.

'At the end of the table was a young man called d'Alton, he went in for being funny, he is very short and small, dark, with a *very* curly moustachio which he twirls with pride. . . .

'There was an old man close by fishing with a bamboo. After some time he caught a beautiful fish about one foot six long, then killed it and put [it] in a nitch in the rock. . . . He was so pleased with his success that he began smoking a cigar.'

His tone is one of controlled astonishment which sometimes lifts the story very agreeably to the edge of farce.

'Aunt Aggie said she thought it would be a good idea to go to the sphinx on camels, directly she mentioned this word fifteen camels were on us, all making the most awful noise when sitting down. We were all seized by at least four men who pulled us in four different directions. I got to a Camel and an Arab said it was a lady's one, which it was not so I was hussled off and two men came and lifted me into the air and put [me] on a camel at this moment the sheik interfered and I got onto the one that was supposed to have had a lady's saddle. It was rather a ghastly sensation when the camel got up and you thought you were going to tumble off. We walked on our camels to the sphinx where we dismounted and walked to a place just opposite its face. Although its nose had entirely gone it looked as if all its features were there. What an exquisite face it is – how solemn – how majestic you look, your eyes looking out into the desert with that beautiful expression always on your face so collosal and so perfect. You, who have been there for thousands and thousands of years, you, who have gazed and gazed at that endless sea of sand ever since you existed, tell me oh tell me how to look with that sublime expression on your face at all that comes and all that goes, careless of everything for ever.'

Such a passage contains many of the Stracheyesque ingredients that were to make up his mature style: the wonderfully comic vision; the dramatic narrative gift; the romantic and rhetorical rhapsodizing which, slightly overpitched, seldom quite brings off the effect for which it strives.

The mood of all his later diaries is entirely different. Those that were the 'outcome of excitements' – for example, those of August 1905 and of May 1919 – are never sustained. It was so much more intriguing, in the real meaning of that word, to whisper his secrets to people rather than commit them coldly to paper. For Strachey was to find his natural balance by becoming involved, simultaneously, with two types of people: the lover and the confidant. He fell deeply in love about half-a-dozen times during his life, and parallel to this band of inamoratos there stretched a line of brother and sister confessors to whom he poured out the narrative of his passion. The first of these intimate friends was Leonard Woolf; and he was succeeded by John Maynard Keynes, James Strachey, Ottoline Morrell, Carrington and Mary Hutchinson. These people eclipsed his diaries, which would have disappeared altogether had his amatory arrangements worked out more tidily. As it was, lovers and confidants sometimes became entangled or else involved with other parties who were already interdependent, forming love-atoms of astonishing molecular complexity. Then there were other times, of course, when Strachey was alone. It was during these solitary periods that his diaries reappear.

Not until he got to Cambridge did Strachey find anyone whom he could trust as his confessor. Before that, at Leamington and Liverpool, he had relied on diaries alone. At Leamington, for instance, when he became infatuated with another boy, he put down his thoughts and feelings about it in a secret book. This book gives us a glimpse into his life at a crucially formative stage, and is of great biographical interest. But from Strachey's own point of view, this diary was not an ideal method of describing such episodes. It could be lost, could run the risk of being read by unsympathetic strangers. The thought of such dangers was inhibiting. One could go so far, and no further.

The Liverpool diary is a cry for love. 'The truth is, I want *companionship*,' he writes. He had no real friends, and was desperately lonely. At times his isolation seems almost to have obliterated his personality, extinguished his sense of being – but the diary flourished. He began it, he tells us, 'in the veriest dog days imaginable', for a special purpose. 'I hope it will fulfil the office of safety-valve to my morbidity, which otherwise will become too much to put up with and will have to be abolished.' But there are some amusing sketches of academics and of middle-class society in Liverpool, and a quite unromantic description of

the slums which seemed to mirror back at him all his physical
self-disgust:

> 'Nearly every street is a slum in this town, except those with the
> fine shops. Here is nothing intermediate. Hardly anyone lives
> in the town if they can possibly help it. Pitt Street was pain-
> ful to me in the extreme; it stank; dirty 'furriners' wandered in
> groups over it; and a dingy barrel-organ rattled its jargon in
> the yard. . . . I met an old man today, haggard, and pitiful to
> behold. His cheeks were a hectic red, and his eyes looked out
> on me with the weary, desolate expression of one lost and drift-
> ing. He tottered along the road in an access of decrepitude, his
> ragged overcoat clutched over his frail form. . . .
>
> '. . . In the afternoon walked down to the docks and thence
> to the landing stage. The crowds of people were appalling. The
> landing stage blocked; and *all* hideous. It gave me the shivers
> in two minutes, and I fled. My self-conscious vanity is really
> most painful. As I walk through the streets I am agonised by
> the thoughts of my appearance. Of course, it is hideous, but
> what *does* it matter? I only make it worse by peering into
> people's faces to see what they are thinking. And the worst of
> it is I hate myself for doing it.'

Solitude, failure, the '*absolument rien*' of Liverpool life, and
especially the conviction of his own outcast ugliness – these are
the dominant themes of this diary. 'When I consider that I am
now 18 years of age a shudder passes through my mind and I
hardly dare look at the creature those years have made me.' This
is a far cry from the gingerbread figure of Bloomsbury legend, the
'extravagant old stage duchess whinnying and trumpeting her
pronouncements over the teacups' as P. N. Furbank amusingly
pictured him. It is also very far from the Strachey who was shortly
to establish himself, by sheer force of character, as a pre-eminent
figure at Cambridge, and to delight so many people with his wit
and gaiety. Here he reveals the darker side of himself. 'I wonder
if I shall ever fall "in love". I can't help smiling at the question –
if they only knew – if they only knew! But it is a tragedy also.'
This is the other face of that comedy which made up so much of
his high-stepping life, a face unseen even by some of his friends

who consequently did not take his love-affairs very seriously. Love was the only refuge from the sort of intense loneliness he delineates here, his only method of relinquishing all that he hated in himself. It was important.

Strachey's Liverpool diary appears to have been successful for a time in redressing the balance between the glamour of his fantasies and the degrading spectacle he felt he made of himself in public. But in the end it seems only to have increased his self-preoccupation, and he abandoned it.

The last journal of his life, 'A Fortnight in France', was also written in solitude – but this was a solitude of his choosing. By now he was able to contemplate his own image with a certain stylized equanimity.

'Looking at myself in a shop-window mirror I saw for the first time how completely grey my hair was over my temples. So that has come at last! I was beginning to think it never would. Do I feel like it? Perhaps I do a little – a very little. A certain sense of detachment declares itself amid the agitations that continue to strew my path.'

This journal is by far his most polished performance as a diarist, and shows what he might have achieved in this vein had his life turned out differently. It is a marvellously fluent piece, full of wit and tenderness, remembrances of loves past and speculations over the future, all effortlessly interwoven. Perhaps better than anything else he wrote, 'A Fortnight in France' conveys the peculiar charm that entranced so many men and women who knew him, and that is often so elusive on paper. His stream of consciousness, intensified by solitude, is not entirely uninhibited; there is something slightly contrived: but that was the man. There is little sign, too, of the stomach cancer that, within five months, would kill him – just some fatigue and a lengthening detachment from life (he is very much the spectator). The vacuous boredom of his early days is long since past – he had experienced almost too much. Like Hazlitt, he had 'had a happy life', and there is much sheer entertainment in these pages, mixed with some wistfulness. Describing the wine cellars of Reims, he wrote:

'In the middle of the endless avenues, about half a dozen slaves – sweet creatures – sat bottling and corking the wine. Impossible to speak to them, as the odious cripple who was showing me round gave no possible opportunity for any such thing. All I could do, as I vanished down one of the avenues, was to wave my hand to them – and I'm glad to say they waved back.'

At the beginning of the Liverpool diary, Strachey warns us that 'there will be little recorded here that is not transitory, and there will be much here that is quite untrue. The inquisitive reader should he peep between the covers will find anything but myself – who perhaps after all do not exist but in my own phantasy.' This, of course, was a defensive gambit; all these diaries throw searching beams of light into strange corners of his character. But what is true is that they do not portray the whole man.

His other autobiographical writings – pieces such as the facetious 'First and Last Will and Testament' and his address to the Conscientious Objectors' Tribunal – show him in a more public role. The most important of these are his two long autobiographical essays 'Lancaster Gate' and 'Monday June 26, 1916', both of which he read out to the Memoir Club.

The Memoir Club was founded in March 1920. Besides Strachey, it consisted of twelve members: Clive and Vanessa Bell, E. M. Forster, Roger Fry, Duncan Grant, Maynard Keynes, Desmond and Molly MacCarthy, Adrian Stephen, Saxon Sydney-Turner and Leonard and Virginia Woolf. The club had developed out of an earlier play-reading and Novel Club invented to bring Desmond MacCarthy to the point of writing his novel, which had collapsed once it was discovered that MacCarthy was speaking spontaneously from blank sheets of paper. It was joined later by some members of the Caroline Club, founded by David Garnett and Francis Birrell as a rival to the Novel Club.

Over a period of thirty-six years the Memoir Club would meet, two or three times a year, dine at a restaurant, and then listen to one or two of its members reading aloud some reminiscences. Several of the group had been Cambridge 'Apostles', so it comes as no surprise to learn that 'absolute frankness' was insisted upon. But being older now and a little less severely

Apostolic than before, this frankness was mitigated by some discretion. One of the long-term achievements of the club was the part it later played in bringing into existence books such as David Garnett's and Leonard Woolf's autobiographies, Virginia Woolf's biography of Roger Fry, and possibly even Desmond MacCarthy's *Humanities*. The two brilliant papers Keynes delivered have been published in book form as *Two Memoirs* (1949) and these and other memoirs will almost certainly be of great service to the official biographies of Keynes and Virginia Woolf by Robert Skidelsky and Quentin Bell respectively, to the forthcoming history of Bloomsbury by Noël Annan, and to Paul Levy's study of G. E. Moore and the Apostles.

Strachey read 'Lancaster Gate' to the Memoir Club in 1922. His *Queen Victoria* had been published the year before, and he was now at the height of his fame and literary powers. With the single exception of *Elizabeth and Essex*, all his books were based on the essay form. Although he longed to write drama and lyric poetry, it was the essay that suited his style and stamina best. He was, in fact, one of the most talented essayists in the English language, and 'Lancaster Gate' must be accounted one of his finest essays. Its remarkable evocation of atmosphere, its passages of superb comedy, its analysis of the physiological effects produced on him by this pink and black pile have been orchestrated together by a masterly hand. Here is the clue to Strachey's attitude towards the Victorians. The centre of this house, and its most characteristic feature, he tells us, was the drawing-room.

'When one entered that vast chamber, when, peering through its foggy distances, ill-lit by gas-jets, or casting one's eyes wildly towards the infinitely distant ceiling overhead, one struggled to traverse its dreadful length, to reach a tiny chair or a far-distant fireplace, conscious as one did so that some kind of queer life was clustered thick about one, that heaven knows how many eyes watched from just adumbrated sofas, that brains crouched behind the piano, that there were other presences, remote, aloof, self-occupied, and mysteriously dominating its scene – then, in truth, one had come – whether one realised it or no – into an extraordinary holy of holies. The gigantic door, with its flowing *portière* of pale green silk, swung and shut behind one. One stepped in the direction of the three distant windows covered by their pale green limitless curtains, one looked about, one of the countless groups of persons disintegrated, flowed towards one, one sat and spoke and listened; one was reading the riddle of the Victorian Age.'

Here also is the clue to so much in his life. 'To reconstruct, however dimly, that grim machine, would be to realize with some real distinctness the essential substance of my biography,' he writes. And in reconstructing it, he unconsciously shows it as a womb in which his very soul was entangled, and out of which he had to be born again in order to achieve any sort of freedom and fulfilment.

Strachey remained acutely susceptible to architecture all his life, from the 'lovely musharabiyeh windows and sweet arches' of an Egyptian mosque, to Blenheim which, he told Mary Hutchinson, is 'entrancing, and life-enhancing. I wish it were mine. It is enormous, but one would not feel it too big. The grounds are beautiful too, and there is a bridge over a lake which positively gives one an erection.' Every building he subconsciously compared with Lancaster Gate. But his description of the place is not objective – an estate agent would be prosecuted for it. He magnified its size because of its extraordinary effect upon him; and he exaggerated certain features of his home life because he was an hysteric given, in all his writing, to dramatic extremes. It is more than possible that this hysteria formation had its origins in the influence of Lancaster Gate upon him. Yet his exaggerations are not untruthful. 'The life that began then – my Lancaster Gate life – was to continue till I was twenty-eight,' he writes, '– a man full grown – all the changes from childhood to adolescence, from youth to manhood, all the developments, the curiosities, the pains, the passions, the despairs, the delights, of a quarter of a century having taken place within those walls.' No one could guess from reading this sentence the large amount of time he had spent away from his home – his boarding schools, his holidays in Rothiemurchus, his frequent travels in France and Italy, his two years at Liverpool, six years at Cambridge. Yet the presence of

Lancaster Gate did pervade these years, and however long he might stay away, however far he might go, he could not escape its magnetic field. So strong was this influence upon him that, years after he had left the house, he continued, with a curious iteration, to dream the same dream about it.

'For some reason or another – one of those preposterous and yet absolutely satisfying reasons which occur in dreams – we are back again once more, just as we were, in Lancaster Gate. We are in the drawing-room, among the old furniture, arranged in the old way, and it is understood that we are to go on there indefinitely, as if we had never left it. The strange thing is that, when I realise that this has come about, that our successive wanderings have been a mere interlude, that we are once more permanently established at number 69, a feeling of intimate satisfaction comes over me. I am positively delighted. And this is strange because, in my working life, I have never for a moment, so far as I am aware, regretted our departure from the house, and if, in actuality, we were to return to it, I can imagine nothing which would disgust me more. So, when I wake up, and find myself after all at Gordon Square or Tidmarsh, I have the odd sensation of a tremendous relief at finding that my happiness of one second before was a delusion.'

The second paper he read to the Memoir Club, 'Monday June 26, 1916', was not written specifically for this group, which had not yet been formed. Like 'Lancaster Gate', it is an autobiographical fragment of lasting value, yet in every other respect it is quite dissimilar. For here Strachey breaks new ground as a writer. 'To come close to life!' he writes. 'To look at it, not through the eyes of Poets and Novelists, with their beautifying arrangements or their selected realisms, but simply as one actually *does* look at it, when it happens, with its minuteness and its multiplicity and its intensity, *vivid* and complete! To do that! To do that even with a bit of it – with no more than a single day – to realise absolutely the events of a single and not extraordinary day – surely that might be no less marvellous than a novel or even a poem, and still more illuminating. ....' Abandoning his usual Procrustean technique, he gives a minute reconstruction of a day on which nothing in particular happens, a day spent with friends in talk and strolls and tea and ingenious stratagems concocted for the pursuit of love and in the cause of personal relationships. Instead of compression, of prefabricated and well-rounded shape – what Max Beerbohm called 'the serpent swallowing its own tail' – he uses a linear, even a tangential method of composition, similar in some ways to that of Virginia Woolf. Everything is set down with trace-like exactitude and with an unsparing analysis of motives, especially his own; yet as an evocation of Bloomsbury it will probably convert no one. Those who detest the group will be confirmed in their antipathy by this picture of a life of crowded leisure and of easy privilege in the midst of war. But others will undoubtedly be fascinated by what is a unique view of this gifted circle, a spontaneous and brilliant piece of writing, without parallel in Lytton Strachey's career.

Virginia Woolf: A Suitable
Case for Biography?

The first volume of Quentin Bell's biography of Virginia Woolf*
takes us up to the spring of 1912 when, at the age of thirty, she
agreed to marry Leonard Woolf.

The third child of Leslie Stephen by his second marriage,
Virginia came to believe that the rival streams of her mother's and
father's traditions 'dashed together and flowed confused but not
harmonized in her blood'. From her mother she inherited her
sensitivity and artistic taste: from her father intellectual power and
a neurotic conscience. She was educated at home and the influence
of her father was especially strong.

Leslie Stephen's career was an epitome of Victorian intellectualism. Brought up in the faith of the established church, he had
gone up to Cambridge and entered Holy Orders. Then, turning
to agnosticism, he left for London and a career in literature.
Founder of the *Dictionary of National Biography* and author of
critical and philosophical works, he had grown celebrated as a
skilled expositor of the agnosticism that permeated Victorian
thought after Darwin's *Origin of Species*. Less tough than Thomas
Huxley, less bleak than Herbert Spencer, he shared with many of
the brilliant scholars who were his friends a core of poetry en-
cased within the hard shell of pedantry.

For these dons, judges and headmasters, earnest rationalists all
of them, who moved so magisterially within their cathedral closes,
quadrangles of ancient colleges or the secluded squares of Ken-
sington, nursed, beneath their assured exteriors, fears about the
stability of this world as well as the existence of the next.

* *Virginia Woolf: A Biography. Volume One, Virginia Stephen, 1882–1912* by
Quentin Bell.

Increasingly they found their happiness at the circumference of their lives, at remote places where the railways could now conveniently carry them – the coast of Cornwall or the mountains of Switzerland where they might again sense the mystery of life that had so logically been explained away behind their desks at home.

Leslie Stephen was already in his fiftieth year when, as the result of a contraceptive failure, Virginia was born. The days of his athletic feats on the river or struggling up big peaks between Swiss guides were over, though relics of these exploits – the dusty cup on the mantelpiece, the rusted alpenstocks that leant against the bookcase – encumbered their gloomy house at Hyde Park Gate. Yet he was still capable, while on holiday, of going on a 'potter' of thirty miles or so. In the summer the family often went to Talland House at St Ives 'at the very toenail of England', and here Virginia was at her happiest. These childhood summers left sea-memories that haunt her novels – especially *Jacob's Room*, *To the Lighthouse* and *The Waves* – in their images, rhythms and colours, the blues and greens, that shine through her work and give it a translucent glow.

London, by contrast, was overcast. If the sea symbolized the poetry of life, Hyde Park Gate came to represent the threat of death, madness and disaster. Virginia's upbringing, though outwardly secure, was interspersed by a series of traumatic shocks. From an early age her half-sister Laura had shown disconcerting symptoms of mental instability; then her cousin J. K. Stephen, following an accident, also began to go mad, violently pursuing Virginia's half-sister Stella Duckworth. Since 1888, when he suddenly collapsed, Leslie Stephen's health had not been good. He was looked after devotedly by Julia, his wife, until, worn and harassed, she suddenly died in 1895. 'Her death,' declared Virginia, 'was the greatest disaster that could happen.'

The period between her mother's death and that of her father nine years later was filled with darkness. The lease of Talland House was sold and Virginia suffered the first of a series of nervous breakdowns that were so dreadfully to punctuate her life. When in 1897, within a year of her marriage, Stella Duckworth died, the old man came increasingly to rely on his two daughters Vanessa and Virginia. Lovable to his friends, he was ruthless with his family, inflicting on them a savage emotional blackmail. The Stephens were devoted to catastrophe. Like all their tragedies, his illness was accompanied by a chorus of female lamentations that magnified and funereally enriched his last agonizing months.

For Virginia this time was made more horrible by the improper advances of her half-brother, George Duckworth. 'I still shiver with shame,' she wrote many years afterwards, 'at the memory of my half-brother, standing me on a ledge, aged about six or so, exploring my private parts.' Now, while her father lay dying of cancer three or four floors below, George would fling himself upon Virginia's bed, kissing and embracing her in order, so he later explained, to administer comfort. The result was, Quentin Bell writes, that 'in sexual matters she was from this time terrified back into a posture of frozen and defensive panic'. She felt her life had been spoilt before it had begun.

Her father's death in 1904 was followed by another of Virginia's breakdowns: the birds sang piercingly in Greek while King Edward VII, among the azaleas, swore in the foulest language. The absurdity reached a pitch of nightmare, and she attempted to commit suicide by throwing herself out of a window. But Leslie Stephen's death – as with a similar situation in *The Years* – had given his children freedom. By moving into Bloomsbury they escaped the galling interference of their relations and started a new life by meeting their brother Thoby's Cambridge friends – Clive Bell, Lytton Strachey, Leonard Woolf and others who form the nucleus of the Bloomsbury Group.

The chronicle of disaster, however, was not yet at an end. Following a visit to Greece, Thoby died of typhoid. One partial result of this was that Vanessa Stephen agreed to marry Clive Bell. Virginia was half-pleased, half-distressed; but when Vanessa had a child, she was undisguisably jealous and to injure her sister embarked on a prolonged and pointless flirtation with Clive Bell.

Men as lovers played no part in Virginia's imagination. It was with women she tended to fall in love – with Madge Vaughan, Violet Dickinson and even her sister Vanessa. The love she felt for them was akin to that of a daughter for her mother. When

Hilton Young proposed marriage, it was no more than a game to her: nothing real. But when Lytton Strachey proposed, she briefly accepted because, since he was homosexual, she might enjoy with him an affectionate brother-and-sister marriage unthreatened by the horror of sex.

She wanted to be married. To remain a spinster would, in the eyes of the world, be 'failure', and she was acutely aware of this. The Strachey experiment came to nothing, but in 1912, after some hesitation, she accepted a proposal from Leonard Woolf. 'The obvious advantages of marriage stand in my way ... I feel no physical attraction to you,' she assured him. '... And yet your caring for me as you do almost overwhelms me. It is so real, and so strange.'

The facts of this first part of her life explain why she veered off from reality into fantasy and how this fantasy, which she tried to substitute for reality, became her creative stimulus. It is usually assumed, too, that it was the centre of her madness; but since the dangerous times would come at the end of her novels, it seems that the threat of being sucked back into the actual world was what she really feared.

Some biographers are like actors, almost assuming the identity of their subject. Quentin Bell is not a biographer of this school. He writes as if from the position of a close and sensible friend – an impression that is strengthened by his curious use throughout this book of the first person singular. We get near Virginia Stephen but do not have the sense of what it must have felt to be her. Professor Bell's method has been to assimilate a vast amount of information and produce a narrative admirably lucid and succinct, that is linked together by his conclusions on this information. His powers of summary are excellent and his accuracy unimpeachable.

He is not a great dramatic biographer, and he passes over some of the extraordinarily dramatic scenes, such as the death of Leslie Stephen, very swiftly. Nor has he 'gone adventuring' into literary criticism or psychological speculation. His purpose, he writes, has been 'purely historical', and in putting together an account of Virginia Stephen's life that is absolutely authentic, he has achieved this purpose with complete success.

*   *   *

'I've got a confession to make. I'm going to marry Leonard Woolf. He's a penniless Jew,' Virginia Stephen abruptly announced to her friend Violet Dickinson. Two months later, on 10 August 1912, they were married at St Pancras Registry Office, after an engagement which, in the words of her sister Vanessa, was 'an exhausting and bewildering thing even to the bystanders'. In Virginia's own mind, so Quentin Bell tells us at the beginning of the second volume of his biography,* this 'seemed a very good way of getting married' to the strange wild man, her husband. During the ceremony a thunderstorm broke out and the half-blind Registrar, temporarily deprived of most of his faculties, began muddling the names – at which Vanessa interceded to ask how she should go about changing the name of Quentin, her younger son. Despite this confusion, Virginia and Leonard at length emerged officially married into the rain.

Iceland was where they had planned to enjoy their honeymoon: but eventually they set off in the more orthodox direction of the Mediterranean. It was a trying time. The heat was bad; the food was not good; and Virginia, who was reading Charlotte M. Yonge, found it impossible to respond physically to Leonard. Although she cheerfully continued expecting to have children, she also confessed to Ka Cox that 'I might still be Miss S.' There seemed some unfathomable inhibition that made male lust, even when compounded with love, if not horrific, quite incomprehensible to her. The physical act of intercourse was not even funny: it was cold. Leonard, who must have hoped to thaw her sexual frigidity, regretfully accepted the facts and soon brought the word in line with the deed by persuading her that they should have no children. It was a sensible decision for, though she could never contemplate her sister's fruitfulness without envy, children with their wetness and noise would surely have killed off the novels in her: and it was about novel-writing that she cared most.

After five years of marriage, so Quentin Bell indiscreetly reveals, Leonard, 'whose passionate nature was never in doubt', took a mistress. Her name was the Hogarth Press and, despite some odd deviationist experiments in the Bloomsbury manner,

* *Virginia Woolf. A Biography. Volume Two, Mrs Woolf, 1912–41* by Quentin Bell.

he would consent to share her with no man. For Virginia the press was, at least for a time, therapeutic: she could escape from being a novelist and become a compositor and packer. She needed to escape. From the end of 1912 onwards she had suffered from acute anxiety, from depression, gnawing headaches and nights of sleeplessness in which the sense of her own futility, like a weed, rose to terrible proportions. The tortured intensity with which she had written her first novel, *The Voyage Out*, followed by a disillusioning *douche* of cold proofs, was breaking her up. Within herself she carried a more-than-ordinary tiredness, impossible to reach. In September 1913, overcome with guilt and misery, she attempted to kill herself – and nearly succeeded.

Her recovery was slow; agonizingly slow and intermittent. She was afflicted with states of garrulous mania, with comas, bouts of monstrous physical self-aversion, and a virulent animosity towards Leonard. 'She won't see Leonard at all,' Jean Thomas recorded, 'and has taken against all men. She says the most malicious and cutting things she can think of to everyone and they are so clever that they always hurt.'

The gradual improvement in her health was assisted by the good notices her novel received, which acted as certificates of her sanity. Even so, it was not until the autumn of 1915 that she could begin once more to follow a normal life. These two lost years, spent largely in the land of her own delusions, overshadowed the rest of her career and affected the pattern of her marriage. Leonard, who had come under very considerable strain, took to politics and gardening as part-time escapes into less intense areas of reality. Since she might easily relapse into madness, and each attack threatened to be more difficult to recover from, he had to watch her vigilantly and get to know her illness with the real intimacy of enemies. Praise and encouragement were oxygen and hydrogen to Virginia, and he supplied them in measured quantities continually, blowing away the irrational pain, the sense of failure that threatened to lay waste her life. To outsiders he was cast as the family dragon – a part that in some ways suited his temperament well. He had to make sure that Virginia led as vegetative an existence as possible, supported by good food, cushioned with plenty of rest. She must avoid too many visitors and anything that might tire her physically or mentally. Yet she was a born writer. Living, breathing, meant writing to her, with all the awful agitations and agonies so incomprehensible to non-writers. 'Nothing is real unless I write it,' she once admitted. And so Leonard trained himself to spot the smallest symptom of an oncoming attack, and take quick action to avoid it. Over the years, while she gave birth to a unique series of novels, essays, short stories, he acted as their midwife, making sure after each book was born that she could come back and face the ordeal of writing another.

Yet the threat of madness was always present. 'I feel certain I am going mad again,' she wrote to him on the morning of Friday, 28 March 1941. 'I feel we can't go through another of those terrible times. And I shan't recover this time. I begin to hear voices, and I can't concentrate. So I am doing what seems the best thing to do . . .' She made her way across the water meadows to the river, forced a large stone into her pocket, and drowned herself. Her last sentence, reminiscent of Hazlitt's dying words, is a tribute to her own indomitable courage and the unwavering devotion of Leonard: 'I don't think two people could have been happier than we have been.'

*   *   *

Reviewers of biographies tend to treat the subject not the book. But Quentin Bell's biography prompts many questions about literary biography as a whole. The high standard achieved in the first volume has been maintained – indeed his scholarship, especially at the moment when he establishes, not beyond question, Virginia's possible failure to smoke a pipe in Sicily, tops American summits. He has charted the where-and-when of her life with studied accuracy; his Chronology is definitive. Yet now the full work is before us, its total impact seems curiously muffled, as if Virginia has been too elusive to be caught by such a straightforward approach.

Literary biography is an opportunity for the subject to write, in collaboration, a posthumous work. But in this biography, Virginia has not collaborated with her 'old and valued collaborator in fiction Mr Quentin Bell'. Her own biography of Roger Fry may, in some sense, provide a reason. It was an ungrateful task, hemmed in by the unspoken censorship of the Fry sisters, and it plagued her. Although she felt that revision was the hardest, saddest part of writing, she re-wrote this book ten or fifteen times: 'fearful niggling drudgery', she called it. According to Leonard Woolf, 'she could deal with facts and arguments on the scale of a full-length book only by writing against the grain, by continually repressing something which was natural and necessary to her peculiar genius'. But there were also repressions demanded from without. 'How, how to deal with love so we're not all blushing?' she asked Vanessa, whose adulterous passion for Fry was one of the aspects not touched upon in the biography. The harm such inhibitions did to the book is very well analysed by Quentin Bell:

> 'A crucial period of Roger's life was made tremendous by Cézanne and by Vanessa. I doubt whether Virginia could have given the whole of Roger's feelings and of his adversaries' feelings about Cézanne. Vanessa she did understand, and she might have described her love affair with Roger beautifully; but she was prevented from doing so. Thus in the end she was thwarted both by what she knew and by what she did not know.'

Although Leonard Woolf dismissed *Roger Fry* as 'merely analysis, not history', it is by no means a bad book. It brought back Fry to those who had known him, though it did not, I think, bring him fully alive for the general reader. This, too, is the degree of success attained by Quentin Bell's franker and more thorough book on Virginia. There are, for instance, very few visual descriptions of people – those who knew Virginia's friends will be able to see them in their mind's eye, while for the rest of us there are the illustrations. To paraphrase Leonard Woolf, this book is not biography, merely history: that is to say it is external. To look at Virginia from the outside is specifically Quentin Bell's aim, for he shares something of her attitude to biography.

> 'Many scenes have come and gone unwritten since, it is to-day 4th September [1927, she wrote in her diary]. A cold grey blowy day, made memorable by the sight of a kingfisher and

by my sense, waking early, of being again visited by "the spirit of delight". Rarely, rarely, comest thou, spirit of delight. That I was singing this time last year; and so poignantly that I have never forgotten it, or my vision of a fin rising on a wide blank sea. No biographer could possibly guess this important fact about my life in the late summer of 1926. Yet biographers pretend they know people.'

To this passage, which, it may be argued, is in part self-contradictory, Quentin Bell gives his enthusiastic support. 'They [biographers] don't, or at least they ought not to,' he writes. 'All that they can claim is that they know a little more than does the public at large and that, by catching at a few indications given here and there in recollections or writings, they can correct some misconceptions and trace, if they are very skilful or very lucky, an outline that is consistent and convincing, but which, like all out-lines, is but tenuously connected with the actual form of the sitter in all lights, poses, moods and disguises.'

Of course it is true that no biographer is omniscient, and that there is no scientific method he can call on to calculate the whole truth about everything. The claim that Quentin Bell makes for biographers, however, is in imaginative terms a modest one, need-ing much goodwill, a lot of energy and some basic literary com-petence to perform. In a letter to Shena Simon, Virginia Woolf wrote of her *Roger Fry*: 'If I could have shirked all the relations, I might have said more – but as it is, No, I don't think one can so disregard human feelings: – a reason not to write biographies, – yet if one waits the impression fades.' Quentin Bell has not been confronted with these difficulties to the same extent. He has not attempted to write a 'personal' biography, so that there is little to lose by fading impression. More time has elapsed and in that time the whole climate of biography has altered. Even so, tactful and sympathetic as he is, there is at least one person in his book who will have been offended by what he has written. Quentin Bell's defence – and he is nice enough a man to feel he needs one – is that the offending passages were absolutely relevant to Virginia Woolf's life. Many other matters could have been mentioned, but they were not so central and could therefore legitimately be omitted. So the old problem still remains, though a shift of emphasis has taken place. Relevance, on a strict factual basis, has become the criterion.

Biography, though it interested her, was not Virginia Woolf's métier – she punished herself and indirectly those near her in the cause of fiction: rightly so. For others, a small enough band, who believe obstinately in biography as a possible form of literature, this question of relevance is crucial. What is relevant to a biographer must be what excites him, what encourages within him his best writing. For the aim of all biography is to recreate a world into which the reader may enter and where he can experience certain feelings and thoughts, some of which will remain with him after the book is closed. Techniques must differ, but the universal method must be for the biographer, who lives so long with his subject, to discover exactly what their relationship is, and then give that relationship a literary pattern, a living shape. Quentin Bell's relationship with his aunt was already settled long before he began writing, and did not alter during the course of his biography. He first knew her, of course, when he was a child, and Virginia, he tells us, was extremely good with children. When, in 1964, he was first asked by Leonard Woolf to undertake this book he declined on two grounds: that, as an artist and a professor in the history and theory of art, he knew too little about English literature; and that as Virginia Woolf's nephew he was partly disqualified, Bloomsbury having written too exclusively about itself already.

The first objection, a modest one, was easily met by the decision to include no formal literary criticism in the book. This was surely correct, not because of Professor Bell's stoutly maintained ignorance (which I fancy is very much exaggerated), but because there has been a very great deal of critical attention given to her books and, perhaps even more important, Virginia herself 'distrusted academic criticism altogether'.

The second objection was swallowed back once Quentin Bell realized that he could not stomach the alternative idea of some intrusive stranger peering at Virginia, probing, possibly for years, to make up his biography of her. She would have hated this and, as Leonard Woolf had suspected, Quentin Bell felt he could not expose her to such treatment. Already what some outsiders had written grated horribly on him, not necessarily because it was hostile, but because the tone was inappropriate, giving room for all sorts of misunderstandings. As her nephew he was in a privileged position which he could use to eliminate the kind of error so easily picked up by people who had never known her.

So, with eager reluctance, he set to work. But his difficulty was, at least in the modern climate of writing, that he did not feel himself by temperament to be a biographer at all. In his previous book on Bloomsbury, published in 1968, he had written: 'I am not required nor am I inclined to act as Clio's chambermaid, to sniff into commodes or under beds, to open love-letters or to scrutinize diaries. On the present occasion I shall leave Bloomsbury linen, whether clean or dirty, unaired.' On this subsequent occasion he has steeled himself and done what he has conceived to be his duty; he has steered a course very skilfully between his inclinations and our expectations. It has been extremely hard work over a long period but, to some degree, it is still a compromise biography. His own reaction has been very similar to Virginia's after *Roger Fry*. 'Something of a nightmare,' he admitted to Janet Watts; '. . . the sense of failure is very acute. Though people have been very nice about it, and I'm beginning to cheer up a bit.'

It was never Quentin Bell's intention to raise up a work of piety: simply a book of flat accuracy. But the tone throughout is one of watchful protectiveness. At the beginning of the second volume he informs us that Clive Bell, 'giving vent to his frustrations, had said some very bitter things indeed' about Virginia following her engagement. What were they? We are not told, even though, at a later stage, Virginia herself declared that such exasperated outbursts usually contain much insight. Throughout both volumes there are many examples of sentences beginning: 'It is unnecessary to describe the process . . .' or 'The circumstances of that schism do not concern us . . .'. At one point we are specifically referred to an important letter that cannot, 'at present, be published'. Again, it is the problem of 'relevance'. Such non-necessities and matters of unconcern are not normally paraded before the reader, and the fact that they are here indicates, I think, that the paraphernalia of the biography has become something of a paper wall separating Virginia from the reader. When, for instance, we read in volume one that her letters to Emma Vaughan were 'lively productions' yet are allowed to see not a single quotation from them, there is only one conclusion that can be drawn: that this biography is not constructed to be, except in outline, complete in itself; that it is part of a wide-ranging publication programme, stretching probably over years and involving re-edited diaries, volumes of selected letters and various recollections that will, like a cluster of dots, form a mosaic of books to give us the composite picture of Virginia Woolf. Such a programme may well be very sensible, but it cannot be good for the biography if, to avoid the overlapping of material, it acts as a limiting force, robbing us of quotations and even paraphrase.

Another symptom of biographical protectiveness is Quentin Bell's use of the first person singular. He does not use it intimately, but to fix a mood of unassertiveness. Yet it is a watching I, looking both at Virginia and at us, the readers, measuring the distance, warning us from coming too near.

This protectiveness is naturally stimulated whenever Virginia comes under attack. We are not given the full thrust of these attacks since that would trespass into literary criticism. In the first volume Quentin Bell suggested that Virginia was not given to malice. It is a point of view that needs, to sustain it, the sort of ingenuity that admirers defending Proust from the charge of snobbery are driven to employ. Maliciousness and snobbery are blunt words, vague and inexact, and there is no doubt that there are whole areas they cover which do not apply to these writers. But defences of this sort are apt to end up as definitions. In his second volume, Quentin Bell gives an illustration of the type of occasion on which Virginia has been undeservingly credited with malice: her part (described in David Garnett's edition of Carrington's *Letters* as 'unscrupulous') in the affair between Carrington, Ralph Partridge and Lytton Strachey. Quentin Bell's explanation of her conduct is able and at least partly convincing. Her advice, he tells us, was genuine, though perhaps she did not know all the up-to-daie facts. Yet he fails to quote an unpublished letter that she wrote to Vanessa Bell at the time which, by any standard, must surely be relevant to the argument: 'Ralph has a fixed and gloomy look which reminds me of his father, the suicidal colonel. I imagine (but for God's sake don't shout this about Gordon Square) that there's been a crisis. Anyhow, I hope so. I hope they're all at daggers drawn.' There lies the poison which seeped into her advice. Quentin Bell could explain Virginia's hopes and motives perfectly reasonably: but how could anyone explain away the *tone* of such a passage?

No one should want to. During her life Virginia needed protection. 'No atmosphere round me,' she noted poignantly in her diary. '... I have no protection ... And I want to burst into tears.' It is no more than natural that her nephew should seek to provide this protection: it would be curious were it otherwise. Nevertheless I think this aim is misguided for a biographer. That part of her that needed protection is dead; the writer lives, and it is the biographer's part to celebrate the living writer – not, certainly, through piety, but not by protective custody either. For she suffered what almost every genuine writer suffers, only more than most. And if, under the strain and tension of her work, she was ungenerous, egotistical, malicious and at times something of a mischief-maker, then these superficially unpleasant vices, as well as the 'sympathetic' illnesses, testify to the great risks she would take in her fierce dedication to literature. She hurt others because she was in pain herself; she did not write novels without tears. Therefore she needs no excuses, for one can only protect the woman by diminishing a little the novelist. It is, of course, true that she did not herself always justify some of her feelings. They were, she wrote, 'not creditable, nor lovable'. But then the writer would come into herself: 'There was something noble in feeling like this; tragic, not at all petty'. The first statement was written when her faith in her novelist's art faltered for a moment and 'nothing matters'; the second and truer reaction came when that faith was restored.

She cared more about writers than other people, and to some extent treated life as raw material for literature. She would not, I believe, object to being treated as raw material herself. There is a striking example of this preference in her differing attitudes to two contemporary fiction-writers, Vita Sackville-West and

Katherine Mansfield. Vita Sackville-West loved her, and to a degree this feeling was returned: their relationship, Quentin Bell concludes in considering the case for 'the prosecution', may not have been entirely 'innocent'. But it was not love in the accepted sense that Vita Sackville-West inspired in Virginia: it was an eternal curiosity. She was not blinded but open-eyed, weaving her fantasies about this strange figure, experimenting perhaps a little, and using their affections in the composition of *Orlando*. There is no call for prosecution or defence: the writing is there. Who can doubt this when they read her words, the words of her diary, spun about the phenomenon that was her friend:

> 'I like her and being with her and the splendour – she shines in the grocer's shop in Sevenoaks with a candle lit radiance, stalking on legs like beech trees, pink glowing, grape clustered, pearl hung. That is the secret of glamour, I suppose . . . There is her maturity and full breastedness; her being so much in full sail on the high tides, where I am coasting down backwaters; her capacity I mean to take the floor in any company, to represent her country, to visit Chatsworth, to control silver, servants, chow dogs; her motherhood (but she is a little cold and off-handed with the boys) her being in short (what I have never been) a real woman. Then there is some voluptuousness about her; the grapes are ripe; and not reflective.'

No one who enjoys language can fail to relish such passages as this, or to admire the way she makes the words obey her – the music and the movement so beautifully controlled, and the discipline never squeezing them so that they lose part of their force. Then, so many good monosyllables and when the long word comes, so right. Each sentence seems to finish just as it is about to be overfilled; and we are carried on.

Katherine Mansfield has something of this gift. She, too, touched Virginia's heart – though Virginia never wrote of her as she did of Vita. One was a subject for her pen, odd and remote from her own world; the other a creature like herself, an outcast, a writer. 'A queer effect she produced of someone apart, entirely self-centred; altogether concentrated upon her "art": almost fierce to me about it' – these words of Virginia Woolf's about

Katherine Mansfield express what many people felt about Virginia herself. As a person, she did not really like Katherine Mansfield; certainly she felt moments of jealous rivalry, of malice and antipathy: they were a form of back-handed compliment not always easy to appreciate. '... she stinks like a – well, civet cat that had taken to street walking. In truth, I'm a little shocked by her commonness at first sight; lines so hard and cheap.' By Vita Sackville-West, a lady of high lineage, she was fascinated; but although she recognized in her a certain literary heritage, very romantic to play one's mind over, she recognized, quite frankly, that Vita wrote with a 'pen of brass'. So it was for Katherine, who 'seems to me an unpleasant but forceful and utterly unscrupulous character', that Virginia nevertheless reserved her real admiration. 'The inscrutable woman remains inscrutable – I'm glad to say; no apologies or sense of apologies due ... I find with Katherine what I don't find with other clever women – a sense of ease and interest, which is, I suppose, due to her caring so genuinely if so differently from the way I care, about our precious art.'

Virginia Woolf is a particularly difficult subject for a biographer, if only because, as her sister observed, she 'lives in a world of her own'. From politics, from what others (especially in the 1930s) tended to think of as 'the real' world, she seemed isolated. 'It is not catastrophies, murders, deaths, diseases that age and kill us,' she wrote in *Jacob's Room*, her most political novel; 'it's the way people look and laugh, and run up the stairs of omnibuses.' Though she made gestures at exercising a social conscience, she did not believe that writers had the power of changing society, of abolishing the British class system. 'The rising novelist is never pestered to come to gin and winkles with the plumber and his wife,' she pointed out. 'His books never bring him into touch with the cats'-meat man, or start a correspondence with the old lady who sells matches and bootlaces by the gate of the British Museum.' This attitude irritated some Left Wing intellectuals who considered her politically sterile. For her part, she did not believe that novels should be judged by sociological criteria, or that writers were some breed of politician *manqué*. Since few of the working class read literature, and in any case, according to Croce, all change in history comes from the top downwards, books would have to be valued for their governmental repercussions – and authors must surely be seen as the most ineffective members of the community. She did not believe this for, whatever the social issues, the moral problem of the novelist is a private matter: to write what he does best.

What Virginia Woolf did best was something unique and quite removed from politics. 'Life is a luminous halo,' she wrote, 'a semi-transparent envelope surrounding us from the beginning of consciousness to the end.' It seemed, sometimes, as if she were only half-born into the actual world, the world that is cluttered up with newspaper headlines and important to-ing and fro-ing; as if her wraith-like spirit never completely possessed her body. The probing, innocent curiosity she felt about her life, though often passionate, appeared strangely bloodless. In place of the direct involvement that was denied her, she posed a string of improbable questions. What must it feel like to be a king? – a bus conductor? – men and women walking together at a railway station, safe and happy? She speculated endlessly upon the unknown; and for her the unknown was often the commonplace.

Her novels are intricately charted extensions of her method of self-examination. Between periods of importance flies the moment of significance, and it is this moment she catches, holds up for us to see. Like a bat, relying on sound waves alone to tell it the geography of its surroundings, she put together a vision of life full of wisps and fragments – a shadow, a silhouette, a twig in the wind, the mark on a wall. Whatever flies too fast for us each day, what impresses itself only on our subconscious minds – this was her ordinary material as a novelist. Her best books, by virtue of their perfect style, hold in equilibrium sanity and madness, reality, delusion, the concrete and the dream. But it is the dream that gives them their special floating quality. They are immersions into the neurasthenic depths of her nature which, like that of Coleridge, was subterranean. As an ordinary land-animal she was ill-adapted, at times even absurd; but as some deep-sea creature, whose habits and moods could not be properly understood on the bright matter-of-fact surface of things, she entered her natural kingdom. There are many exquisite vignettes scattered through her pages that convey her sensibility with a lyrical, muted radiance, seeming to tremble from refracted rays of sunlight playing far below the green waves to the soundless bed of the ocean.

In Quentin Bell's biography we are shown the wide blank sea, and now and then, on the horizon, a fin rising. We see something of what it was like looking at her, less of what it was like for her looking at us. Her view was somnambulistic, tenuously connected with waking reality. 'She lives,' wrote Clive Bell, 'in a world of fantastic daydreams, half in a world of solid reality, half in a Victorian novel.' In the first volume of Quentin Bell's book we are given something of the Victorian novel: in the second, the solid reality – only it was not real to her. 'My present feeling is that this vague and dream-like world, without love, or heart, or passion or sex, is the world I really care about, and find interesting,' she wrote to Madge Vaughan in 1907. 'For, though they are dreams to you, and I can't express them at all adequately, these things are perfectly real to me.' We do hear her voice in this biography, but it is distant. For we have the letter of the truth rather than the spirit, the duty not the joy. Her vegetable life, 'the outer life of work and activity', has been very well excavated: here is the paraphernalia of the writer's existence – the ink and illnesses, royalties, reviews, the quires, queries and long afternoon walks, all nailed down with unswerving chronology. Her own corporeal existence, from which she always tried to escape, has been painstakingly resurrected. What else could Quentin Bell have done? It must be acknowledged that his problem was a stiff one. To have plumbed her inner life of emotion and thought 'which meanders darkly and obscurely through the hidden channels of the soul', he would have had to take a step on his own initiative; to present what Virginia herself called 'that queer amalgamation of dream and reality, that perpetual marriage of granite and rainbow', he would have had to evolve a biography as daring and difficult as one of her own novels. As it is, she has slipped through his fingers, and he has given us, faultlessly, the expected not the real thing.

Roger Fry

Upon the climate of British painting in the first half of this century, the influence of Roger Fry was enormous – 'in so far as taste can be changed by one man', writes Lord Clark, 'Fry changed it'.

He would have preferred to be a great artist: 'How I hate writing,' he once told Gerald Brenan, 'and how I like painting.' But his pictures, carefully painted with the dead hand of intellectuality, were disappointing. 'I try all ways to tap that side of me, I mean the instinctive and subconscious but I have undoubtedly a damned active mind which often "butts in" when it isn't wanted,' he explained. In his introduction to Fry's letters, Denys Sutton agonizingly warns us that 'his contribution as a painter should not be overvalued; but its consistency deserves praise'. His courage stood him in better stead as a critic, for he was always prepared to chance his arm with unfashionable opinions. But it was as a teacher, in particular a lecturer, that he had genius.

Brought up in a strict Quaker family, he went in 1886 to Cambridge where he was later initiated into the Apostles, that very secret society to which the origins of the Bloomsbury Group may be traced. 'I never was so happy in my life before,' he wrote. '. . . In fact I am quite drunk with mere existence here.' He found himself in an atmosphere ringed with romantic homosexuality and innocent intellectualism – something completely different from his home. What he valued most was the freedom, which enabled him to develop from his father's son into an individual, and it was this that made Cambridge 'the only place where a man is permitted truly to live'. Here, on the road between Trinity and King's, he was suddenly converted from Natural Science to Art,

* *Letters of Roger Fry* edited with an introduction by Denys Sutton.

writing to reassure his horrified father that though 'the possibility of landscape-painting without figures is quite untenable . . . there is no reason at all why one should draw from the female figure'.

Having decided to continue with painting, Fry made the first of many visits to Italy, studying and copying old masterpieces, and hardly able to keep still for excitement. If only Cambridge could have been transplanted to Rome or Florence, what great works he and his friends could have produced! The following year he began studying at the Académie Julian in Paris, but in the autumn of 1893 his paintings were rejected by the New English Art Club. It was then that he turned to criticism.

Although he persisted with his painting, it was from his writings, his lectures and his administrative work that he earned money. For several years he was associated with the Metropolitan Museum in New York, but though initially he found society there 'very friendly and accessible', he did not like America: it was all big talk and big money – an inhuman place. When in 1910 he was dismissed – 'a vile deed', he called it – he was not altogether sorry, for by then he had become 'fed up with the crass stupidity of public bodies'. He was out of official life for good – 'but you know', he told a friend, 'that if I can earn enough money to live without this kind of distinction I am perfectly content'.

This turning-point in his career coincided with a crisis in his private life. One of the most endearing things about Fry was the frequency with which he fell in love. Although he had blossomed in the homosexual climate of Cambridge, he was himself exclusively heterosexual – to the sentimental regret of his Apostolic brother Lowes Dickinson. In 1896 he had met Helen Coombe, an art student, 'and fell completely in love in one afternoon's talk'. In a letter to her, he wrote: 'I'm afraid you'll have to love me after all because I want you to so very much.' They were married within the year. But shortly afterwards she began to suffer from a mental illness that by 1910 had become so serious that she had to be permanently consigned to a home.

He was forty-three, without a job or a wife, horribly lonely and at sea over the prospect of remaking his life. He looked far older than his age, yet eight years later Aldous Huxley was observing that 'for a man of over fifty [he] is far the youngest person I have ever seen'. In the interval he had brought about a revolution in British art and established himself as the leader of modern British artists. It was an astonishing achievement.

Fry's early correspondence is rather schoolmasterish and packed with descriptions which, he blandly admits, 'are generally a bore'. But as soon as he involves himself with living artists, the letters grow more lively, though writing, he tells D. S. MacColl, 'always is something of a labour to me'. His best letters are usually to the women he loved, for to them he would write more in the style he talked. The first of these was Vanessa Bell, the last Helen Anrep – both of whom 'invited' ideas out of his head about art. By himself he was no art-politician. His Omega Workshops nearly ruined him and attracted the sort of personal antagonism from artists that was always taking him by surprise. In order to protect himself he tried to develop 'such a crust that no one will break through'. To his enemies, such as Tonks, he seemed ruthless and obstinate, an authoritarian with prodigious energy and a Hitler of the art world. It was only with women, on whom he was dependent in a childlike way, that he revealed what lay beneath this crust. 'On the surface I'm rather efficient and capable,' he once wrote to Helen Anrep. '. . . But at bottom I am rather helpless and love to feel how much I can just lean on you.'

In the opinion of Clive Bell, Fry was 'one of the few men of genius who ever made a real synthesis of the attitudes of artist and scientist'. Yet his weakness as an interpretative critic lay in the lack of synthesis between artistic and human values – Quentin Bell remembers him describing the agonized body of Christ upon the cross as 'this important mass'. He had, of course, his blind spots – Turner, Delacroix, Klee: but his chief peculiarity was an extreme eagerness to believe the most implausible theories – a gift that earned him the nickname 'Old Credulity'. 'If you sent him a gilded turd in a glass case he would probably discover some strange and potent rhythm in it,' Augustus John once advised John Quinn, 'and hail you as a cataclysmic genius.' There were a number of artists, led astray by this eloquent credulity and his inability to adapt general theories to particular talents, who were said to have been 'rogered' by Fry – almost certainly Duncan Grant and possibly also Augustus John, whom Fry saw as another Watts. But there was a strength even to his naïvety, for he persisted in it to the point of wisdom and would not be deterred by fear of ridicule. 'I have no admiration for people who won't risk being thought fools,' he once wrote to Helen Coombe.

These letters leave one with an increased respect for Fry's scholarship, his unbribable honesty and deep devotion to art. Mr Sutton has read widely and worked with patience to prepare these volumes. It is therefore disappointing to record that his editing is not always very adept. He has lavished on these volumes much window-scholarship – many too many black-and-white illustrations of doubtful relevance which must greatly inflate the price; and a number of footnotes that ferret out the identities of such people as Diderot, Gibbon and Bernard Shaw. He has written a very long and interesting introduction to which it is necessary to refer back when reading the letters again and again. One has only to compare this method with that of Dan H. Laurence's *Collected Letters of Bernard Shaw* to see the advantages of dividing such a book into sections and giving the reader information, when necessary, between letters. Nevertheless, one must be grateful to Mr Sutton for having given us a work that will be of permanent value.

Delacroix

At a dinner for writers and artists some time ago, my neighbour – an author – dolefully remarked that you could pick out the writers from among the gathering at a single glance: they were the ones with the sad faces. The general truth of his observation would seem to be confirmed by this edition of Delacroix's sparkling letters.* Was there ever a literary artist of equivalent stature who maintained so happy an equilibrium? That Delacroix experienced the same sort of difficulties which confront most authors is apparent from much of this correspondence. 'I am a prey to a state of nerves that makes me like an hysterical woman,' he confided to a friend. 'Solitude, and my still precarious health and perhaps, as I believe, a particular crisis in my temperament, make me want and not want, and turn the simplest matters into something monstrous.' The choice, so often, seemed between anxiety and boredom. 'What ardour I must bring to my study to alleviate that *ennui*,' he wrote. Then his mood would change and he longed for the peace of indifference, for apathetic serenity. 'Alas, that state of mental health is unknown to me,' he told George Sand. 'I am continually wounded by a thousand pinpricks at which most men would laugh. The slightest trifles make me happy, while on the other hand I have mountains of worries.' It was no wonder he complained of being unable to 'govern myself' and of being 'always either up in the air or down in the depths'.

Yet, to judge from his letters, it is at this very self-government that Delacroix excelled. The strong contradictory impulses between the claims of society and the individual, between passion and patience, body and mind, nature and human nature he kept

* *Selected Letters 1813–63* by Eugéne Delacroix edited and translated by Jean Stewart with an introduction by John Russell.

in superb suspension. How was it done? 'Whatever I happen to be doing in the way of painting gives me such pleasure that it comforts me for all the ills, great and small, that life incessantly offers,' he explained. 'Living alone, and deprived of great joys, but also free from the sometimes excessive griefs which one suffers through members of one's family, I have plenty of time to give to that art which will delight me as long as I live.' It is this quality of enjoyment that resolves the contradictions and carries him through, a sensuous physical enjoyment in the applic aion of paint. Sometimes the work overtired him, sometimes it disappointed him. Many sacrifices had to be made. It placed a barrier between him and the appreciation of pleasures he would otherwise have relished. For if his work did not go well, everything was spoiled. 'It seems to me that one should have fulfilled one's task in order to enjoy with a clear conscience the good things that nature offers one. A great argument for work!' Guilt so mantled him that even a cigar was 'an agent of corruption'. Yet despite the price that had to be paid, he was in no doubt that 'I'm fortunate to practise an art in which I find such true enjoyment and interest'.

These letters form a valuable complement to Delacroix's famous *Journal*. They cover other periods of his life and many subjects other than his painting. Since he turned to his diary mostly in moods of uncertainty or pessimism, these letters also reveal different facets of his personality, above all his extraordinary adjustment to the rigours of the artist's life. They have been selected from some six volumes in French with a view to showing all the varied aspects of his temperament. Very occasionally letters will overlap and some incident is described twice – but only when such descriptions are extremely good. One feels that the editor, Miss Jean Stewart, has a loving knowledge of her subject. Her translation is marvellously fluent and sympathetic, warm yet very exact.

As a young man Delacroix was dazzled by the twin dreams of love and ambition – was not one the raw material for the other? He is always falling in love as everyone, except rogues, must. In the brief intervals when he is not in love he feels dead and the world is empty. 'I am miserable, I am not in love with anyone,' he writes to his friend Charles Soulier during one of these profit-less spells. 'I cannot be happy, lacking that delicious torment. I have only vain dreams that disturb me and satisfy nothing at all. I was so happy when I was unhappily in love! There was something exciting even in my jealousy, and in my present state I am no better than a living corpse. In order to live truly, in my own way, that is to say through my feelings and passions, I am obliged to seek these joys from painting, to wrest them from my art by force. But this is not nature's way, and when I fall back on my empty heart, weighed down by an *ennui* that I've beguiled and distracted by artificial means, I feel only too well that my flame needs sustenance and that I should paint very differently if I were kept constantly in suspense by the sweet excitement of love.'

To keep his heart filled with this fuel of love he needed to involve himself in life; but to paint great pictures he needed seclusion and detachment. Expressed crudely, the problem was that the more you put into women the less you can put into your work. Yet if you cut yourself off entirely you have nothing with which to charge your work. Delacroix succeeded perfectly in balancing his appetite for sex with his appetite for work. His erotic feelings were sublimated on to the canvas, so that he almost made love in terms of paint. 'It is an amazing thing,' he noted in his diary in April 1824, 'but although I wanted to make love to Laurie all the time she was posing for me, I lost all heart for it the moment she began to leave.' The synthesis between the opposing demands of love and work came to him in the form of fantasy. The essence of this was a trick of time. He would expose himself to delicious and terrible moments, then quickly retire. 'It often happens to me that a mental experience, of whatever sort, only affects me after the event, and when I am by myself or withdrawn into the seclusion of my own mind I feel the effect all the more powerfully because the cause is removed,' he told his friend Achille Piron. 'That is when my imagination gets to work and, unlike sight, it makes things seem larger the further away they are. I reproach myself for not having fully enjoyed the moment that chance had granted me; I build fantastic castles in the air, and go off roaming and wandering on the "boundless and shoreless sea of illusions".'

The urge to paint which gave him this self-control was very strong and, at first, as generously romantic as the urge to love. 'Pray heaven that I may be a great man,' he exlaimed to Achille Piron; 'and may heaven do the same to you.' But he was not vain. Fame, popularity, the approval of critics did not obsess him. 'The praises of others have never made more than an imperfect impression on me,' he told J.-B. Pierret. His criticism of his friends' work is never flattering, but sympathetic, and usually constructive in suggesting improvements. He was not unaffected by criticism, but does not seem to have allowed himself the artistic licence of paranoia. 'It's this terrible *Art* which is the cause of all our sufferings, not to mention all the envious and spiteful rascals who look askance at our wretched works before they're done,' he complained to George Sand. 'Fortunately we do them partly for our own sakes, very little for the sake of posterity, which I haven't the honour of knowing, but chiefly to help us forget our troubles a little.'

To steer clear of these troubles, Delacroix was always praying God to 'make me become as unsociable as possible', always proclaiming that 'I am going to become a recluse'. In his excellent introduction to this volume John Russell warns us that we can be misled by this repeated longing 'for a modest, withdrawn, slippered existence'. A letter from Prosper Mérimée to Stendhal recounting an orgiastic evening with six girls running through some gymnastic exercises in *puris naturalibus* describes Delacroix as 'beside himself – puffing and blowing as if he wanted to take on the whole six of them at once'.

Delacroix distrusted critics. Most often they wanted to prove something, valuing only by their artificial rules and in terms of schools and movements, and discounting beauty for its own sake. So much of what painters did was, in any event, irrelevant to judgments in words. Undeniably Delacroix's imagination was luxuriously romantic, and, along with Berlioz and Victor Hugo, historians have placed him as one of the most brilliant members of the Romantic Movement in France. Such labelling, though not inaccurate, tends to blur Delacroix's individuality, to reduce him in the interests of consistency. In many respects he was austerely unromantic: his manners were polite and rather self-conscious;

his way of life often very frugal, his clothes sober, his appearance ultimately unByronic. The music of Berlioz he called 'an appalling row, a kind of heroic mish-mash'; and of Victor Hugo he said that 'he never came within a hundred miles of truth and simplicity'. Elsewhere, in a letter to Madame Cavé, he wrote: 'Truth is so close to the parody of truth that it is not surprising that they are often mistaken for one another: which caused the ruin and confusion of the so-called Romantic school, or rather, as you say, the word school means nothing; truth in the arts concerns only the person who writes or paints or composes, in any *genre* whatsoever.' Many of his tastes – his preference for the simple style of Saint-Réal over Chateaubriand's rhetorical inflation – appear to have more in common with the Classical tradition. He possessed, too, a vein of philosophical self-mockery inimical to pure romance. 'I have taken up horse riding,' he writes on one occasion. 'Mr Elmore, who has shown me the utmost kindness, is my riding-master. I show great aptitude. I even looked like breaking my neck on two or three occasions. But it all helps to form one's character.'

Delacroix was a natural writer. His letters are written in a prose that waits to be loaded with every nuance of what he wishes to give, that carries often in a single sentence humour and seriousness, pathos, intelligence and much charm. It waits, but it also moves, rhythmically, perfectly attuned to its meaning.

Success came to Delacroix at last in 1857 when, after twenty years and six failures, he was elected to the Institut. He was almost sixty and had six years to live. 'You say quite rightly that this success, twenty years earlier, would have given me far greater pleasure,' he wrote to Constant Dutilleux. 'I would then have had a chance to prove myself more useful than I can be to-day, in such a position.' He had never played art-politics – 'what do petty rivalries matter: I have never worried much about them,' he told Paul Huet – but he was an ambassador of painting and took recognition by the Establishment with graceful responsibility. In these last years the numbness of old age affected him increasingly. He was constantly unwell; nothing was left of love; many of his friends had died; he was a prey to disillusionment – to 'the despair of maturity'. Yet age was one more stimulus for work, and he felt 'firmly convinced that the mind grows towards perfection'. Nothing enchanted him now except painting. Painting was life – the supreme tonic that gave him resignation and real satisfaction. And so, when the man died, the painter still lived on.

Brave Face, Hideous Place

Among those books that an enterprising publisher might well reissue, perhaps in an abridged edition, are William Rothenstein's three volumes of memoirs, *Men and Memories*. Anyone interested in British art between the 1880s and the 1930s will know how indispensable a source book this is, how readable, and how well for the most part it has stood the test of time.

What Will Rothenstein succeeded in doing for an earlier age, his elder son Sir John Rothenstein has done equally brilliantly for the period between the 1920s and the 1960s. Like his *Modern English Painters* – a third volume of which is in preparation – his autobiography comprises both an invaluable reference book and a highly entertaining, often amusing personal narrative.

In *Summer's Lease*, the first and possibly the most perfectly co-ordinated of these autobiographical volumes, Sir John relied on his memory and on a number of letters that happened to have survived from the first thirty-seven years of his life. Thereafter he has had a daily diary and a far greater accumulation of correspondence on which to draw, and one of the results is that his book has become a less private affair, spread over a wider canvas. The second volume, *Brave Day: Hideous Night*, which covered his years as keeper of the Tate, showed him to be an enlightened and hard-working patron of twentieth century art. But it also revealed him as a better writer than administrator. In this third volume,* which overlaps in chronology with the second and tilts the balance back to a more private narrative, Sir John candidly admits his shortcomings as an administrator.

'I demand high standards; I am in general fairly quick to discern anything amiss; I am, I believe, fairly quick, too, to dis-

* *Time's Thievish Progress*: Autobiography III by John Rothenstein.

cern solutions to problems. But for the means of remedying the one and of "implementing" the other I am often at a loss.'

To some extent, and especially in the discrepancy between his private and public selves, Sir John resembles his father very closely. Will Rothenstein began his career as a promising artist, but he did not, I think, fulfil this promise, becoming instead a figure somewhat comparable to Hugh Walpole in literature. 'For myself,' he wrote to his wife, Alice, 'I want to paint my pictures and live within my means. I am slow and unproductive; but above all things I am an artist, and I dread the growing complexities.' Yet these complexities continued to multiply and his painting dwindled; for the loneliness of the painter's life neither suited nor satisfied him, and he moved more and more into art-politics. 'No-one among his contemporaries had shown such perceptive generosity towards his brother artists of succeeding generations, from Augustus John and Epstein to Henry Moore and Ceri Richards,' writes Sir John. This is completely true, yet he was never the popular figure he deserved to be. What was the secret of this gift for unpopularity? Partly, I believe, it was due to the prevalent ill-will of the competitive art-world; partly to certain defects of personality. He felt he lacked charm; his tone could vary disconcertingly between the lofty and the obsequious; he was suspected of chasing celebrities; and he attracted much inverted gratitude. But partly, too, it may have been that he felt some measure of self-dissatisfaction at having neglected the painter in himself for the patron – dissatisfaction, like happiness, being contagious.

Sir John has something of the same division between his public and private roles. He describes very well the sudden emptiness he felt on leaving the Tate, where his interests, affections and entire way of life had been so intimately involved. 'So I walked out into the street as into a void ... Suddenly, after a third of a century, to have no public function is a strange sensation; I missed even activities peripheral to my duties at the Tate which – when I had thought of them at all – I had thought of as drudgery.' The prospect of being able to give more time to his writing was not sufficient compensation, and he soon took up another public appointment, the chief result of which has been the publication of that useful series *The Masters* – 'a logical continuation', as he describes it, 'of my efforts at the Tate to make the most serious artists widely known'.

In these efforts, throughout his career, he has been remarkably successful. Since his writing has been directed to much the same aim as his work as official patron, he has succeeded rather better than his father in reconciling the private and public aspects of his life, and in concealing what, at a certain level, I suspect they both share; a lack of self-confidence.

> Private faces in public places,
> Are wiser and nicer
> Than public faces in private places,

W. H. Auden tells us. But they are seldom so diverting. Sir John's book is packed with public faces in private places, with the accounts of friendships that sprang up between himself and the artists with whom he dealt in his official capacity. The book opens with a marvellously tender and charming description of Matthew Smith, a 'pale melancholic man, peering helplessly through thick-lensed glasses, whose body was so inert that its movements left his suit uncreased', yet whose presence was so paradoxically invigorating and whose pictures so startlingly ripe and audacious. There follows a whole gallery of vivid pen-portraits of artists and writers – Augustus John, over drinks, growling: 'There's a girl who's going to join us. Sturdy little thing ...'; H. G. Wells at the Café Royal, jaunty in his dapper clothes, yet with an air of exasperated melancholy, his 'large eyes, luminous with intelligence and a diffused benevolence that gave dignity and light to his commonplace features'; Wyndham Lewis, destitute in Canada, writing for a job; 'Is there some old, much-bombed lighthouse that needs a Keeper? Have they been asking for someone, on nights of Blitz, to accouch the Zebras at the Zoo?; Francis Bacon, followed everywhere by his teddy-boy acolytes, substituting, in place of his sitter, a chimpanzee; and many more, including, perhaps the most affectionate of all, Edward Burra, living silently with his mother in Rye, their house full of conventional golf-clubs, macintoshes and fishing tackle, his studio, in bizarre contrast, decorated with the enlarged photograph of a leper far gone in his fearful decay – the word decay being frequently on Burra's lips 'as a term, moreover, of approbation'.

When Churchill once asked him what he thought of Graham Sutherland's famous portrait of him, Sir John replied that he had deliberately avoided seeing it, 'being determined not to involve myself in the controversy in the slightest degree'. In his anxiety not to risk controversy, he is sometimes over-polite in this book, having a tendency to award marks to artists for good manners and gratitude. At the Tate he had grown accustomed to arousing hostility which caused him some distress and even despair. Like his father – both of them capable of delivering a telling upper-cut on occasion – he feels keenly the ingratitude of artists.

Occasionally, in this volume, he is tempted to write 'for the record' as he puts it. But his disquisition on the Tate trustees, or the passages he devotes to refuting details in Maurice Collis's life of Stanley Spencer, though interesting, are less good than his evocations of personal friendships, and might well have been relegated to footnotes or appendices. However, these are tiny blemishes in Sir John's considerable achievement. He has written a rich and rewarding work that will delight all those interested in the artists of our day.

Wilson Steer

———◆———

The painter Philip Wilson Steer was built upon a pattern very dear to his fellow countrymen. He was a large, genial, small-headed, slow-moving man, very easy-going, incurious and inarticulate. People loved him for his modesty – you'd never guess he painted, especially since he locked up his painting equipment in a cricket bag, explaining: 'I get better service that way.' They admired him for his refusal, while in France, to learn a syllable of the French language; they were reassured by his teaching methods at the Slade – an interminable silence, then 'How's your sister?'; they relished his impassioned valetudinarianism, his longevity, his stubborn feasting off steak and linseed tea. His virtues were total shyness and a monumental calm. Despite his eye for painting pretty girls, he was triumphantly unromantic; and as England's most avant-garde painter he remained, very properly, a deeply conservative man.

Mr Laughton casts a sideways disapproving glance at this legend of the man, but it hardly obtrudes on his austere investigations into Steer the painter.* The most extreme quality of Mr Laughton's book is its carefulness. His research is painstaking and his narrative is set in a concrete of sensible footnotes. He edges carefully forward testing for dates, establishing the exact locale of the pictures, noting the brushwork, quoting the reviews, pointing to possible influences. Upon Steer's painting *The Bridge at Étaples*, a 'minor masterpiece', he delivers over five hundred words and produces three plates to prove, convincingly, that it was not painted at Étaples. But he does not reveal how this makes it a masterpiece. Later, he defines the word 'masterpiece' in the context of his study as 'a completely unified and substantial state-

* *Philip Wilson Steer 1860–1942* by Bruce Laughton.

ment of a visual experience, *which no artist but Steer could be expected to paint*. We have everything in this book except the experience.

Mr Laughton's writing has a bespectacled tone: his prose is passive, impersonal, with plenty of good negatives, nice qualifications – but not too much of the adventurous originality he urges on his subject. Yet in this sea of scholarly expertise, a personal theme suddenly breaks surface. Mr Laughton detects a tug-of-war in Steer between his orthodox temperament and his painter's eye. Hating anything contentious, he had no desire to reject tradition; yet as a painter he could not help experimenting. His experiments in the French Impressionistic style, which many think his most outstanding work, were castigated by the critics, especially by D. S. MacColl his friend and biographer. Mr Laughton concludes that the combined opinion of English critics in the 1890s discouraged Steer and had a deleterious effect on his painting.

No one who has seen Steer's tender and delicious portraits of Rose Pettigrew could fail to recognize that he loved her. From her 'Memoir of Wilson Steer', which Mr Laughton publishes for the first time as an Appendix to his book, it appears that they were briefly engaged when she was fifteen or sixteen. Rose Pettigrew's 'lively powers of expression are left to speak for themselves and the reader to judge for himself', Mr Laughton tactfully comments. It is a movingly egocentric piece of writing, relentlessly trivial, full of ruthless sentimentality. Poor Steer!

One could have wished for a better index, more colour plates, and some discussion of Steer's influence on Gore and Innes. Nevertheless this is a serious and authentic work that complements and in some respects supersedes MacColl's biography, and no one who cares for English painting should miss it.

Damn and 'Blast'! The Friendship of Wyndham Lewis and Augustus John

The long, precarious friendship between Wyndham Lewis and Augustus John was unique in both their careers. Neither was an easy man; both had undeniable personalities; and in the course of their relationship they struck sparks off each other that light up peculiar corners of their characters.

John, who was four years older than Lewis, made his name far earlier. In 1898, the year that Lewis went up to the Slade School of Fine Art, John had left with honours thick upon him, in particular the Summer Composition Prize for his picture 'Moses and the Brazen Serpent'. Three years later he had already become something of a cult-figure among the students, and the walls of the Slade, Lewis recalled in *Rude Assignment*,

> 'bore witness to the triumphs of this 'Michelangelo' ... A large charcoal drawing in the centre of the wall of the life-class of a hairy male nude, arms defiantly folded and a bristling moustache, commemorated his powers with almost a Gascon assertiveness and fronting the stairs that led upwards where the ladies were learning to be Michelangelos, hung a big painting of Moses and the Brazen Serpent ...
> '... One day the door of the life-class opened and a tall bearded figure with an enormous black Paris hat, large gold earrings decorating his ears, with a carriage of utmost arrogance strode in, and the whisper 'John' went round the class. He sat down on a donkey – the wooden chargers astride which we sat to draw – tore a page of banknote paper out of a sketch-book, pinned it upon a drawing board, and with a ferocious glare at the model (a female) began to draw with an indelible pencil. I

joined the group behind this redoubtable personage. John left us as abruptly as he had arrived. We watched in silence this mythological figure depart.'

It was about a year later that the two painters were formally introduced by William Rothenstein. Lewis by then was a good-looking, shy, gloweringly ambitious young man, who drew with thick black contours resembling the lead in a stained-glass window. He could be relied upon to act unpredictably, yet in the opinion of Professor Tonks, who taught him at the Slade, he possessed the finest sense of line of any student there. Rothenstein took him to John's flat at 18 Fitzroy Street (which Lewis himself was later to occupy) probably in the summer of 1902 – 'there was a noise of children', Lewis afterwards recalled, 'for this patriarch had already started upon his Biblical courses'.

John had by now attracted a great deal of steam to himself, and for a time Lewis, made heady by this atmosphere, became his most formidable disciple. They stimulated and exasperated each other in about equal measures. Lewis was much impressed by all that John had so rapidly achieved. His success in art and with women appeared phenomenal, and by associating with him, Lewis seems to have felt, some of this success might rub off on him. John, on his side, was flattered by Lewis's veneration. Here was someone mysterious and remarkable, a poet hesitating between literature and painting, whose good opinion of him served to increase John's self-esteem. He seemed a valuable ally. Whatever else John felt, he was never bored by Lewis, whose dynamic progress through life was conducted as if to outwit some invisible foe. This involved a series of improbable retreats – to Scandinavia even, where he would find a letter from John asking: 'Tell me Lewis what of Denmark or – is Sweden safe?'. Such places were not only safe, Lewis would hint in his replies, but the arenas of unimaginable conquests.

Very aware of his friend's superior education, John strove to match Lewis's 'calligraphic obscurity' by what he called 'linguistic licence' – a fantastic prolixity that he thought the intellectual tenor of their relationship demanded. The result was an exchange of letters, part undiscoverable, part indecipherable, covering over fifty years, that is almost complete in its comic density. Both were flamboyantly secretive men with bombardier tempers, and their friendship, which somehow endured all its volcanic quarrels, kept being arrested by declarations that it was at an end – an event upon which they would with great warmth congratulate themselves and each other. Yet such was the good feeling generated by these separations and congratulations that they quickly came together again when all the damning and blasting of their complicated liaison would start up once more.

Their correspondence, on both sides, is extremely generous with offensive advice which they attempted to make more palatable by adding the odd 'mon vieux' or 'old fellow'. John frequently intends to return Lewis's letters by post in order to get him, in the most friendly way of course, to 'admit [that] no more offensive statement could be penned'; but almost always he mislays the letter or, in his first fit of uncontrollable fury, flings it irrecoverably into some fire or sea. He is constantly being dumbfounded by Lewis's reminders to lend him money coupled with his forgetfulness in repaying it; and by his insistence that John was influencing mutual friends to his discredit. His style grows more and more convoluted in grappling with these groundless charges until it becomes blameless of almost all meaning. Then, suddenly, the clouds clear and in a succinct moment of retaliation he announces that Lewis's drawings 'lack *charm*, my dear fellow'.

The whole relationship is bedevilled by ingenious misunderstanding. Each credits the other with Machiavellian cunning, while assuming for himself a superhuman naïvety. Lewis is amazed that John never invites him for a drink; John is perplexed that Lewis is never able to visit him – when he does so, John is always out; while Lewis, on principle, never answers his door-bell. They make elaborate plans to meet on neutral territory, but then something goes wrong – the wrong time, the wrong place, the wrong mood. Lewis becomes increasingly irritated that John so seldom writes. John becomes irritated because when he does write his letters go astray, Lewis in the meantime having moved in darkest secrecy to some unknown address – such as the Pall Mall Safe Deposit. The letters which do arrive express very adequately this irritation fanned, in Lewis's case, by eloquent invective and in John's by a circumlocution that marvellously avoids answering the most innocent of Lewis's enquiries. It is a most stimulating exchange.

Lewis's drawing of John, which is reproduced in *Blasting and Bombardiering*, is not among his best work; John's portraits of Lewis are. An early etching shows a handsome, not ungentle face, though its moodiness is undisguised, and conveys the impression that John liked him, certainly thought him no fool. This etching, and one other, were done in January 1903, and a little later that year at Matching Green in Essex John painted an excellent oil portrait of Lewis, full of Castilian dignity displayed, as John Russell has observed, 'in a moment of repose'.

Lewis's description of John as a great 'man of action into whose hands the fairies put a brush instead of a sword' – a description which John himself was to define as rubbish – was a tribute to his physical personality. But on close companions the force of this personality was one of disintegration. In 1906, when the two of them were in Paris, Lewis wrote to his mother: 'I want to do some painting very badly, and can't do so near John . . . since his artistic personality is just too strong, and he is much more developed, naturally, and this frustrates any effort.' Partly because of this frustration, Lewis turned to his writing, being known by John as 'the Poet'. John respected Lewis's talent as an artist – in about 1910 he bought Lewis's *Porte de Mer*; and a little later Frank Rutter remembers John 'standing in admiration for fully twenty minutes before Wyndham Lewis's "Night Attack".' But it was as a writer that he chiefly recommended him to others. Early in 1910 he is writing to the American lawyer John Quinn to say that 'my friend Lewis . . . is writing for the English Review and hopes to publish a book of poems in the autumn. I think he is certainly the most gifted of the young writers.' This veneration for Lewis's writings was genuine and lasted throughout his life. In 1930 he writes to him for publication: 'In your "Apes of God" you have, as it were, suspended upon magical wires colossal puppets, whose enlarged and distorted features may be attributed to those of not a few contemporary figures known to fame, infamy, and myself. Some of these you, from your own superabundance, have endowed with unexpected intelligence; others, by an ingenious operation of trepanning, you have bereft of what wits they had or could lay claim to. These grandiose toys you manipulate with a gargantuan and salutary art unexampled in our or in any other time I know of. Your readers and especially, I feel, your subjects, must be compelled, before the work of criticism begins, to salute with a wide and comprehensive flourish the lofty genius of the author. . . . This act of homage and surrender I now myself perform.' Later still he praised very highly *The Childermass, Self-Condemned* and *The Revenge for Love.*

Lewis is equally full of public praise for John. It was John, he writes, who 'inaugurated an era of imaginative art in England'. Even in the 1940s and 1950s when John's powers were very much in decline, Lewis always notices his paintings favourably; and when John's autobiography *Chiaroscuro* appears, Lewis reviews it well in *The Listener.* Such acts, which really belong to the field of artistic trade unionism, seem to proclaim a friendship of enviable sweetness.

In fact they got on best when apart. During the years 1906 and 1907 when John was jostling between Paris and London, and Lewis was on the move between England, France and Germany brewing up his Dostoievsky cocktail *Tarr,* they saw a good deal of each other and their relationship rapidly over-ripened. John's romantic admiration of his disciple now began to evaporate and what was left mingled curiously with lumps of more indigestible emotion. They would go off to night-clubs together, or sit drinking and talking in a café in the Rue Dareau recommended by Sickert for its excellent *sauerkraut.* 'Not that I find him absolutely indispensable,' John conceded in a letter to Alick Schepeler, 'but at times I love to talk with him about Shelley or somebody.' Lewis himself, it seems, preferred to talk of Apaches and 'to frighten young people' with his tales of them. But what chiefly amused John were his friend's odd and ineffectual love-affairs. These formed part of his material for *Tarr,* whose theme became sex and the artist, displacing the stated one of its hero's spiritual progress. If the male artist, Lewis seems to argue, finds much in his work that other men seek of women, then it follows that he must be particularly discriminating in his affaires, scrupulously avoid sentimentality and all other false trails that lead him away from reality. It was a theme nicely attuned to John's own predicament, and almost certainly it formed part of their regular conversations. John understood very well the conflict between artistic integrity and appetite for life, knew that overlapping territory between inspiration and gratification. 'I am like the noble, untaught and untainted savage who, embracing with fearful enthusiasm the newly arrived Bottle, Bible and Whore of civilization, contracts at once with horrible violence their apoplectic corollary, the Paralysis, the Hypocrisy and the Pox ... So far I have been marvellously immune.'

Lewis's immunity, however, seemed far stronger. Prudence, suspicion and an aggressive shyness ringed him about like some fortress from which he seldom escaped. His affaires often appeared to be no more than word-affairs, though the words themselves were bold enough. 'Lewis announced last night that he was *loved*!' John reported to Alick Schepeler. 'At last! It seems he had observed a demoiselle in a restaurant who whenever he regarded her sucked in her cheeks slightly and looked embarrassed. The glorious fact was patent then – l'amour! He means to follow this up like a bloodhound. In the meanwhile however he has gone to Rouen for a week to see his mother, which in my opinion is not good generalship. He has a delightful notion – I am to get a set of young ladies during the summer as pupils and of course he will figure in the company and possibly be able to make love to one of them.' But when not in the vein to be amused by Lewis's eccentricities, John would quickly get needled. It was almost as if his own romanticism was being caricatured. 'The poet irritates me,' he admitted, 'he is always asking for petits suisses which are unheard of in this country and his prudence is boundless. What a mistake it is to have a friend – or, having one, ever to see him.'

In later years they made this mistake less often. But the romance of war drew them together again when, in the winter of 1917–18, they rather improbably found themselves occupying a large château near the Vimy front. Lewis appeared there as an ex-battery officer; John, to his evident confusion, as a Canadian Major. For both of them it was an untypically peaceful time – guns were everywhere, but for painting not firing. John, Lewis noticed with approval, did not neglect the social side of military life and was everywhere accorded the highest signs of respect, largely on account of his beard. 'He was the only officer in the British Army, excepting the King, who wore a beard,' Lewis wrote. 'In consequence he was a constant source of anxiety and terror wherever he went. Catching sight of him coming down a road any ordinary private would display every sign of the liveliest consternation. He would start saluting a mile off. Augustus John – every inch a King George – would solemnly touch his hat and pass on.'

On one occasion, after a specially successful party, the two war-artists commandeered a car and careered off together almost into enemy lines. It was the closest John ever got to the fighting, and Lewis, the ex-bombardier, was soon poking fun at his friend's mock-war experiences. But John, observing that Lewis had quickly retreated home after their exploit, pursued him vicariously. 'Have you seen anything of that tragic hero and consumer of tarts and mutton-chops, Wyndham Lewis?' he asked a mutual girl-friend. 'He is I think in London, painting his gun-pit and striving to reduce his "Vorticism" to the level of Canadian intelligibility – a hopeless task I fear.'

A little later John was to join him back in London. Tiring of the stalemate of war, he had suddenly struck out, connecting with the chin of one of his allies, a notorious Canadian captain. A court martial was avoided by the intervention of Lord Beaverbrook, and John was hurried back to paint his war-picture, modestly entitled 'Fraternity', which now hangs in the Imperial War Museum.

Though Lewis was to blast many things, such as gypsydom, which John popularly represented, the clan John was safe. Augustus's son, Henry John, contributed to *The Enemy* and when he died in 1935, Lewis suggested 'some sort of book, assembling fragments perhaps of Henry's writing, to commemorate the promise of this young life'. Four years later, when Augustus's sister Gwen died, Lewis proposed bringing out a volume of her and Augustus's pictures and was only prevented by certain copyright difficulties from carrying this out.

Between the wars they corresponded tirelessly, made many

secret plans for private meetings, but were not much connected
in the public mind until, in 1938, they suddenly hit the headlines
together. It was this year that Lewis completed his famous portrait
of T. S. Eliot – much admired by Eliot and himself. In the spring
it was submitted to the Royal Academy which, much to Eliot's
relief and Lewis's indignation, rejected it. On learning this, John
at once issued a statement, full of powerful negatives, for the
press. 'I very much regret to make a sensation, but it cannot be
helped,' he began. 'Nothing that Mr Wyndham Lewis paints is
negligible or to be condemned lightly. I strongly disagree with
this rejection. I think it is an inept act on the part of the Academy.
The rejection of Mr Wyndham Lewis's portrait by the Academy
has determined my decision to resign from that body . . . I shall
henceforth experience no longer the uncomfortable feeling of
being in a false position as a member of an institution with whose
general policy I am constantly in disagreement. I shall be happier
and more honest in rejoining the ranks of those outside, where I
naturally belong.'

This statement provoked an extraordinary response in the
press in Britain, America and, breaking through the walls of art
insularity, France. 'Premier May Be Questioned' ran a headline in
the *Morning Post*. Elsewhere, with more bewilderment, it was
reported that the Academy itself had received no notification of
John's resignation. In fact he had written a formal letter to the
President of the Royal Academy, Sir William Llewelyn, three
days beforehand, but neglected to post it. 'After the crowning
ineptitude of the rejection of Wyndham Lewis's picture I feel it is
impossible for me to remain longer a member of the R.A.,' he
told Llewelyn. Although in all the press announcements John confessed to great 'reluctance' in coming to his decision, he had in
fact been searching round for an avenue of escape from the
Academy, partly because he disliked Llewelyn. The Eliot portrait provided him with a perfect motive, and he wrote to Lewis
to thank him. 'I resign with gratitude to you for affording me so
good a reason.'

Lewis was delighted and suggested that all sorts of politico-
artistic activities should issue out of this rumpus, including the
formation by the two of them of a new *Salon des Refusés*. But

John demurred, 'being more than occupied with my show'. This show, of John's Jamaican pictures, Lewis reviewed enthusiastically in *The Listener*. 'As one passes in review these blistered skins of young African belles, with their mournful doglike orbs, and twisted lips like a heavyweight pugilist, one comes nearer to the tragedy of this branch of the human race that one would in pictures more literary in intention, such as Gauguin would have supplied us with. . . .

'Mr John opens his large blue eyes, and a dusky head bursts into them. He has his brushes and his canvas handy. His large blue eyes hold fast the dusky object, while his brushes stamp out on the canvas a replica of what he sees. But what he sees (since he is a very imaginative man) is all the squalor and beauty of the race – of this race of predestined underdogs who have never been able to meet on equal terms the crafty white man or the even more crafty Arab.

'In describing Mr Augustus John's assault upon these Negro belles – his optical assault, as his large blue eyes first fall upon them in Jamaica – I was indicating what is, in fact, a good deal of his method of work. Nature is for him like a tremendous carnival, in the midst of which he finds himself. But there is nothing of the spectator about Mr John. He is very much part of the saturnalia. And it is only because he enjoys it so tremendously that he is moved to report upon it – in a fever of optical emotion, before the object selected passes on and is lost in the crowd.'

In a letter to Lewis, John thanked him for this article. 'It does me a lot of good to have such a generous and understanding tribute from a man of your critical ability and I am proud of it.' But he was not too proud to overlook the many *double entendres* Lewis had used, and never for a moment lowered his guard. Instead, he delivered a neatly placed blow just below the belt when he let it be known that he had not seen the portrait of Eliot at the time of its rejection, but that on doing so later felt inclined to agree with the Academy. Two years later, Llewelyn having left, he was re-elected to become what Lewis described as 'the most distinguished Royal Academician . . . of a sleeping-partner order'. To the end this jousting between them continued. They conversed, for the most part, by a series of back-handed compliments, of which perhaps the finest is Lewis's 'I thank you quite unaffectedly for having knocked a good deal of nonsense out of me, and am only sorry that I was not able (owing to my tender years and extravagant susceptibilities) to have rendered you a similar service'. Such complimentary abuse, punctuated by sudden extraordinary acts of kindness, seems to show a strange discrepancy between their public and private exchanges. When Lewis went blind, John boasted that he sent him a telegram expressing the hope that it would not interfere with his real work: *art-criticism*. And when pressed to explain this unsympathetic message, he declared that he wasn't, through sentimentality, going to lay himself open to some crushing rejoinder. In fact his letter was not unsympathetic. 'I hope you will find a cure as did Aldous Huxley,' he wrote. 'Anyhow indiscriminate vision is a curse. Although without the aid of a couple of daughters like Milton, I really don't see why you should discontinue your art criticism – you can't go far wrong even if you do it in bed. You can always turn on your private lamp of aggressive voltage along with your dictaphone to discover fresh talent and demolish stale.' At other times he treats this blindness as a gift of which Lewis has taken full advantage. 'I have been *entranced* by this,' he writes to him of *Rotting Hill* (10 December 1951), '... and delighted to see that your present disability has in no way impaired your powers of observation, but rather heightened them.'

Lewis receives these 'impertinent' congratulations with an appreciative silence. He never once alluded to his blindness, preferring to make any accusation more obliquely: 'Dear John, I'm told you've mellowed.' John hotly denied the charge, but Tristan de Vere Cole remembers him taking Lewis out to dinner shortly before his death, seeing that his food was properly cut up, deferring to him in their conversation and exerting all his charm for Lewis's entertainment. At the end of John's essay on Lewis, 'Elephants with Beards', which appeared in *Finishing Touches* after both of them were dead, there is a gruff, almost grudging note of admiration for his old adversary: 'The heart which he had so successfully disciplined was now allowed to make its appearance at moments, though never vocally. Lewis was incapable of pathos, and practised to the end the reserve of a philosopher.'

In retrospect, the course of their friendship seems like an endless sparring match conducted in private so as to train them for real encounters against 'the Enemy'. For it was a common enemy they fought, and they go down fighting on the same side.*

* Mr Geoffrey Grigson, who 'often listened to Wyndham Lewis discussing Augustus John', has objected (*Listener*, 13 July 1972) to what he calls this pious signing off. 'Lewis,' he writes, 'was sardonically aware that John had made a pact with social success at the expense of painting, and had gone over – like so many English artists – to the other side. But Lewis stuck to his friends (to more ambiguous ones than John) and there was a limit to what he would write about them publicly.' In their conversations, he recalled, 'Lewis hedged on John as an artist. He would say – if one protested, "Wasn't John really a vulgar art-school draughtsman with a provincial mind?" – that John was an Eye; and that the results were all right if the Eye, unallied as it might be to intelligence or imagination, happened to fall on the right object, such as a flamboyant dahlia.' It must be left to the reader to decide whether Lewis's forbearance was with John or with Mr Grigson.

Dorelia: an Obituary

————◆————

Dorelia John, who died this summer [1969] in her late eighties, is well-known to anyone familiar with the work of Augustus John, whose drawings and paintings of her, over a period of sixty years, can be seen in many British and American art galleries.

She was a woman of extraordinary beauty, yet of a beauty, and personality, so unusual that it is curiously difficult to describe. Beauty is not rare, but what was rare about Dorelia was the enigmatic power and magnetism that gave her beauty its depth.

One of seven children – four sisters, three brothers – Dorelia McNeil came from a Scottish family which had originally lived in the Western Highlands. All of them were remarkably good-looking. It was said they partly owed these looks to Spanish blood. While she was still very young, Dorelia took a job as typist in a lawyer's office near Streatham. In the evenings, she went to classes at the Westminster School of Art, and it was here she got to know several artists working in London.

One of these was Gwen John, Augustus's sister. On an impulse the two girls decided to walk to Rome, starting out in the summer of 1903, as Mary Taubman has described, 'carrying a minimum of personal belongings and a great deal of painting equipment. They found the going slow.' Occasionally they would manage to get lifts in carts, and once in a motor-car, 'till it broke down'. They journeyed up the Garonne, sleeping under haystacks, trudging from village to village, encountering several adventures, and doing drawings of people in return for food or a little money.

By the autumn they had reached Toulouse where they hired a room, as Gwen told Ursula Tyrwhitt, 'from a tiny little old woman dressed in black ... she is very very wicked'. It was here that Gwen did three marvellous portraits of Dorelia, all painted on to the canvas without previous studies – *The Student, Dorelia in Black,* and *Dorelia by Lamplight at Toulouse* which is, wrote Edwin Mullins, 'among the most exquisite and intimate studies ever painted by a British artist'.

'We shall never get to Rome, I'm afraid,' wrote Gwen. 'It seems further away than it did in England.' Instead they returned to a hotel in Paris, and over the next three years, apart from a short stay in Belgium, Dorelia divided her life between England and France, earning her living by modelling and making dresses. Much of this time was spent with Augustus and his first wife Ida, an ex-Slade student and close friend of both Dorelia's and Gwen's. 'Dorelia is angelic as always,' Ida wrote during this period to William Rothenstein. '. . . Gwen John is mysterious and flame-like and *impitoyable.*' And, at about the same time, in a letter to William Rothenstein's wife Alice, Gwen John described Dorelia as 'simple and good' – both high terms of praise in her vocabulary.

There are many stories of how Dorelia and Augustus met. Dorelia first set eyes on his commanding figure at an exhibition of Spanish paintings at the Guildhall – but he did not see her. A popular story was that, a little later, he overtook her in a London street, looked back and was unable to avert his gaze almost for the rest of his life.

What quality was it that so mesmerized him? Above all, it was perhaps her serenity – something he so conspicuously lacked, and the source of which, in her, both baffled and attracted him. Dorelia, or Dodo as everyone was to call her, was not an intellec-tual; she was not particularly witty or articulate; she was certainly not sentimental. It was her *presence* that was remarkable, her peace-giving quality and her deep common sense. 'She has more common sense,' Augustus wryly remarked to John Quinn, 'than would be needed to fit out a dozen normal people.'

Her high cheek-bones, dark complexion, downward-curving mouth, the grace of her panther-like movements, so intensely feminine, and her simple peasant quality – all these helped to inspire him as an artist. But it was her equanimity, her unending tact and efficiency upon which he relied at various crises in his life. For if he was like a great man-o'-war, braving the highest seas, she was the anchor that saved him from dashing himself upon the uncharted rocks.

When, in the spring of 1907, Ida John lay dying of puerperal fever after the birth of her fifth son Henry, it was Dorelia who came and took charge; and after Ida's death, it was Dorelia who brought up four of Ida's sons, in addition to her own growing family. This, too, was the year that Augustus painted his most celebrated picture of her, *The Smiling Woman*, of which Roger Fry wrote: 'Here at last Mr John has arrived in painting as definitely as he has long ago done in his drawings.'

The houses in which the prolific John family lived from this time on were her creations and the most eloquent expressions of her personality. The rich colours, the arrangements of flowers, the delicious Provençal meals, the almost pagan love of the beautiful, so unplanned and so unpretentious – all these were hers. They were not tidy places, these houses – Lord David Cecil remembers leaving his hat on the floor one evening, and returning six weeks later to find it unmoved – nor was the régime formal: guests were seldom introduced to one another, and might be confronted by a deep animal silence from the whole John pack. But the atmosphere had a magic quality that cast its spell on almost everyone – so much so that more than one visitor who came for tea stayed on for several weeks, or months, and in one case for over a year.

Perhaps the most individual of all her houses was Alderney Manor, near Poole, into which the family moved in the summer of 1911. Alderney was a strange house, a sort of long castellated bungalow of cardboard colour, looking like a toy Gothic castle. It was set in fifty acres of land, and was a marvellous place for the children to grow up. Dorelia let their hair grow long and golden, shaped into low fringes; and they ran wild among the heaths and streams, dressed during the winter in pink pinafores, brown corduroy knickers, red socks, black boots; and, in summer, naked. They were not pampered, but put to work sawing logs, grooming the horses, collecting the hens' eggs, even making the milk into butter with a hand-operated churn, and, most arduous of all, answering the patriarchal summons: 'Come and sit!'

Alderney seemed to flow with milk and honey. Under Dorelia's management it became almost a self-supporting community, and to the herds of cows and pedigree pigs, the ponies, donkeys, miscellaneous dogs, endless cats, she added twelve hives of dangerous bees.

But her chief passion was for flowers. Almost every kind of tree and shrub flourished at Alderney with an abnormal vigour – ilex and pine, giant rhododendron and chestnut. 'The peculiar charm of that garden was its half-wild appearance,' wrote Romilly John in his delightful memoirs. 'The grass was seldom as closely shaven as orthodoxy demands, and great masses of lavender and other smelling plants sprawled outwards from the concentric beds, until in some places the pathways were almost concealed. Tangled masses of roses and clematis heaved up into the air, or hung droopingly from the wall. The pond in the middle became hidden by the high screen of flowering vegetation ... In summer the composite smell of innumerable flowers hung upon the still air. The wall was overtopped most of the way by a thick hedge formed by the laurels that grew outside, and a eucalyptus, which had escaped the frosts of several winters, lifted high into the air its graceful and silvery spine.'

Dorelia's influence extended far beyond the walls of this garden, affecting many she never met. For three decades her taste in clothes became the fashion among art students. She took no notice of the genteel manners and sophisticated fashions of London or Paris, or of the brash styles that succeeded them. Her style was original, peculiar to herself. Sometimes she would wear a broad-brimmed straw hat, with its sweeping line like those of the French peasants. Her long dresses that reached the ground, high waistline, tight bodice with long tight sleeves, so memorably caught by Augustus in some of his lyrical Welsh panels, was a uniform copied by nearly all the girls at the Slade, and a symbol, in their metropolitan surroundings, of an unsevered connection with country things, with the very soil of the country. But no one could carry it off with such dignity, such hypnotic fascination as Dorelia herself.

In the spring of 1927, the John family moved to Fryern Court, a Georgian manor-house near Fordingbridge in Hampshire. Here, interspersed with many trips to Provence where they had a small farmhouse, Augustus and Dorelia lived the rest of their lives. For over thirty years Dorelia did her best to guard Augustus against distractions from his work. Some intruders were met with silent generosity, in a manner sympathetic but firm; to others she was coldly polite; to others again invisible. At all times she carried her secrets well. Her presence, one of generally cheerful detachment, was always felt – a mixture of formidable common sense and absolute vagueness on the many matters that did not concern her. Almost invariably she seemed aloof, but then something trivial would startle her into laughter – the incompetent way someone cut a slice of bread – she would put up her hands to her face and *hoot* with amusement.

In October 1961 Augustus died. Dorelia continued to live at Fryern, enveloped by the rough, lavish and romantic atmosphere she had given the place. She still wore the same style of clothes, radiated the same extraordinary natural grace, travelled regularly to France. But in the last year of her life she grew frailer, was less able to feed and prune her flowers – and this frustrated her.

On the evening of 23rd July, 1969, Romilly, Dorelia's son, found her fallen on the dining-room floor, and she was put to bed. She died soon afterwards in her sleep, quietly, without fuss.

Index